Promoting Inclusive Practice

Promoting Inclusive Practice

Christina Tilstone, Lani Florian
and Richard Rose

London and New York

First published 1998
by Routledge
11 New Fetter Lane, London EC4P 4EE

Simultaneously published in the USA and Canada
by Routledge
29 West 35th Street, New York, NY 10001

Reprinted 2000, 2002 by RoutledgeFalmer

RoutledgeFalmer is an imprint of the Taylor & Francis Group

© 1998 Christina Tilstone, Lani Florian and Richard Rose;
individual chapters, their authors

Typeset in Garamond by Routledge
Printed in Great Britain by
St Edmundsbury Press Ltd, Bury St Edmunds, Suffolk

British Library Cataloguing in Publication Data
A catalogue record for this book is available from the British
Library

Library of Congress Cataloging in Publication Data
A catalogue record for this book is available from the Library of
Congress

ISBN 0-415-18067-8

Contents

Illustrations

TABLES

FIGURES

Notes on contributors

Caroline Broomhead, after training to teach business studies, taught in community schools and developed a particular interest in integration and inclusion before moving into special education. She is now head of High Birch School, Rochdale, for children with moderate, severe or complex learning difficulties, and brings to her position as a regional tutor on The University of Birmingham's Distance Education Course (Learning Difficulties) a particular interest in the role of staff development in improving the quality of education for pupils with special educational needs.

Richard Byers, an independent consultant on curriculum development for pupils with learning difficulties, is a part-time lecturer in special educational needs at the University of Cambridge School of Education and at the Centre for the Study of Special Education at Westminster College, Oxford. He has written extensively on curriculum design and development.

Ted Cole is Research Fellow (Emotional and Behavioural Difficulties Project) at The University of Birmingham. His publications on special education include *Apart or A Part?* which has received wide critical acclaim.

Allan Day is head teacher of Southall Special School, Telford, for pupils with moderate learning difficulties, language difficulties and autism, which was named a 'Highly Effective Special School' in 1996. He has published articles on special school and mainstream links and on curriculum development.

Lani Florian is a lecturer and consultant in special education with particular expertise in inclusive education. She has conducted research on the characteristics of inclusive schools and has published a number of articles on this topic. She has a wide range of experience in schools and in higher education. She was Legislative Assistant to the US Senate Subcommittee on the Handicapped during the 99th Congress where she had staff responsibility for the development of PL 99–457, the federal law which established the US early intervention programme for infants and toddlers with disabilities and their families.

Liz Gerschel is an inspector, trainer, consultant, adviser and writer with a wide experience in education in both the UK and the West Indies. She works extensively with the staff and governors of both special and mainstream schools on a variety of issues, including: special needs; assessment; behaviour management; and responses to bullying and harassment.

Penny Lacey is a lecturer in education at The University of Birmingham and co-ordinator of an interdisciplinary course for staff working with children or adults with profound and multiple learning difficulties. She has published widely on support services and the curriculum and on multidisciplinary teamwork.

Claire Marvin is a teacher in the assessment nursery of a special school, and a part-time lecturer in education at The University of Birmingham. She has taught in a wide range of schools, both in the UK and abroad, and has written material for The University of Birmingham's Distance Education Course in Learning Difficulties.

Geoff Read is deputy head teacher of Derrymount School, Nottingham, an all-age school for pupils with special educational needs. From 1993 to 1995 he was Research Fellow (learning styles and learning preferences) at The University of Birmingham.

Christopher Robertson is senior lecturer in special education in the Special Needs Research and Development Centre at Christ Church College, Canterbury. He has had wide experience of teaching pupils with severe and profound and multiple learning difficulties.

Richard Rose is senior lecturer in special education at Nene University College, Northampton, having previously held a number of posts in schools, and headship of a special school. Until recently he was inspector for special education in Northamptonshire. He has made contributions to several journals and is co-author of three previous books including *Planning the Curriculum for Pupils with Special Educational Needs*.

Jonathan Steele is the head teacher of a school for children with severe learning difficulties. His publications include articles in major research journals in the UK, Europe and the USA.

Christina Tilstone is senior lecturer in special education, and programme of study tutor for the distance education course for teachers of pupils with learning difficulties (severe and moderate), at The University of Birmingham. She has taught children with severe learning difficulties in a variety of settings and has worked in teacher education, both in the UK and abroad, since 1983. She has published widely on aspects of special educational needs and is currently editor of the *British Journal of Special Education*, a leading special needs journal

Jan Tyne taught in mainstream and special schools for twenty years before beginning work with organisations actively committed to the development of better services for adults with learning difficulties. She is now director of a small (non-profit-making) agency, which aims to seek better futures and opportunities for people with disabilities.

Alan Wiltshire is head teacher of an all-age school for pupils with severe learning difficulties. He has been involved in local education authority in-service education and training courses, for which he has published supplementary material.

Jim Wolger. After serving as a police officer with the Metropolitan Police, Jim taught in mainstream schools, retrained in craft, design and technology, and then taught in special schools before his appointment as head teacher of Rosemary Special School (SLD), London.

Foreword

The focus of this book is on inclusive educational practice for pupils with learning difficulties. The theme of inclusion is a particularly timely one: the 1994 Salamanca Statement from UNESCO called on national governments to adopt the principle of inclusive education for all children, and the new Government in the UK has responded to this in a recent consultative Green Paper (DfEE, 1997). The term inclusion is, however, open to different interpretations. The significance of the particular perspective adopted in this book can perhaps best be highlighted by a comparison with earlier characterisations of integrated educational provision.

It is now twenty years since the Warnock Committee gave its carefully qualified support to the principle of integration for pupils with special educational needs (DES, 1978). The Committee distinguished between three main forms of integration, which it described as: 'locational', where special units or classes are attached to, or share a site with, mainstream schools; 'social', where the unit's pupils 'eat, play and consort with other children, and possibly share organised out-of-classroom activities'; and 'functional', where, in addition to social contacts, those with special educational needs join the regular school classes on a full- or a part-time basis (DES, 1978, paragraphs 7.6 to 7.11).

It was, as the Committee acknowledged, a basic and oversimplified model and perhaps inevitably it encouraged a greater emphasis on *where* a pupil was placed rather than on the *quality* of his or her educational experiences. It also reinforced a perception which was current at the time that integration concerned only those pupils who had traditionally been educated in segregated provision. In the years following the publication of the Warnock Report, it became evident that significant shifts in thinking were needed on both of these dimensions.

The Fish Report for the ILEA in 1985 was representative of concerns among many people working in special education that integration must be conceptualised as a dynamic process rather than simply as a state of placement. That is, it should imply 'continued and planned interaction with contemporaries' (ILEA, 1985). While a focus on social interaction with peers is clearly important it is not the only aspect of the quality of children's educational experience that needs to be addressed. There is evidence that in some early approaches to integration the social dimension could be given such priority that it distracted attention from other significant educational goals. Further, it has become apparent that constructive and sustainable relationships between pupils with special educational needs and their peers involve mutual perceptions of shared experiences of a kind that may require the provision of well-planned collaborative learning activities. Accordingly, there has been an increasing recognition of the interconnectedness of the Warnock Committee's categories of social and functional integration. This is evident, for example, in the governmental Green Paper, which states that: 'By inclusion, we mean not only that pupils with SEN should, where possible, receive their education in a mainstream school, but also that they should join in fully with their peers in the curriculum' (DfEE, 1997, p.44).

Such a perspective automatically leads to some questioning of the traditional view that integration is only the concern of those pupils who have in the past been educated in segregated settings. Dissatisfaction with a narrow interpretation of integration as the 'problem' of the minority, where success equates to 'fitting a child' into a system which was not designed with his or her needs in mind, was signalled as early as 1981 by Hegarty and his colleagues (Hegarty et al., 1981). It has been this dissatisfaction with the way in which the term 'integration' has often been understood that has provided a significant impetus to a change in the use of terminology away from 'integration' and towards 'inclusion'. The very notion of inclusion acknowledges that there is a risk of exclusion to be redressed. Further, the term carries with it a recognition that it involves everyone: that is, the principle of inclusive educational practice is one that applies to all pupils, and its implementation therefore has implications for the design of a curriculum and organisational strategy in schools which is responsive to the full range of diversity among pupils.

Thus the change in terminology represents an explicit attempt to move thinking and practice beyond some of the narrow and confining frameworks that had become associated with the use of the word integration. Nevertheless, although there is a remarkable degree of consensus among many countries about the desirability of the principle of inclusion, it is evident that a range of possible interpretations of the principle continues to exist. It is for this reason that the editors of this book are to be congratulated in making clear from the outset the definition of inclusion that they and their contributors adopt. Derived from the work of Inclusion International, their perspective on inclusion emphasises the promotion of informed choices and active participation in the community throughout an individual's life. The aim of the book is to demonstrate how this can be promoted during the school years.

Lani Florian elaborates on this concept of inclusion from both historical and international perspectives with great clarity. In doing so, she demonstrates vividly how far our thinking has progressed in recent years. This is not to suggest that the implementation of inclusive practice has generally kept abreast of these shifts in thinking, however. The editors present a persuasive analysis of the principles which must underpin an inclusive approach. At the same time, though, they note the real tensions that are inherent in the attempt to realise an inclusive ideal, incorporating genuine recognition and valuing of diversity, within a legislative framework which emphasises competition focused on league tables or academic achievement.

Other chapters in the book address the issues involved at a whole school level. Christina Tilstone provides a detailed exposition of the changing relationship between what she refers to as the *vision* and the *reality* of inclusion. Never losing sight of the primary principle of promoting quality educational and life experiences, she draws attention to the almost paradoxical role of special schools and their staff in the process. We frequently hear of the vested interests of the 'special sector' in maintaining segregation, and yet it is notable that within the current climate of pressures on mainstream schools, special school staff play a very significant role in initiating and maintaining inclusive experiences for their pupils. The Green Paper (DfEE, 1997) refers to the need to strengthen links between special and mainstream schools, and there is no doubt that within a changing context which aims to support greater inclusion, staffs from both will need to embrace new forms of collaboration.

Several contributors focus on questions of classroom practicalities, whether these are in mainstream or special contexts. One of the principles which underpins the Code of Practice (DfEE, 1994) is that pupils have a right to be involved in the development of provision to meet their needs and that such involvement contributes to more successful learning. Richard Rose makes a strongly argued case for active pupil participation in the assessment and learning process as a means of facilitating high quality inclusive education. The role of schools in preparing young people for lifelong learning within the community and their transition to adulthood is particularly emphasised in this part of the book. It must be seen as crucial that approaches for the involvement of pupils with learning difficulties in decision making and review procedures are well established by the time that transition planning begins. Rose provides a thorough discussion of strategies that schools might adopt.

The editors share an admirably clear and informed vision of the issues that are involved in the promotion of inclusive educational practice for pupils with learning difficulties. They have brought together a team of contributors who have between them an extensive and varied range of practical experience in special education as well as a wide knowledge of current developments and research in the area. As a result, the book as a whole succeeds in combining philosophical debates on inclusion with a rigorous evaluation of their theoretical underpinnings, and relating these in accessible ways to direct applications for the development of effective school practice.

Sally Beveridge
School of Education
University of Leeds

REFERENCES

DES (1978) *Special Educational Needs* (The Warnock Report), Cmnd 7212, London: HMSO.

DfEE (1994) *The Code of Practice on the Identification and Assessment of Special Educational Needs*, London: HMSO.

DfEE (1997) *Excellence for All Children: Meeting Special Educational Needs. Green Paper*, London: HMSO.

Hegarty, S., Pocklington, K. and Lucas, D. (1981) *Educating Pupils with Special Needs in the Ordinary School*, Windsor: NFER-Nelson.

ILEA (1985) *Educational Opportunities for All? (The Fish Report)*, London: ILEA.

Acknowledgements

As editors of this book we are grateful for the support and advice received from family, friends and colleagues. We are indebted to our contributors, the regional tutors on The University of Birmingham's distance education course for teachers of children with learning difficulties. It is their work which has inspired and informed much of the content of the book. Particular thanks must go to Norman Brown, Jill Porter, Noreen Stacey, and other colleagues at The University of Birmingham. Similar gratitude is owed to staff from Nene University College, Northampton, especially to Michelle McManamon for computer wizardry. The support and encouragement of Philip Burke of the University of Maryland Department of Special Education, and Judy Sebba of the University of Cambridge School of Education, who have always been prepared to listen and to give advice despite their heavy schedules, is very much appreciated. Nina Stibbe and her colleagues at Routledge kept faith with our approach, and responded to our many demands.

Finally, our thanks to Sara Rose, Martyn Rouse and Philip Tilstone, just for being there and for being wonderful!

Chapter 1

Pragmatism not dogmatism

Promoting more inclusive practice

Lani Florian, Richard Rose
and Christina Tilstone

Few areas of education have undergone the kind of development that has characterised special education over the past twenty-five years. The recent movement for the full inclusion of all pupils in mainstream schools is but one example of development where philosophical thought outpaces practice. Over the past ten years, a philosophy of inclusion and its associated meanings has been gaining momentum in many parts of the world (UNESCO, 1996). Although there are those who might argue that a book written by special educators cannot be about inclusion because the vocabulary, and indeed the nature of the profession, is focused on difference (see Florian, 1998), we take a more pragmatic view. It is the emphasis on *difference* that precludes some children from attending mainstream schools and perpetuates the continuation of a separate segregated system of special education. However, to suggest that the elimination of a separate system of provision will necessitate the development of a more responsive mainstream system is to forget that special schools were created to cater for pupils unable to be accommodated in mainstream schools. The complex social and historical reasons for this have received much attention in the literature (see e.g. Barton, 1988; Cole, 1989; Lazerson, 1983; Skrtic, 1991; Tomlinson, 1982). We believe that special educators, meaning those with expertise about the education of pupils who experience difficulty in learning at school, are important players in promoting more inclusive practice. That the term inclusion has found its way into several important international policy documents creates an unprecedented opportunity for improvement in the lives of people with disabilities. Though it has sparked as much debate as consensus, the notion of inclusive education has served to focus the field of special education on issues of quality and outcomes as never before. This book is about moving forward from where we are. It explores some of the theoretical and practical problems associated with inclusive education. The context for much of the discussion is the United Kingdom. However, many of the topics have wide applicability and relevance to the situation in other countries.

Since the Warnock Report in 1978, it has been assumed in the UK that about 20 per cent of school-aged children will have special educational needs requiring additional help at some point in their school careers. Furthermore, approximately 2 per cent of children will have severe physical, sensory, intellectual or emotional difficulties, some of which will remain with them throughout their lives. Historically this 2 per cent of children have been excluded from mainstream schools, receiving their education in special schools instead. In recent years, a growing sense of injustice regarding the *idea* of segregated special schooling for these pupils has led to calls for more inclusive educational opportunities as a matter of human right and equal opportunity. To date, efforts to decrease the number of pupils with special educational needs excluded from mainstream schools have taken two distinct routes. One is characterised by the attempt to *integrate* children from special schools into mainstream schools and classes through a range of provision whereby pupils with special educational needs spend part of the school day with peers of roughly the same chronological age (i.e. Beveridge, 1996; Lewis, 1995). The second and more recent approach currently under investigation has focused on improving the capacity of mainstream schools to accommodate diversity amongst their pupils (i.e. Booth *et al.*, 1997; Hopkins *et al.*, 1996).

At the same time, there has been increasing rhetoric about the immorality of segregated provision. Ideas about more inclusive schooling are appearing in education policies in many parts of the world. In the UK, they are central to the government's education policies and have been incorporated into the recent education consultation documents of the new Labour government. One of these policy documents, *Excellence in Schools* states: 'Where children do have special educational needs there are strong educational, social and moral grounds for their education in mainstream schools' (DfEE, 1997a, p.34). The other, *Excellence for All Children* (DfEE, 1997b), endorses the 1994 UNESCO Salamanca World Statement on Special Needs Education which calls for the inclusion of pupils with special educational needs in mainstream schools. In addition, both papers call for stronger links between special and mainstream schools. The appearance of this type of rhetoric in government policy documents has put pressure on special education professionals to undertake a critical examination of the methods and means by which they work. Many have come to believe, indeed many have always believed, *philosophically*, in the right of children with special educational needs to the same educational opportunity as that available to other children. This opportunity has included access to mainstream schools and to the curriculum offered by those schools. What has not been so easy to agree are the terms of this access. The problem is not so much with the idea, as with uncertainty about the practice.

Uncertainty about practice stems from the conflict which arises when policies clash. Special education policy has been based on a deficit model of individualisation which regards people with disabilities as inherently flawed, and therefore requiring specialised instruction to meet individual need. Inclusive education is based on a social model which recognises the value of people with disabilities and the positive contributions they make to society. However, it is needs-led provision which characterises special needs legislation as well as other policies such as the Code of Practice (DfEE, 1994). In a review of major legislation affecting pupils with special educational needs, Lindsay (1997) noted that 'there is a clear sense of commitment to children with SEN. This is not simply a welfare-caring approach, but rather one that has gradually extended their legal rights' (p.25).

In the USA, Lipsky and Gartner (1997) have compared the movement towards more inclusive education for children with disabilities with the process of racial desegregation. Although pupils with disabilities are members of a minority group, the extent to which their oppression by the dominant culture can be redressed by models of racial equality has been questioned by advocates who wonder about the extent to which policies aimed at protecting individual rights against discrimination based on skin colour can promote true inclusion of people with disabilities (Zola, 1989). People with disabilities and members of racial minority groups are not directly comparable, even though both groups have been discriminated against in society. To be excluded from the educational mainstream because of the colour of one's skin is very different than to be excluded because the mainstream curriculum is irrelevant to one's needs. Full inclusion of *all* pupils with learning difficulties requires changes to the curriculum and the manner in which it is delivered. Consistent with this view, Hart (1996) has argued that the Code of Practice with its emphasis on documentation and stages of assessment may have inhibited inclusive practice. Full inclusion will not be achieved until education reform policies stop treating selected children as members of any minority group. The need is for flexible reform policies which are inclusive of all.

This book is about promoting inclusive practice. It takes the reality of daily life of school-aged children with learning difficulties as its starting point. In doing so, it takes a broad view of inclusion, emphasising that the ways in which we approach pupils, the perspectives we adopt and the efforts we make to provide for them the opportunity for an ordinary life are critical factors in implementing policies of inclusion. To explore these factors we have invited regional tutors on The University of Birmingham's distance education course for teachers of children with learning difficulties to write about ways in which inclusive practice can be promoted. The tutors have recent practical experience and a wide knowledge of current developments and research in their specialist fields of study. They work or have worked in mainstream and special schools, and as educational psychologists, LEA advisers, school inspectors and university lecturers. All of them are committed to the idea that people with learning difficulties are entitled to the same chance for a good life as anyone else.

The number of pupils with severe learning difficulties who are already included in mainstream schools is not known as school records in the UK do not tend to identify pupils by disability category. However, close to 90,000 pupils (1.4 per cent of all 5–15 year olds) are enrolled in English special schools (Norwich, 1997) suggesting that many of the resources and much of the expertise currently available are not in mainstream schools. There is much work that needs to be done before the reconfigured role for special schools (as community special schools which support their mainstream counterparts) envisaged in government policy becomes reality. Part III offers the ideas of several special school heads about how to move practice forward. Some of these ideas are untested, others are currently under review (i.e. Sebba and Sachdev, 1997). Ainscow (1997) has suggested that the instructional methods developed in special schools may not transfer to inclusive settings. We are aware of Slee's (1996) warning that recommendations for inclusive practice should avoid becoming 'a misleading veneer for old special educational practices' (p.29). Whilst it is easy to criticise the obstacles to inclusion which exist through the maintenance of a segregated system of special schools, we recognise that many contributions have been made to the education of pupils excluded from mainstream schools by the professionals working in them. Much of the innovative teaching practice which has influenced the raising of standards and expectation with regards to pupils with learning difficulties has its origins in special schools. The most well-documented British example can be found in the work which has assured access to the National Curriculum for pupils with severe learning difficulties (e.g. Carpenter et al., 1996; Sebba et al., 1993; Tilstone, 1991).

Research studies on inclusive education tend to be non-categorical, making it difficult to differentiate what works for whom, when and how. Part I looks at processes within mainstream schools from a school improvement perspective. The school improvement perspective on inclusion focuses on expanding a school's capacity to respond to all its pupils. However, successful inclusion also requires that teachers' views about pupils who experience difficulty are consistent with an expectation of learning and achievement. Attitudes are difficult to change, yet our experience suggests that when schools recognise that pupils respond positively to being involved in decision-making processes, increased participation in many aspects of learning is possible. Pupils need to feel wanted and respected in the classroom, and the marginalisation of pupils on the grounds that they are in some way different is a major obstacle to changing the current educational climate. Teachers who are prepared to accept that each child is an individual, and will therefore have specific needs at various times, are already making a contribution in the move towards more inclusive classrooms. By so doing they communicate to pupils that they respect them as individuals, understand that their learning needs are specific to them, and that together they should strive to gain the highest possible standards. The pupil who has a clear understanding of teacher expectations is more likely to be able to respond in ways which are appropriate to the achievement of individual targets, and to the requirements of a mainstream classroom. As has been noted elsewhere (McConkey, 1994; Tilstone,1997), special school staff will have an important role to play in changing attitudes by preparing communities to accept differences, particularly through planned personal contact. Parts I and II include chapters on curriculum, pupil participation, teaching methods, the relationship between policies of inclusion and equal opportunities, and the conditions necessary for successful inclusive practice.

We also look at systemic issues of school change and multidisciplinary teamwork, as well as conceptual issues to do with challenging behaviour and teaching and learning styles. Two chapters in Part IV consider life after the school years. The relationship between inclusive education and quality of life is explored in the final chapter. Quality of life

> is not something a person simply has or received, but something the individual actively works to create along with other people, as long as certain basic conditions are fulfilled. Living a 'good life' means that one is able to determine the course of one's own life and has the opportunity to create an existence based on one's own dreams, visions, wishes and needs.
>
> (Holm *et al.*, 1994, p.10)

The idea of participation as inclusion is a theme throughout the book. As discussed in the following chapter, inclusion is not only about attending mainstream school or getting a job. It is about the *opportunity to participate* in daily life. It is about living with *integrity* in whatever social form that might take. Christie (1989) has argued that the full inclusion of people with the most severe learning difficulties into industrialised societies is unlikely to protect them from the indignities associated with being the dependent clients of a professional class of caretakers. He suggests that inclusive living is a way of life that acknowledges the interdependence of people; a way of life where people with and without learning difficulties live and work together.

An attempt to apply this concept of inclusivity was made recently by the Committee on Students with Learning Difficulties and/or Disabilities in its report, *Inclusive Learning* (FEFC, 1996). Faced with the challenge of extending the opportunity to participate in further education to people with learning difficulties and/or disabilities, the twelve-member committee articulated an approach to learning that includes people with learning difficulties *because it is appropriate to all students*. The term 'inclusive learning' was used to emphasise redesigned provision where the needs of students with learning difficulties and/or disabilities are seen as 'cognate with those of all learners' (p.5). The term refers to the match between the needs of the learner and the demands of the course. As used in the report, inclusive learning refers to how colleges effect this match and not necessarily to whether or not a course is 'integrated'. Variations on this notion of inclusive learning are explored in Part II.

A CAVEAT

Two important areas not addressed in the text are teacher education for inclusive practice and early intervention. They are discussed briefly below.

A key issue in promoting inclusive practice must be a reappraisal of the training provided to teachers and other professionals. The pace at which we move towards inclusion will inevitably be dictated not only by legislation, but through the means by which we equip teachers to meet the more complex needs of pupils moving from special to mainstream schools. Preparation of teachers for the challenges ahead must begin with initial teacher training, and permeate through the entire profession through the provision of well-planned and delivered in-service training (Mittler, 1992). Movement towards such changes will require that institutes of higher education work in tandem with schools and LEAs to address the problems which teachers will meet in their classrooms. All teachers need to be equipped with the skills required to address special needs issues, and it is therefore essential that initial teacher training gives a higher priority to making effective changes. It has, however, been recognised (Jordan and Powell, 1995; Rose, 1997) that many existing teachers are apprehensive about teaching pupils with ever increasing degrees of complexity. It is therefore essential that a large part of the focus of future training must come from within a continuing professional development model which responds positively to teacher-led demand. The shift from a special school model of service delivery to a whole school approach for meeting special needs will require new and systematically applied models of teacher education and development (Thomas, 1997).

By taking daily life for school-aged children as our starting point we do not wish to suggest that what happens in the early years before schooling starts is unimportant. On the contrary, we know that this is a very important time and that decisions taken in the early years have implications for schooling as well as life after the school years are over. However, the focus on inclusion during these years is family centred and services to children tend to emphasise developmental rather than educational interventions. As a result, issues of inclusion take on different connotations when applied to the early years. For example, the natural environment for children under 5 is home. Unlike schooling, day care, pre-school, and other early intervention programmes are not universally available to all children. Thus, issues of access and participation are different. Families may have choices about where to send their school-aged children to school but they do not choose whether or not the children attend. Parents have a legal duty to send their children to school. In the early years, the choices a family may make about intervention are not so much influenced by legal duty as their views on childrearing, disability and its causation, change and intervention, health and healing, family and family roles, and communication and language patterns (Hanson *et al.*, 1990).

In the chapters that follow our contributors offer their ideas about meeting so-called special educational needs in ways that are consistent and true to the principle of inclusion. Various chapters examine different aspects of inclusive education with special emphasis on the needs of pupils with severe learning difficulties. Our aim has been to examine research and practice about the process of inclusive education in a real-world context of an existing network of special schools, and a largely unchanged system of mainstream schools operating in the competitive climate of marketplace reforms (Rouse and Florian, 1997). The book is divided into four parts: inclusive schooling, inclusive learning, a reconfigured role for special schools and, finally, inclusive practices for life after school.

ACKNOWLEDGEMENTS

Thanks are due to Christopher Robertson of Canterbury Christ Church College for his generous contribution to our discussion on issues pertaining to quality of life.

REFERENCES

Ainscow, M. (1997) 'Towards inclusive schooling', *British Journal of Special Education* 24(1): 3–6.

Barton, L. (ed.) (1988) *The Politics of Special Educational Needs*, London: Falmer Press.

Beveridge, S. (1996) 'Experiences of an integration link scheme: the perspectives of pupils with severe learning difficulties and their mainstream peers', *British Journal of Learning Disabilities* 24(1): 9–19.

Booth, T., Ainscow, M. and Dyson, A. (1997) 'Understanding inclusion and exclusion in the English Competitive System', *International Journal of Inclusive Education* 1(4): 337–55.

Carpenter, B., Ashdown, R. and Bovair, K. (eds) (1996) *Enabling Access: Effective Teaching and Learning for Pupils with Learning Difficulties*, London: David Fulton.

Christie, N. (1989) *Beyond Loneliness and Institutions*, Oslo: Norwegian University Press.

Cole, T. (1989) *Apart or A Part? Integration and the Growth of British Special Education*, Milton Keynes: Open University Press.

Department for Education and Employment (1994) *Code of Practice on the Identification and Assessment of Special Educational Needs*, London: HMSO.

Department for Education and Employment (1997a) *Excellence in Schools*, London: HMSO.

Department for Education and Employment (1997b) *Excellence for All Children: Meeting Special Educational Needs*, London: HMSO.

Department for Education and Science (1978) *Special Educational Needs, Report of the Committee of Enquiry into the Education of Handicapped Children and Young People* (The Warnock Report), London: HMSO.

Florian, L. (1998) 'Debating the implementation of inclusive education policies: an examination of some practical problems', *Support for Learning* 13(3): 105–8.

Further Education Funding Council (1996) *Inclusive Learning*, Report of the Learning Difficulties and/or Disabilities Committee, Coventry: FEFC.

Hanson, M. J., Lynch, E. W. and Wayman, K. I. (1990) 'Honoring the cultural diversity of families when gathering data', *Topics in Early Childhood Special Education* 10: 112–31.

Hart, S. (1996) 'Towards an inclusive Code of Practice: re-interpreting responsibility and entitlement in the staged assessment process', in L. Florian and M. Rouse (eds) *School Reform and Special Educational Needs: Anglo-American Perspectives*, Cambridge: University of Cambridge Institute of Education.

Holm, P., Holst, J. and Perlt, B. (1994) 'Co-write your own life: quality of life as discussed in the Danish context', in D. Goode (ed.) *Quality of Life for Persons with Disabilities: International Perspectives and Issues*, Cambridge, MA: Brookline Books.

Hopkins, D., West, M. and Ainscow, M. (1996) *Improving the Quality of Education for All*, London: David Fulton.

Jordan, R. and Powell, S. (1995) 'Skills without understanding: a critique of a competency based model of teacher education in relation to special needs', *British Journal of Special Education* 22(3): 120–4.

Lazerson, M. (1983) 'The origins of special education', in J. G. Chambers and W. T. Hartman (eds) *Special Education Policies: their History, Implementation and Finance*, Philadelphia: Temple University Press.

Lewis, A. (1995) *Children's Understanding of Disability*, London: Routledge.

Lindsay, G. (1997) 'Values and legislation', in G. Lindsay and D. Thompson (eds) *Values into Practice in Special Education*, London: David Fulton.

Lipsky, D. K. and Gartner, A. (1997) *Inclusion and School Reform: Transforming America's Classrooms*, Baltimore: Paul H. Brookes.

McConkey, R. (1994) *Innovations in Educating Communities about Disabilities*, Chorley: Lisieux Hall Publications.

Mittler, P. (1992) 'Preparing all initial teacher training students to teach children with special educational needs: a case study from England', *European Journal of Special Needs Education* 7(1): 1–10.

Norwich, B. (1997) *A Trend towards Inclusion: Statistics on Special School Placements and Pupils with Statements in Ordinary Schools, England 1992–96*, Bristol: Centre for Studies on Inclusive Education.

Rose, R. (1997) 'The focus of future training', *Eye Contact* 19: 5–7.

Rouse, M. and Florian, L. (1997) 'Inclusive education in the market-place', *International Journal of Inclusive Education* 1(4): 323–36.

Sebba, J. and Sachdev, D. (1997) *What Works in Inclusive Education?*, Ilford, Essex: Barnardos.

Sebba, J., Byers, R. and Rose, R. (1993) *Redefining the Whole Curriculum for Pupils with Learning Difficulties*, London: David Fulton.

Skrtic, T. (1991) *Behind Special Education: a Critical Analysis of Professional Culture and School Organisation*, Denver: Love Publishing.

Slee, R. (1996) 'Inclusive schooling in Australia? Not yet!', *Cambridge Journal of Education* 26(1): 19–32.

Thomas, G. (1997) 'A blueprint for the future: special educational needs and teacher education in the 21st century', in J. Dwyfor Davies and P. Garner (eds) *At the Crossroads: Special Educational Needs and Teacher Education*, London: David Fulton.

Tilstone, C. (ed.) (1991) *Teaching Pupils with Severe Learning Difficulties*, London: David Fulton.

Tilstone, C. (1997) 'Changing public attitudes', in B. Carpenter, R. Ashdown and K. Bovair (eds) *Enabling Access: Effective Teaching and Learning for Pupils with Learning Difficulties*, London: David Fulton.

Tomlinson, S. (1982) *The Sociology of Special Education*, London: Routledge & Kegan Paul.

UNESCO (1996) *Legislation Pertaining to Special Needs Education*, Paris: UNESCO.

Zola, I. (1989) 'The necessary universalizing of disability policy', *Millbank Quarterly* 67(2): 401–27.

Part I

Inclusive schooling

Chapter 2

Inclusive practice
What, why and how?

Lani Florian

The inclusion of pupils with learning difficulties in ordinary schools and classrooms is part of a large world-wide human rights movement which calls for the full inclusion of all people with disabilities in all aspects of life. In this chapter, Lani Florian summarises the current state of knowledge and practice on inclusive schooling for pupils with learning difficulties.

The concept of inclusive education enjoys a high profile around the world by virtue of its incorporation into the policy documents of numerous international organisations, most notably the United Nations. Standards of UN policies such as those embodied in the UN Convention on the Rights of the Child (1989), the UN Standard Rules on the Equalisation of Opportunities for Persons with Disabilities (1993) and the 1994 UNESCO Report on the education of children with disabilities (Salamanca Statement) all affirm the rights of all children to equal education without discrimination within the mainstream education system. Although this means different things in different places there is a universality to the underlying human rights philosophy of inclusion which suggests that the concept is destined to persist rather than represent the latest educational fad or bandwagon. For this reason, the study of the education of pupils with learning difficulties is rightfully placed in a context of inclusion.

Within special education, the term inclusive education has come to refer to a philosophy of education that promotes the education of all pupils in mainstream schools. The Centre for Studies of Inclusive Education articulated the principles of this philosophy as follows:

- all children have the right to learn and play together;
- children should not be devalued or discriminated against by being excluded or sent away because of their disability or learning difficulty;

- there are no legitimate reasons to separate children for the duration of their schooling. They belong together rather than need to be protected from one another.

(CSIE, 1996, p.10)

However, there is a gap between policy and implementation which must be acknowledged and addressed. How it is that there can be so much philosophical agreement on rights and yet so much divergence in practice is not well understood. Culture explains some but not all of the differences as many of the differences between policy and implementation are as much *within* as *across* cultures. The acknowledgement of rights embodied in policy and the practical implementation of that policy is confounded by many variables such as other competing policies, the struggle over limited resources, and the prescriptive and centralised nature of special education. Indeed, in an international review, Loxley and Thomas (1997) identified these among eight common themes which characterise current special education policy.

Initially in education circles, ideas about the inclusion of pupils with disabilities in mainstream classrooms began to emerge from North America in the mid to late 1980s when Canadian provinces started to develop programmes which focused on including all children with disabilities in mainstream class settings (Aefsky, 1995). In the USA, a growing awareness of the variability among states and local education authorities in their interpretation of the legal mandate to provide educational opportunities for pupils with disabilities in the least restrictive environment (i.e. the mainstream classroom) led to calls for greater understanding and generalisation of the conditions that enabled some states to educate more pupils in these settings (Danielson and Bellamy, 1989). Over the past ten years, the concept of inclusive education has been gaining momentum. The term was introduced in the UK about five years ago with the launch of annual inclusion conferences aimed at extending and refining ideas about integration (Hall, 1996).

FROM INTEGRATION TO INCLUSION: MORE THAN A CHANGE IN TERMINOLOGY

Lewis (1995) suggested two reasons why ideas about integration were in need of refinement in the UK. One is that, over time, the term integration had become too narrowly interpreted as a placement without any regard to the quality of that placement. The second and more complex reason has to do with a critique of the concept of normalisation, a key influence on integration policies throughout the world. Twenty years ago, the influential Warnock Report (DES, 1978) described the process of integration as locational, social or functional. These qualifying terms referred to the sharing of the same site by special/ordinary school provision (locational integration);

shared out-of-classroom activities (social integration); and joint participation in educational programmes (functional integration). Here, the task of integration has been about how to join in the mainstream, how to become like others. How to become like others is at the heart of the concept of normalisation. Normalisation is widely understood as 'making available to all persons with disabilities, patterns of life and conditions of everyday living which are as close as possible to or indeed the same as the regular circumstances and ways of life of society' (Nirje, 1985). For many years advocates believed that the concept of normalisation could be achieved by the process of integration. The problem was that integration, by virtue of being a process of joining, first assumed that the exclusion of people with disabilities from ordinary life was acceptable. Although a key influence on special education, the concept of normalisation has not been without critics (Jenkinson, 1997). Criticisms include the claim that the concept involves a 'denial of differentness' and asks whether the concept itself has contributed to a devaluing of people who are different (Peters, 1995).

When the International League of Societies for Persons with Mental Handicap (ILSMH) announced in April 1996 that it had adopted a new name, Inclusion International, the organisation noted: 'This new name expresses a hope for the future. It is a hope that goes beyond the hope of the past of simply integrating people. . . . The word inclusion acknowledges a history of exclusion that we have to overcome' (p.1). Two phrases confirm Lewis's observations about dissatisfaction with the term integration and provide a rationale for the new term, inclusion. These are: (1) that the term inclusion 'goes beyond simply integrating people', and (2) that it 'acknowledges a history of exclusion that must be overcome'. Overcoming a history of exclusion requires fundamental changes in thinking about 'patterns of life and conditions of everyday living'. The task for inclusion is to redefine these things so that people with disabilities are valued for who they are because of rather than despite difference.

A DEFINITION

Many definitions of inclusive education have been advanced. A selection of these definitions, presented in Table 2.1, range from 'extending the scope of ordinary schools so they can include a greater diversity of children' (Clark *et al.*, 1995, p.v) to 'a set of principles which ensures that the student with a disability is viewed as a valued and needed member of the community in every respect' (Uditsky, 1993, p.88). Some definitions focus on human interaction: for example, Forest and Pearpoint (1992) see inclusion as a way of dealing with difference while Uditsky emphasises valuing all children as members of the school community. Others (i.e. Ballard, 1995; Clark *et al.*, 1995; Rouse and Florian, 1996) adopt an institutional perspective and focus on organisational arrangements and school improvement. To date, none of the proposed definitions have gained currency in the field suggesting that a truly satisfactory definition has yet to emerge.

Table 2.1 Definitions of inclusion

Being with one another ... How we deal with diversity, How we deal with difference (Forest and Pearpoint, 1992)

Inclusive schools are diverse problem solving organisations with a common mission that emphasises learning for all students (Rouse and Florian, 1996)

Being a full member of an age-appropriate class in your local school doing the same lessons as the other pupils and it mattering if you are not there. Plus you have friends who spend time with you outside of school (Hall, 1996)

A set of principles which ensures that the student with a disability is viewed as a valued and needed member of the school community in every respect (Uditsky, 1993)

Inclusion can be understood as a move towards extending the scope of 'ordinary' schools so they can include a greater diversity of children (Clark et al., 1995)

Inclusive schools deliver a curriculum to students through organisational arrangements that are different from those used in schools that exclude some students from their regular classrooms (Ballard, 1995)

Increasing participation and decreasing exclusion from mainstream social settings (Potts, 1997)

Inclusion describes the process by which a school attempts to respond to all pupils as individuals by reconsidering its curricula organisation and provision (Sebba, 1996)

An inclusive school is one which is accepting of all children (Thomas, 1997)

Recently, it has been suggested that inclusion is 'the process of increasing participation in and decreasing exclusion from mainstream social settings' (Booth *et al.*, 1997; Potts, 1997, p.4). This is consistent with Inclusion International's more specific 1996 definition which we have adopted to guide the development of this text:

> Inclusion refers to the opportunity for persons with a disability to participate fully in all of the educational, employment, consumer, recreational, community, and domestic activities that typify everyday society.

This definition is the only one we are aware of to transcend the concept of normalisation. It does so by using language that emphasises participation over normalcy. The opportunity to participate is quite different from making available patterns of life and conditions of everyday living. Opportunity to participate implies active involvement and choice as opposed to the passive receipt of a pattern or condition that has been made available. Locational, social and functional integration are things that are made available. They are easily contrasted with inclusion, which cannot be made available because by definition it requires participation. As advocate Micheline Mason noted: 'inclusion is not something that can be done to us. It is something we have to participate in for it to be real' (Pugh and Macrae, 1995).

For pupils with learning difficulties, the full opportunity to participate in the educational activities that typify everyday society will ultimately require education reform policies that do not treat them as members of a minority group. Unfortunately, the movement for inclusive education will not change the underlying reality of an education system unable or unwilling to meet the needs of all children. To the extent that children are labelled, special education will not change as a social construction. In the meantime, teachers will have to satisfy themselves with the knowledge that a philosophy of inclusive education can be applied in mainstream schools and classrooms. Research has demonstrated that under the right conditions, positive outcomes, though difficult to achieve, are possible for all pupils.

IF INCLUSION CANNOT BE MADE AVAILABLE, HOW CAN IT BE ACHIEVED? A SUMMARY OF CURRENT RESEARCH AND A REVIEW OF REVIEWS

Research on inclusive education (Katsiyannis et al., 1995; O'Hanlon, 1995) suggests that its meaning may be contextual. In other words, the meaning will take different forms in various places depending on the situation. Differences in context result in different pictures of inclusive education despite the fact that many jurisdictions base arguments for inclusive education on human rights. However, despite these differences, there is a great deal of agreement in the literature about practice.

Giangreco (1997) identified common features of schools where inclusive education is reported to be thriving. These features are:

- collaborative teamwork;
- a shared framework;
- family involvement;
- general educator ownership;
- clear role relationships among professionals;
- effective use of support staff;
- meaningful Individual Education Plans (IEPs);
- procedures for evaluating effectiveness.

This is consistent with other research (i.e. Hopkins et al., 1996; Lipsky and

Gartner, 1997; Rouse and Florian, 1996; Sebba, 1996) which links inclusive education to the development of effective schools. The emphasis is on changing school structures so that schools are able to accommodate a greater range of pupils.

In general, the research on inclusive education does not differentiate effects among different groups of pupils. Pupils with learning difficulties may be included in studies of inclusive practice but less frequently are they the focus of the study. Recently, two reviews summarising research on integration and inclusion for pupils with severe learning difficulties appeared in the special education literature. One (Farrell, 1997) involved a wide-ranging review of research on the effects of integration on children with severe learning difficulties (SLD). The second (Hunt and Goetz, 1997) was more narrowly focused on research investigations that included the full-time placement of children with severe disabilities in mainstream schools. Obviously, the parameters the reviewers set themselves resulted in the identification of different sets of studies for review but, surprisingly, there was no overlap on references between the two reviews.

Both Farrell and Hunt and Goetz found a diversity of methodologies utilised in the studies; however, the focus of the reviews was different. Hunt and Goetz were interested in evaluating the state of research on inclusion and pupils with severe disabilities. Farrell wanted to examine selected areas of the research literature because they were thought to be relevant to inclusive education. He reviewed the research on:

- the role of support workers in facilitating integration;
- effect of integration on communication and linguistic interaction;
- relevance of curriculum differentiation;
- effects of integration on children without disabilities;
- attitudes of mainstream teachers and LEA staff towards integration.

Hunt and Goetz identified practices which emerged from triangulation across studies. These were:

- parent perceptions of the pursuit and impact of inclusive educational placement;
- issues and practices in inclusive schools and classrooms;
- educational achievement outcomes in inclusive classrooms;
- social relationships and friendships in inclusive settings;
- the cost of inclusive educational placement.

It is interesting to note the agreement on areas of practice across the two reviews. The ways in which people work together to adapt the curriculum, their attitudes towards pupils with learning difficulties and concern about the social and academic outcomes for all pupils emerge in both reviews as critical features of inclusive education.

Although Farrell did not review research on the effects of parental involvement, Hunt and Goetz found it to be a major force in the development of inclusive options for pupils with SLD. They reviewed several studies which found the willingness of parents to 'take on the system' as leading to the establishment of inclusive education as a placement option.

Interesting issues and practices in inclusive schools and classrooms emerged from the reviews. Hunt and Goetz found these centred on the development of positive attitudes among staff, a positive identity among pupils and staff consensus on the value that all children belong in mainstream schools. Farrell's review suggested there may be a relationship between the severity of the disability and attitude although teachers who had experience working with pupils with SLD tended to be more positive.

Another common practice identified by Hunt and Goetz involves a reconceptualisation of teaching roles and responsibilities to enable collaborative teaming for curriculum development and instruction. To accept the idea that inclusion represents the opportunity to participate rather than something that can be made available requires changes in professional thinking and practice. Just as disabled people are asking philosophical questions about why they should accept definitions developed and imposed on them by others, professionals must begin the process of examining their own role in imposing limits on the ways people with disabilities exist in the world. Clarity about professional identity and future mission requires a consideration of the extent to which the separate system of special education itself has disabling effects. John has argued that it

> is one of the main channels for disseminating the predominant ablebodied/minded perception of the world and ensuring that disabled school leavers are socially immature and isolated. This isolation results in passive acceptance of social discrimination, lack of skills in facing the tasks of adulthood and ignorance about the main social issues of the times. All this reinforces the 'eternal children' myth and ensures at the same time disabled school leavers lack the skills for overcoming the myth.
>
> (cited in Oliver, 1988, p.24)

Clearly, it is the reconceptualisation of teaching roles and responsibilities that is directly relevant to the idea of inclusion as an opportunity to participate for pupils with learning difficulties. Farrell found the role of support staff to be key.

> The role of support staff is both complex and crucial . . . if support workers devote their time to the delivery of a carefully planned individual programme . . . opportunities for social interaction with their

peer group become reduced. . . . However, if the support worker devotes time to foster social interaction, this may leave less time for individual teaching. . . . If the child with SLD is simply placed with a group of mainstream children, he or she may be ignored, if the support worker 'joins in', this can influence the 'naturalness' of the interaction.

(p.10)

When teachers and other support staff are able to work together, for example in co-teaching situations, problems associated with the severity of the learning difficulty and the relevance of the curriculum are diminished. But, as Farrell pointed out, school staff need training and support to take on these new roles and responsibilities.

The scant literature on the effects of inclusive education for pupils with learning difficulties on their educational achievement is equivocal. Though it is not possible to generalise from the research to date, a 'no-difference' finding seems to characterise it. The reported 'no-difference' outcome of the Hunt and Goetz review is consistent with Hegarty's (1993) international review of the research on academic and social benefits of integration. He also found no clear-cut academic advantage for mainstream education. However, it is important to bear in mind that the research base is small and it is not yet possible to rule out the effects of confounding variables which have not been subject to analysis. Thus far, no-difference findings have been interpreted as pro inclusion since the impetus for the movement is grounded in human rights. As a result, the absence of differences in educational achievement for pupils with learning difficulties who are placed in inclusive classrooms when compared with the achievement of those in traditional special education programmes is considered supportive of inclusive education.

The social relationships and friendships of pupils with SLD in inclusive settings has received more attention from researchers. Farrell found a majority of studies reported some degree of social acceptance by non-disabled peers. An even more positive picture emerged from the Hunt and Goetz review. Through case study analyses of friendship, researchers reported that when parents of pupils without disabilities and their teachers were supportive of inclusive education, friendships based on reciprocity (as opposed to the 'tutorial' relationship) were possible. Studies using ratings of social competence reported that levels of acceptance of pupils with SLD varied despite the level of social competence, suggesting that some children with disabilities are more popular than others. Farrell found younger and more able children were more likely to be successfully included. However, the Hunt and Goetz review revealed certain interventions appear promising in their power to increase social interaction and friendship among pupils with SLD and their peers without disabilities. This is an important finding because Farrell's review concluded that the 'degree of social and linguistic interaction between the children with SLD and their peers in integrated settings is limited and tends to be didactic and one way in nature' (p.10). Interventions which enhance participation are essential.

The cost of inclusive education is an important and difficult area to research. Hunt and Goetz argue that any analysis of cost should include a consideration of effects on pupils. In other words, if, as it is possible to argue from this review, children with SLD are, at the very least, no worse off academically, and have the opportunity to participate in mutually satisfying interpersonal relationships with peers, then the cost of inclusive education represents good value for money.

Although Farrell concluded that some form of segregated provision would always be necessary, a careful reading of his review shows that he is referring specifically to limitations on the extent to which a curriculum can be differentiated and relevant. He does not argue for the continued segregation of children in special schools. Rather, he says *full functional integration* can never be a viable option for all children with SLD throughout their school lives' (p.11). Farrell argues that a relevant curriculum for a child with profound and multiple learning difficulties (PMLD), for example, will necessarily emphasise subjects not included in the National Curriculum. The segregated provision that Farrell refers to is with respect to the curriculum and not the location in which the curriculum is delivered. Indeed, he concludes with a plea for resource-based models of integration as part of what mainstream schools offer to enable 'full-time integration for some children while providing segregated education with opportunities for social integration for children with profound and multiple difficulties' (p.11). McInnes (1988) concurs. He argues that the local school can be a viable option for pupils with multisensory impairments if the right support system is established. In his examples, support systems depend on access to specialist teachers who understand the effects of multisensory deprivation on learning and can develop interventions. The extent to which the environmental conditions of the ordinary classroom must be adjusted for these pupils may not be possible at all times. Environments which facilitate communication, and promote cognitive development and concept formation, must also be available.

CONDITIONS

The teaching methods and practices associated with the provision of inclusive education are easier to identify than to implement on a wide scale. Despite a great deal of agreement about the practice of inclusive education difficulties in doing so remain. Giangreco (1997) has noted that the criticisms of inclusive education are often criticisms of poor quality or partial implementation efforts. It is also possible that the teaching methods available to support inclusive education are neither sufficiently refined nor understood to overcome the variability in implementation efforts. For example, it is possible to interpret some of Farrell's findings in terms of a failure properly to implement inclusive education practices. Though 'effective use of support staff' was identified as a commonly agreed practice in inclusive education Farrell concluded this was a difficult area particularly with respect to fostering interaction with non-disabled peers. In his example quoted above, it is clear that if the support worker lacks skill in facilitating interaction then the 'naturalness' of the interaction between the children will be contaminated. It is the lack of skill on the part of the support worker rather than his or her role that results in a misplaced criticism about inclusive education.

Thus, it may be possible that there are a set of conditions which form the basis of inclusive education for pupils with learning difficulties. Such conditions might include:

- an opportunity for pupil participation in the decision-making process;
- a positive attitude about the learning abilities of all pupils;
- teacher knowledge about learning difficulties;
- skilled application of specific instructional methods;
- parent and teacher support.

This review suggests that each of these conditions is necessary but not solely sufficient for inclusive education. All must be in place to avoid implementation failure. For example, a positive attitude alone is not sufficient to achieve inclusive education, though it is a necessary condition. An unskilled teacher, however open minded and willing to try, will fail to provide an appropriate education for pupils with learning difficulties or other special educational needs if he or she is not supported by more experienced colleagues. Likewise, skill in the use of various teaching methods is insufficient without knowledge of pupils' learning difficulties and the belief that such pupils can learn.

Programmes that meet only some of these conditions run the risk of partial implementation and possible failure. Of course, it is possible that programmes that do meet these conditions may also fail, but if the lessons from the research can be applied, the chances are far more in favour of success.

Accepting the idea that inclusion is about participation requires the development of methods which ensure the meaningful participation of people with learning difficulties in the decision-making process. It also requires that the process emphasises participation over placement.

A fundamental respect for the individual must underlie any intervention. As people with disabilities challenge the definitions developed and imposed on them by others, professionals must be prepared for choices that may not be their own. A pupil with a learning difficulty may choose to associate with other pupils with learning difficulties. It is not uncommon for people, as they get older, to identify with others like themselves. It is the acceptance of difference that is the hallmark of inclusive practice.

The relationship between identification with a group and inclusion has been documented by Campbell and Oliver (1996) in their history of the disabled people's movement in Britain. The achievement of inclusive schooling for pupils with learning difficulties has been greatly assisted by the momentum generated by the movement as it becomes increasingly better organised and sophisticated. Although the movement has been criticised for failing to include people with learning difficulties, efforts are being made to address this:

> Through their very open and blunt criticisms about the ways in which we can be exclusive, about the way we run our organisation and the ways we can be quite cliquey, People First are challenging us to continue to open up. We started very exclusively and perhaps we needed to be exclusive at that time. Some people find this opening up very hard, but this is the process of inclusion; it's the process of becoming a mass democratic movement of all disabled people, and not just a bunch of white wheelchair users!
>
> (Campbell and Oliver, 1996, p.203)

CONCLUSION

The critique of the concept of normalisation provides a challenge to the status quo requiring changes in thinking and practice. This chapter has explored this challenge by clarifying the difference between integration and inclusion; elaborating on the meaning of 'opportunity to participate'; and reviewing what is know about the provision of inclusive education for pupils with learning difficulties. A set of conditions necessary to promote inclusive practice were identified to aid implementation efforts and help to bridge the gap between the acceptance of equal rights for all as embodied in policy and the actual achievement of inclusive education.

The literature reviewed here suggests a set of necessary but not sufficient conditions must be in place for the successful implementation of inclusive education policies. These are: an opportunity for pupil participation in the decision-making process, a positive attitude about the learning abilities of all pupils, teacher knowledge about learning difficulties, skilled application of specific instructional methods, and parent and teacher support. To the extent that barriers such as other education laws are incompatible with the establishment of these conditions in mainstream schools (Rouse and Florian, 1997), the range of provision currently available will continue to provide educational opportunity for pupils with learning difficulties. Though it is easy to understand how the separate system of special education evolved in response to the exclusionary practices of schooling, it is much harder to see how current practice depends on a set of practices which require another form of exclusion. To understand this it is necessary to remember that the creation of special education as a separate system was in part a response to the exclusion of pupils with disabilities from mainstream schools. Thus, special education as an exclusive field of study originated in an act of discrimination which now supports a profession. Acknowledging this is a fundamental requirement in moving the debate about inclusive education forward. Consideration of the extent to which special education policy itself leads to possible pupil exclusion, may be useful in illuminating the assumptions underlying and defining the way services are delivered. Practice can then be re-examined in light of the knowledge produced by this line of investigation.

In this way, the development of practice can become a vehicle for change. Thirty years ago innovative professionals were able to demonstrate that all pupils could learn despite policies excluding certain children from school. Though the methods that were developed adhered to a behavioural model emphasising a structural, teacher-directed approach to instruction (Rosenberg and Jackson, 1988), the contribution of special education to the development of instructional methods with applicability to all learners represented a significant advance in extending the right to education for all. Today the same level of innovation is required to demonstrate how all children can learn together. Ainscow (1997) has called upon the profession to develop new ways of working so as to enhance the capacity of mainstream schools to accommodate successfully increasing levels of student diversity.

In the chapters that follow some of the difficult implementation and practical problems being tackled by practitioners committed to the development of more inclusive education are explored in more depth.

REFERENCES

Aefsky, F. (1995) *Inclusion Confusion*, Thousand Oaks, CA: Corwin Press.

Ainscow, M. (1997) 'Towards inclusive schooling', *British Journal of Special Education* 24(1): 3–6.

Ballard, K. (1995) 'Inclusion, paradigms, power and participation', in C. Clark, A. Dyson and A. Milward (eds) *Towards Inclusive Schools?*, London: David Fulton.

Booth, T., Ainscow, M. and Dyson, A. (1997) 'Understanding inclusion and exclusion in the English competitive education system', *International Journal of Inclusive Education* 1(4): 337–55.

Campbell, J. and Oliver, M. (1996) *Disability Politics: Understanding Our Past, Changing Our Future*, London: Routledge.

Centre for the Study of Inclusive Education (1996) *Developing an Inclusive Policy for Your School: a CSIE Guide*, Bristol: CSIE.

Clark, C., Dyson, A. and Milward, A. (1995) *Towards Inclusive Schools?*, London: David Fulton.

Danielson, L. C. and Bellamy, G. T. (1989) 'State variation in placement of children with handicaps in segregated environments', *Exceptional Children* 55: 448–55.

Department for Education and Science (1978) *Special Educational Needs. Report of the Committee of Enquiry into the Education of Handicapped Children and Young People (The Warnock Report)*, London: HMSO.

Farrell, P. (1997) 'The integration of children with severe learning difficulties: a review of the recent literature', *Journal of Applied Research in Intellectual Disabilities* 10(1): 1–14.

Forest, M. and Pearpoint, J. (1992) 'Putting all kids on the MAP', *Educational Leadership* 50(2): 26–31.

Giangreco, M. F. (1997) 'Key lessons learned about inclusive education: summary of the 1996 Schonell Memorial Lecture', *International Journal of Disability, Development and Education* 44(3): 193–206.

Hall, J. (1996) 'Integration, inclusion, – what does it all mean?', in J. Coupe O'Kane and J. Goldbart (eds) *Whose Choice? Contentious Issues for Those Working with People with Learning Difficulties*, London: David Fulton.

Hegarty, S. (1993) 'Reviewing the literature on integration', *European Journal of Special Needs Education* 8(3): 194–200.

Hopkins, D., West, M. and Ainscow, M. (1996) *Improving the Quality of Education for All: Progress and Challenge*, London: David Fulton.

Hunt, P. and Goetz, L. (1997) 'Research on inclusive educational programs, practices and outcomes for students with severe disabilities', *The Journal of Special Education* 31(1): 3–29.

Inclusion International (1996, April) *Inclusion: News from Inclusion International*, Brussels: Inclusion International.

Jenkinson, J. C. (1997) *Mainstream or Special? Educating Students with Disabilities*, London: Routledge.

Katsiyannis, A., Conderman, G. and Franks, D. J. (1995) 'State practices on inclusion: a national review', *Remedial and Special Education* 16(5): 279–87.

Lewis, A. (1995) *Children's Understanding of Disability*, London: Routledge.

Lipsky, D. K. and Gartner, A. (1997) *Inclusion and School Reform: Transforming America's Classrooms*, Baltimore: Paul H. Brookes.

Loxley, A. and Thomas, G. (1997) 'From inclusive policy to the exclusive real world: an international review', *Disability and Society* 12(2): 273–91.

McInnes, J. (1988) *Integration*, Deaf–Blind Education (Jan–Jun), 7–12.

Nirje, B. (1985) 'The basis and logic of the normalisation principle', *Australia and New Zealand Journal of Developmental Disabilities* 11: 65–8.

O'Hanlon, C. (1995) *Inclusive Education in Europe*, London: David Fulton.

Oliver, M. (1988) 'The social and political context of educational policy: the case of special needs', in L. Barton (ed.) *The Politics of Special Educational Needs*, London: Falmer Press.

Peters, S. (1995) 'Disability baggage: changing the educational research terrain', in P. Clough and L. Barton (eds) *Making Difficulties: Research and the Construction of SEN*, London: Paul Chapman.

Potts, P. (1997) 'Developing a collaborative approach to the study of inclusive education in more than one country', Paper presented to the European Conference on Educational Research, Frankfurt am Main, September

Pugh, A. (Producer) and Macrae, I. (Series Editor) (1995) *Old School Ties* [Film], London: BBC Disability Programmes Unit.

Rosenberg, M. and Jackson, L. (1988) 'Theoretical models and special education: the impact of varying world views on service delivery and research', *Remedial and Special Education* 9(3): 26–34.

Rouse, M. and Florian, L. (1996) 'Effective inclusive schools: a study in two countries', *Cambridge Journal of Education* 26(1): 71–85.

Rouse, M. and Florian, L. (1997) 'Inclusive education in the marketplace', *International Journal of Inclusive Education* 1(4): 323–36.

Sebba, J. (1996, Spring/Summer) *Developing Inclusive Schools*, University of Cambridge Institute of Education, No.31, p.3.

Thomas, G. (1997) 'Inclusive schools for an inclusive society', *British Journal of Special Education* 24(3): 103–7.

Uditsky, B. (1993) 'From integration to inclusion: the Canadian experience', in R. Slee (ed.) *Is There a Desk with My Name on It? The Politics of Integration,* London: Falmer Press.

United Nations (1989) *Convention on the Rights of the Child*, New York: UN.

United Nations (1993) *Standard Rules on the Equalisation of Opportunities for Persons with Disabilities*, New York: UN.

United Nations Educational, Scientific and Cultural Organisation (1994) *The Salamanca Statement and Framework for Action on Special Needs Education*, Paris: UNESCO.

Chapter 3

The curriculum

A vehicle for inclusion or a lever for exclusion?

Richard Rose

In this chapter, Richard Rose argues that the ways in which schools view and develop their curriculum will invariably have a major impact upon progress towards inclusion. The National Curriculum is seen as having brought benefits to pupils with special educational needs, but when interpreted in narrow terms it can become a restricting factor which inhibits inclusive practice.

The British government's 1997 Green Paper *Excellence for All Children* emphasises the commitment of national government to move towards increased inclusion. An unequivocal statement at the start of Chapter 4 of this document states

> We want to see more pupils with SEN included within mainstream primary and secondary schools. We support the United Nations Educational, Scientific and Cultural Organisation (UNESCO) Salamanca World Statement on Special Needs Education 1994. This calls on governments to adopt the principle of inclusive education, enrolling all children in regular schools, unless there are compelling reasons for doing otherwise. That implies the progressive extension of the capacity of mainstream schools to provide for children with a wide range of needs.

The document goes on to make recommendations for the actions which LEAs should consider taking, in order to promote and increase opportunities for inclusion. These include a radical reappraisal of the role to be played by special schools, the targeting of existing special needs funds allocated to increase inclusive opportunities, and the registration of all pupils on to the roll of a mainstream school, even where these pupils will receive substantial parts of their education in a special school. Many of the initiatives outlined are to be welcomed, though teachers are understandably concerned with regards to where the funding for change, and the obvious need for additional training, are to be found. This is clearly an area of major concern, yet if the Green Paper demonstrates a major significant weakness, it is in its failure to address the fact that many schools are as yet unable, and in a number of instances unprepared, to provide an appropriate curriculum model which will encourage inclusion. Of all the areas of change which are required for the promotion of inclusion, it is that of attitude which will provide the greatest obstacle.

It is now more than ten years since the introduction of the National Curriculum in England and Wales, and still the debate surrounding its appropriateness and accessibility for pupils with special educational needs continues. If a significant move towards greater inclusion is to be achieved, it must be accompanied by a clear statement of curriculum intent, and an understanding of pupil entitlement which reinforces the rights of all pupils to participate fully in every aspect of school life. Schools have, with good reason, identified legislation fatigue as a major contributor to poor morale within the teaching profession. In recent years staff in schools have been confronted with changes to most of the central tenets of traditional practice, and have been required to respond to a torrent of new initiatives. However, it may reasonably be argued that whilst these changes have caused a certain reluctance amongst some teachers to take on further development, the curriculum structures which are now in place may ultimately make the transition towards inclusive practice much easier. The principle of an entitlement of all pupils to a curriculum which is broad, balanced and well differentiated, and which includes the National Curriculum, has been hard won. For the first time within the education system of England and Wales we have a recognition that all pupils have the right to receive a curriculum which contains some common elements.

Ironically some of the greatest innovation in providing inclusive educational practice in the area of curriculum development has come from within special schools (Fagg et al., 1990; Carpenter, 1995; Byers and Rose, 1996; Ouvry and Saunders, 1996), but it is still possible to find teachers and indeed whole school staff who advocate a curriculum for pupils with special needs which is separate from that which is regarded as an entitlement to all other pupils. If this course of action were to be taken its likely conclusion would be an even greater distancing of pupils in special schools from the mainstream model of provision, and a general slowing down of the principle of inclusion which recognises the right of all pupils to take their place as equals in society. Similarly, if pupils within special schools are not provided with opportunities to address significant elements of the same curriculum as that being provided to their mainstream peers, it restricts the likelihood of those pupils ever making a successful transition into the mainstream. Colleagues who continue to proclaim the merits of a curriculum which is divorced from that which is being provided to the majority of the school population will need to consider with the greatest care the position which they adopt within the continuing inclusion debate.

It would, however, be fatuous to claim that the National Curriculum was designed with a clear view of the needs of pupils with special educational needs in mind. Indeed, it is only as a direct result of the commitment and professionalism of teachers and others working within schools that the National Curriculum has been so successfully adapted and introduced. The wealth of high-quality teaching resources which have been developed to present subjects such as technology, geography and history, which were seldom delivered in depth in the majority of primary schools, has been advanced entirely through the innovation and modifications made by teachers. Even now, after a revision which did make bold efforts in easing access, and after a wealth of publications which give practical advice on adaptation and application (Ashdown *et al.*, 1991; Lewis, 1995; Sebba, 1995a; 1995b; Carpenter *et al.*, 1996; Rose *et al.*, 1996), it is true to say that teachers are continuing to wrestle with the difficulties which confront them in delivering some aspects of National Curriculum content. This being the case, how should we view the curriculum for pupils with special educational needs, and in what ways can it become a positive vehicle for the promotion of inclusion?

WHAT IS AN APPROPRIATE CURRICULUM?

At the heart of any debate concerning the curriculum and its influence upon inclusion must be an understanding of what it is that we expect to achieve through its implementation. The curriculum should not be viewed as an end in itself, but rather as the framework through which we provide a vehicle for learning. A clear definition of curriculum intent must be established before we can begin to address the content which may enable us to move towards meeting the needs of all pupils. The discussion document *A View of the Curriculum*, written by Her Majesty's Inspectorate (HMI) (1980), recognised two juxtaposed requirements of curriculum development. Firstly, it stated the need to reflect the broad aims of education which should apply to all children, no matter what their abilities and needs, and irrespective of the type of school attended. Secondly, the curriculum must recognise the differences in abilities, aptitudes and needs of each individual pupil. The effective curriculum will be the one which not only allows for these differences, but which also enables each pupil to reach his or her potential through a process of collaborative learning, within a school which celebrates the whole range of its pupils' needs. Schools which endeavour to create a climate suitable for inclusion will need to achieve a curriculum balance which addresses the dual purposes described by HMI. Such a demand obviously requires an understanding of the subject content which a school intends to provide. It can be argued as equally important that teachers will need to have an understanding of the ways in which pupils learn, an appropriate structure within which to work, and a variety of strategies and approaches to deliver the curriculum to all pupils. Many of the arguments which have surrounded the relevance, or otherwise, of the National Curriculum have focused upon content and have chosen to ignore the issues of learning and pedagogy. In addressing the two strands identified by HMI, which can be described as the generic curriculum base and the focus upon the individual pupil, teachers will need to make decisions about content, structure and delivery in relation to their own specific school or class population. The decisions which teachers make will inevitably dictate the school's approach to inclusion. As Sebba and Sachdev state: 'Classroom teaching is at the heart of inclusive practice as it directly impinges on every pupil' (1997, p.36).

The promotion of inclusion will depend greatly upon the strategies which teachers adopt to ensure that all pupils participate fully in learning for as much of the time as is possible (see Chapter 9 by Geoff Read). An individual teacher who is not committed to the principles of inclusion has the potential to undermine the development of inclusion throughout the school.

The vital role of the teacher is a theme taken up by Evans (1997) who, in recognising the critical influence of curriculum structure on the development of inclusive approaches, believes that the functional integration of pupils with special educational needs into mainstream classes will not be achieved without considerable curriculum modification. He views the curriculum in broad terms, and in particular focuses upon the need for attitudinal consistency which regards all pupils in positive terms. Each teacher in every school must begin to accept responsibility for a full range of pupil needs and abilities. Evans affirms that: 'A key component of this thinking is that all students are on a continuum of learning ability. That is, from an educational perspective no qualitative distinction is made between the disabled and non-disabled' (Evans, 1997, p.130).

Evans recognises that changes in attitude will not be easily achieved, and suggests that the whole school climate needs to be addressed as a means of influencing the approaches of individual teachers. The model which he presents builds upon the need for whole staff development which addresses the school curriculum at both a philosophical and a practical level. This reinforces the assertion of the effective schools movement that inclusion will be most successful in those schools which define a culture for school improvement which is shared by and values the whole school community (Stoll, 1991; Rouse and Florian, 1996; Ainscow, 1996; 1997).

If the curriculum is to be seen as a positive force in the movement towards inclusion, schools will need guidance with regards to the ways in which they can make positive changes to provide a framework which meets those requirements as described by HMI (above). Curriculum content, structure and delivery will need to provide a focus for discussion with a commitment to take the necessary actions to ensure that all pupils are provided with equal opportunities to learn at a pace which is consistent with their individual needs.

CURRICULUM CONTENT AND STRUCTURE

Williams (1993), in reviewing the factors which determined the successful integration of pupils with moderate learning difficulties into mainstream classes, stated that, if a child was able to access the same curriculum as his or her peers, a major obstacle to mainstreaming would be removed. It is certainly true to say that prior to the introduction of the National Curriculum, many pupils who received their education in special schools worked within a curriculum the content of which was far removed from that provided in mainstream schools. The fact that the majority of special schools are now working within curricula structures which have embraced the National Curriculum should in theory make for a smoother transition of pupils between the special and mainstream sectors. However, it would be nonsense to argue that the introduction of the National Curriculum, and the accompanying notion of entitlement, automatically make for the easier inclusion of pupils into mainstream classes. It would be similarly misleading to suggest that the National Curriculum in its current format is suitable to address the whole needs of all pupils. Indeed, it has been suggested (Peter, 1989) that the rigidity of the National Curriculum structure may inhibit the flexibility required, and the time available, to provide the content which may be deemed necessary to address the specific needs of individual pupils. During the next round of National Curriculum change it will be necessary to ensure that the issue of balance is revisited, and that the original principles outlined in Curriculum Guidance 3 (NCC, 1990) are brought back to the centre of discussion.

In an effort to meet the requirements of the National Curriculum schools have placed an emphasis in their development upon the core and other foundation subjects. Such a move has been understandable, particularly when considering the political emphasis which has been placed upon assessment and reporting within these areas. The notion of school success measured in terms of National Curriculum performance has been largely endorsed by the inspection focus of the Office for Standards in Education (Ofsted) and through the narrowly perceived priorities of politicians. The message which is often conveyed by political leaders, and endorsed by the media, is that the successful school is the one which has achieved good results in relation to National Curriculum requirements. This in turn has prompted an increased competitiveness amongst schools, particularly those who are pleased to trumpet the number of passes achieved at level C or above in examinations at the end of statutory schooling. Little credence has been given to the diversity of population within schools which makes the validity and use of league tables highly questionable. With the promotion of such a climate in our schools, it is hardly surprising that the whole curriculum model which was originally intended when the 1989 Education Act was introduced has been lost. The current climate is such that mainstream schools, with one eye on the local and national league tables, are disinclined to admit pupils whose performance may have an adverse effect upon assessment results. The implications of this situation for the promotion of inclusion are a matter for concern.

If inclusive practice is to be encouraged, the balance of curriculum content will need to be carefully reviewed to address the needs of the pupils in each individual school. Curriculum Guidance 3 (NCC, 1990, p.1) defined the whole curriculum as comprising:

- the ten subjects of the National Curriculum;
- religious education;
- additional subjects beyond the National Curriculum;
- an accepted range of cross-curricular elements;
- extra-curricular activities;
- the spirit and ethos of the school;
- effective teaching methodology;
- efficient and effective management of the curriculum and the school.

Pressure to apply the National Curriculum has resulted in many schools addressing the ten subjects and religious education in such a way that the importance of the other curricular elements has been diluted. For many pupils, including those who have special educational needs, establishing a balance may demand that greater attention is paid to those parts of the curriculum which lie outside of the core and foundation subjects. In welcoming the Dearing review of the National Curriculum in 1994, Richard Byers wrote:

> it will be up to teachers, curriculum co-ordinators and those charged with the responsibility of supporting development in schools to see that the emphasis does not swing entirely in the direction of National Curriculum content and away from whole curriculum issues. Pupils' personal and social development: the cross curricular skills, themes and dimensions; methodological and practice-related notions like group work and problem solving must continue to be seen as being of prime importance.
>
> (Byers, 1994, p.95)

The extent to which this objective has been achieved has varied from school to school, and the approaches adopted have often been influenced as much by the pressures exerted by a competitive marketplace and the interpretations of Ofsted as by the school's own convictions and beliefs.

The National Curriculum has undoubtedly brought advantages to pupils with special educational needs. Many pupils who previously received the narrowest of curricula diets are now experiencing subjects which had been denied to them, and are demonstrating their abilities to assimilate knowledge and apply a wider range of skills. However, in the promotion of inclusion, schools need to examine the content of each subject in order to match this with care to the needs of each individual pupil. Carpenter (1995) has argued that meeting the needs of individual pupils through the process of curriculum delivery holds the key to successful inclusion. It may well be, for example, that for the pupil with special needs attending a science lesson, the established learning priorities may be as much about his or her ability to work collaboratively with a group of peers as it is about achieving a science-focused target. Similarly for a pupil in an art lesson, an individual target may concentrate upon developing fine motor control using a paint brush rather than judging success solely in terms of a finished product. This is not to suggest that teachers should not challenge pupils in relation to the subject content. The skilled teacher of pupils with special educational needs will be the one who is able to make judgements with regards to the fine balance between a focus upon subject content and individual need. Such a teacher will be in a position to develop inclusive practice which extends the opportunities provided to the pupil with special educational needs, whilst at the same time addressing those needs through careful planning in relation to individual targets.

The promotion of such an approach will require a radical shift in the working practices of some schools whose concern has centred more upon outcomes than on the quality of learning experiences provided to all pupils. However, where schools have adopted planning approaches which have integrated targets for addressing the needs of individual pupils within schemes of work, the depth of analysis which this has required has had major benefits for all pupils. Schools have been required to consider the content of the subject to be taught, but have given equal consideration to the relationship of this subject to other curriculum areas such as communication skills or personal and social education (see Chapter 4 by Richard Byers). Furthermore, where these schools have implemented effective monitoring procedures which have analysed both the achievements of pupils and the quality of learning experiences provided to them, it has been shown that they are able to demonstrate an appropriate pace of progress being made by pupils with the most significant special educational needs (Rose and Parsons, 1998; Rose and Wilson, 1998).

CURRICULUM DELIVERY

Whilst access to appropriate content may be seen as of major importance in the promotion of inclusion, this must be accompanied by the application of approaches which ensure effective curriculum delivery. Teachers need to give time in considering how they can best provide effective access for pupils with special needs, but in addition to this the teaching methods deployed need to be well matched to both the subject and the needs of the individual.

The use of classroom support to enable pupils with special educational needs to access mainstream lessons has been a traditional route by which the inclusion of pupils has been achieved, yet this is an area fraught with possible dangers. Welding (1996) has described how support teachers can be successfully used to ensure pupil access and the development of learning confidence. It can, however, be argued that such in-class support where inappropriately used can take the responsibility for management of the pupil away from the class teacher, thus perpetuating the focus upon the special needs of the pupil. In such cases the use of classroom support, far from being a means of promoting inclusion, can become a tool for isolation and exclusion. Carefully planned support which is provided at key times, and has a well-identified purpose of ensuring access and understanding, can enable pupils to participate in the regular school classroom. This contrasts with a system in which the pupil becomes dependent upon the support, and where the class teacher abdicates responsibility for management of the pupil with special educational needs. A common complaint made by special needs co-ordinators in secondary schools is that they are expected to support pupils in classes where they themselves have minimal subject knowledge. Unless the subject teacher accepts responsibility for collaboration with the support teacher in the provision of appropriate methods of access, the pupil may well be denied the curriculum opportunities to which he or she is entitled. Dyson (1994) has put forward a strong argument for changing the nature of support for pupils by suggesting that school improvement strategies which ensure that all teachers accept total responsibility for the full range of pupils in their classrooms would enable teachers to concentrate upon the individual needs of all pupils. Such a move would certainly take us a step nearer to inclusion; however, he is aware that before we reach this stage there is a need for further training and a greater clarification of curriculum expectations with regard to the needs of all pupils.

The role of all teachers in delivering an effective curriculum for pupils with special educational needs is one which will continue to provide fuel for debate. The strategies which have been deemed likely to provide success have received widespread coverage in the education literature. In particular, much has been written about approaches to differentiation (Gross, 1993; Lewis, 1995) and its importance in enabling access for pupils with special educational needs. In many schools, teachers have become proficient in considering how best to adapt and modify materials and approaches to ensure that all pupils can participate fully in lessons. However, there are still schools in which, far from being a supportive mechanism, differentiation comes close to being a discriminative practice. Hart (1992) has expressed her concerns that in some instances differentiation can become a misnomer for the constant withdrawal of pupils from the mainstream of classroom activities. The substitution of different and less demanding tasks which appear to have pupil occupation as a primary objective, and remove him or her from the activities being undertaken by others in the class, denies the pupil a right of access to the curriculum. Lewis (1995) has demonstrated how a wide range of strategies can be used according to the needs of the pupil, the nature of the activity, the context in which it is taught and the desired outcomes. There are occasions in some schools when the only approach to differentiation appears to be through the provision of a modified worksheet. Schools which view differentiation in narrow terms are limiting opportunities for inclusion. There is a need to consider differentiation in direct relation to teaching approaches based upon a careful analysis of pupil learning styles (see Chapter 9 by Geoff Read).

In her more recent work, Hart (1996) has considered an analytical approach to examining the matching of teaching approaches to pupils' learning needs. She advocates positive intervention in considering the individual needs of pupils by identifying deficiencies in a pupil's functioning, or something missed through prior experiences, or restricting in the learning environment, which can be addressed by the teacher. This she describes as *diagnostic thinking*, which enables the teacher to address those particular pupil needs which are remediable and which through intervention can be dealt with in a way which impacts upon pupil achievement. In moving the differentiation debate forward, Hart provides further positive suggestions for ways in which structured approaches to assessment can enable teachers to identify pupil-preferred learning styles and to plan strategies in line with these. This contrasts with many of the traditional approaches to differentiation, which far from beginning with an analysis of pupil needs tend to focus upon the activity and the means by which the pupil can be 'fitted in'. This part of Hart's approach, described as *differential thinking*, provides the teacher with sufficient information to ask key questions and to design teaching methodologies which are child centred but manageable within a mainstream classroom setting. Hart believes that through a change in the ways we view classroom practice, and the adoption of 'innovative thinking', we can raise teacher expectations with regard to the performance of all pupils.

> Innovative thinking is a way of generating new ideas about what might be done in response to concerns about children's learning. It involves probing more closely into the dynamics at work in a particular situation, in the belief and expectation that, if we do so, we can always find

ways of positively influencing and changing a situation that is causing concern – or our perception of it – through the use of our existing resources. It is based on the principle that, because the dynamics of teaching and learning are so complex, any situation is always capable of yielding new insights that will suggest new ideas for practice, if we think in a way that opens up new possibilities.

(Hart, 1996, p.1)

Hart's research was conducted in a mainstream classroom, and provides us with useful insights into the advantages which an analytical approach to teaching that considers learning preferences and teaching styles may have in the promotion of inclusion.

With so much time having been committed to the development of curriculum content in recent years, it is refreshing to find researchers and teachers who are prepared to consider approaches which begin with the pupil. Time spent in considering how the curriculum can best be managed in order to meet the needs of pupils, rather than attempting to fit pupils to one pattern of curriculum delivery, is likely to yield benefits for all pupils. Teachers working to develop inclusive classrooms need to play an active role in researching classroom methodologies which focus upon the needs of pupils. In so doing they must set high expectations for all pupils, and determine the criteria by which they measure success. For pupils with special educational needs this may well require an individual focus which is different from that provided for their peers. Equality of opportunity does not mean that all pupils should receive the same curriculum diet, but rather that they should all be provided with a curriculum which is relevant to their needs through a range of well-planned shared learning experiences.

Good curriculum delivery will depend upon teachers not only having an understanding of the needs of their pupils and the matching of teaching strategies to address these. It will also require effective classroom management skills, the appropriate deployment of resources, a commitment to full pupil participation and the careful use of classroom support. Whilst ensuring that each of these areas is addressed in turn will play an important role in developing an inclusive curriculum, it is not until all have been successfully developed that full inclusion may be achieved. Teachers who work to develop a curriculum which meet the needs of all pupils are developing a vehicle for inclusion. Those who attempt to fit pupils to existing structures are more likely to provide a lever for exclusion.

REFERENCES

Ainscow, M. (1996) 'Towards inclusive schooling', *REACH Journal of Special Needs in Ireland* 9(2): 67–75.

Ainscow, M. (1997) 'Towards inclusive schooling', *British Journal of Special Education* 24(1): 3–6.

Ashdown, R., Carpenter, B. and Bovair, K. (1991) *The Curriculum Challenge*, London: Falmer Press.

Byers, R. (1994) 'The Dearing review of the National Curriculum', *British Journal of Special Education* 21(3): 92–6.

Byers, R. and Rose, R. (1996) *Planning the Curriculum for Pupils with Special Educational Needs*, London: David Fulton.

Carpenter, B. (1995) 'Building an inclusive curriculum', in K. Ashcroft and D. Palaco (eds) *The Primary Teachers' Guide to the New National Curriculum*, London: Falmer Press.

Carpenter, B., Ashdown, R. and Bovair, K. (1996) *Enabling Access*, London: David Fulton.

DfEE (1997) *Excellence for All Children* (The Green Paper), London: The Stationery Office.

Dyson, A. (1994) 'Towards a collaborative learning model for responding to student diversity', *Support for Learning* 9(2): 53–60.

Evans, P. (1997) 'Structuring the curriculum for pupils with learning difficulties', in S. J. Pijl, C. J. W. Meijer and S. Hegarty (eds) *Inclusive Education: a Global Agenda*, London: Routledge.

Fagg, S., Aherne, P., Skelton, S. and Thornber, A. (1990) *Entitlement for All in Practice*, London: David Fulton.

Gross, J. (1993) *Special Educational Needs in the Primary School*, Milton Keynes: Open University Press.

Hart, S. (1992) 'Differentiation – way forward or retreat?', *British Journal of Special Education* 19(1): 10–12.

Hart, S. (1996) *Beyond Special Needs*, London: Paul Chapman.

HMI (1980) *A View of the Curriculum*, London: HMSO.

Lewis, A. (1995) *Primary Special Needs and the National Curriculum*, 2nd edition, London: Routledge.

National Curriculum Council (1990) *The Whole Curriculum. Curriculum Guidance 3*, York: NCC.

Ouvry, C. and Saunders, S. (1996) 'Pupils with profound and multiple learning difficulties', in B. Carpenter, R. Ashdown and K. Bovair (eds) *Enabling Access*, London: David Fulton.

Peter, M. (1989) 'Will the English National Curriculum create learning difficulties or cure them?', *New Era in Education* 70(2): 53–7.

Rose, R. and Parsons, L. (1998) 'Supporting the subject co-ordinator through the process of curriculum monitoring in a special school', *Support for Learning* 13(1): 21–5.

Rose, R. and Wilson, G. (1998) 'Monitoring effectiveness in science for pupils with severe learning difficulties', *The SLD Experience* (Spring edition).

Rose, R., Fergusson, A., Coles, C., Byers, R. and Banes, D. (1996) *Implementing the Whole Curriculum for Pupils with Learning Difficulties*, 2nd edition, London: David Fulton.

Rouse, M. and Florian, L. (1996) 'Becoming effective and inclusive: cross cultural perspectives', in L. Florian and M. Rouse (eds) *School Reform and Special*

Educational Needs: Anglo-American Perspectives, Cambridge: University of Cambridge Institute of Education.

Sebba, J. (1995a) *Geography for All*, London: David Fulton.

Sebba, J. (1995b) *History for All*, London: David Fulton.

Sebba, J. and Sachdev, D. (1997) *What Works in Inclusive Education?*, Ilford: Barnardos.

Stoll, L. (1991) 'School effectiveness in action: supporting growth in schools and classrooms', in M. Ainscow (ed.) *Effective Schools for All*, London: David Fulton.

UNESCO (1994) *The Salamanca Statement and Framework for Action on Special Needs Education*, Paris: UNESCO.

Welding, J. (1996) 'In-class support: a successful way of meeting individual student need?', *Support for Learning* 11(3): 113–17.

Williams, P. (1993) 'Integration of students with moderate learning difficulties', *European Journal of Special Needs Education* 8(3): 303–19.

Chapter 4

Personal and social development for pupils with learning difficulties

Richard Byers

In considering the ways in which schools might address curriculum management, Richard Byers suggests that there is a need to examine the priorities given to personal and social education. Inclusion is unlikely to become a real option until a greater emphasis is given to this important area of pupil need.

For many people working among pupils and students with learning difficulties, the challenge of promoting personal and social development remains a priority. This chapter will explore the nature of this challenge and the extent to which a way forward can be provided if those who seek to develop an inclusive model of the whole curriculum, wherever their work is done, welcome differently abled pupils and students, not in order to absorb them into a forced homogeneity or in order to preserve their differentness in dividing them from the majority, but, in contrast, as agents of development (Ainscow, 1991).

Interestingly, the Ofsted handbooks seem to echo this chapter's concern with inclusive whole curriculum issues. The guidance on the inspection of special schools (1995), for example, states that:

The curriculum of a special school complies with the 1988 Education Reform Act if it:

- is balanced and broadly based;
- promotes the spiritual, moral, cultural, mental and physical development of pupils;
- prepares pupils for the opportunities, responsibilities and experiences of adult life;
- includes the subjects of the National Curriculum as prescribed in regulations;
- provides for religious education in accordance with an agreed syllabus or the school's trust deeds;

- provides for sex education in accordance with the school's policy.

Schools should also provide:

- careers education and guidance (for secondary age pupils), and health education, including education about drug misuse.

(p.77)

I offer this quotation in full because the parallels with Ofsted's mainstream criteria are instructive. The model for the whole curriculum, in Ofsted's view, appears to be remarkably consistent from school to school, whether mainstream or special. It is also interesting to note, without suggesting that this is in any sense a hierarchical view of the curriculum, the way that the National Curriculum (DfEE, 1995) is tucked away amidst issues which, to paraphrase Marland's (1995) thoughts on the 1988 Act, could have been drafted by an enthusiast for personal and social education.

A MODEL FOR THE WHOLE CURRICULUM FOR PUPILS AND STUDENTS WITH LEARNING DIFFICULTIES

The model of the whole curriculum (see Figure 4.1) owes much to the literature on personal and social education (Best *et al.*, 1995) and much to the guidance on curriculum planning provided by, for example, SCAA (1995; 1996) and Byers and Rose (1996). It also owes a great deal to discussions held during a series of meetings at the University of Cambridge School of Education during 1997, where a group of senior staff, working among pupils and students with learning difficulties in a range of contexts, met in order to debate the nature of the whole curriculum for these learners. The model is based on the idea that staff who seek to promote personal and social development for pupils and students with learning difficulties should concern themselves with a series of evaluative questions about each of the aspects of this whole curriculum model. To address only one, or some, of these aspects will be to offer a diminished vision of a curriculum for personal and social development.

Unfortunately, this is not designed to be a two-dimensional model. It is offered here, with apologies for the limitations of print, as a series of words on a sheet of paper, but it would be better presented in three-dimensional virtual reality. I am suggesting that the ethos of the school, discernible in the spirit or atmosphere which characterises the institution, is part of a broader landscape in which the curriculum environment is located. The geology of this landscape may offer a safe and productive site upon which to build, or dangerous and uncertain conditions. Locating a secure bedrock in

Ethos   Spirit   Atmosphere
of the whole school

Rights and responsibilities
Rules in the community

Routines and rituals
in the learning environment

Relationships and respect
in interactions between staff and parents, staff and pupils, pupils and pupils

Curriculum
policy and guidelines
Whole and national
curriculum content

Meeting individual
needs
Priorities in key skills,
attitudes and behaviour

Schemes of work   Individual education plans
Long-term, medium-term and short-term planning

Teaching and learning

Observation, recording and assessment

Accreditation and progress files
Annual report   Annual review

Monitoring and evaluation
Revised policy   Revised priorities
Schemes of work   Plans and targets
and Revised practice

Figure 4.1 Promoting personal and social development within the whole curriculum

the values upon which the curriculum is constructed is a task of primary importance discussed below.

The social climate of the school community, expressed through a system of rules, framed in terms of rights and responsibilities; a matrix of routines and rituals; and a complex web of interactions between staff, pupils and other members of the school community, provide an underpinning for the curriculum. Without a sense of community, set firmly within the school ethos, the curriculum is a construct without a foundation. Upon this foundation the two main structures supporting the learning experience can be established in parallel. Curriculum development entails strategic planning, across year groups and key stages, in a range of subjects and aspects of the curriculum, including personal and social education, for notional groups of pupils. Planning for particular individual pupils and students will secure relevance to their specific needs, including their personal and social development, and continuity across and through the experiences offered by the curriculum.

This model is not intended to be dualistic, however. Although systems of curriculum and individual planning may need to be developed by staff with some clarity about their distinctive purposes, pupils and students enter the classroom each day without great concern for the complex structures which underpin their experiences. At the interface between planning and practice, if this whole curriculum model is operating as intended, pupils will experience teaching and learning as seamless and coherent. They will take the opportunity to grow and develop personally and socially, even as they gain new knowledge, skills and understanding in relation to the curriculum and their individual programmes. If teaching and learning are to flourish in this way, rigorous, but shared and open, approaches to observation, recording and assessment will need to be in place in order to keep track of a potential multiplicity of outcomes for learners. Pupil and student involvement in these processes will lend them significance in terms of personal and social development. This involvement will also enhance the contribution that the recognition and celebration of achievement, through progress files, reports to parents and accreditation, can make to the whole curriculum and to learners' self-esteem.

Maintaining quality in this environment is of crucial importance. The processes of monitoring and evaluation will enable all members of the school community to remain committed to a programme of constant improvement as well as the possibility of the need for more structural renovation. Each of the different levels of this model of the whole curriculum, from the underpinnings up to the decorative flounces, will thus be maintained under review in order to seek ever more effective means of promoting personal and social development for all learners.

Following this swift attempt to lift the whole curriculum off the page and give a sense of its form, subsequent sections now provide a more detailed analysis of each of the aspects of this model in turn, with reference to principles in practice.

Ethos, spirit and atmosphere

The National Curriculum Council (1990) suggested that spirit, ethos and atmosphere should be seen as part of the whole curriculum even though they are 'intangibles'. It is difficult to write a policy for atmosphere, a scheme of work for ethos, or a lesson plan for spirit, yet the ethos, spirit and atmosphere of each school, translated on a constant and consistent basis into practice through the social, cultural, moral, spiritual and physical fabric of the workings of the whole school community, make a significant contribution to the personal and social development of all pupils and students.

If these aspects of the whole curriculum are difficult to fix in words and conscious deeds, they are not entirely mystical. The National Curriculum Council (1990), for example, identified some of the cross-curricular dimensions which 'make a major contribution to personal and social education'. These and other dimensions permeate all aspects of the life of a school and may include, for example:

- a commitment to equality of opportunity regardless of pupils' and students' ethnicity, gender, disability, and cultural or social background;
- the recognition and celebration of the value of the culturally, socially and spiritually diverse nature of our society;
- entitlement to and access to an inclusive whole curriculum which is broad, balanced, relevant and well differentiated;
- participation for all in meaningful learning opportunities in diverse and age-appropriate pupil and student groupings.

Once these dimensions are made explicit through policy statements, their impact upon learners' personal and social development may be tracked through the prevailing culture of the school community; the values upon which that community is founded, and, in terms of this discussion, the values that guide attitudes and approaches to pupils and students with learning difficulties (see Chapter 5 by Liz Gerschel).

If the arguments in favour of an inclusive model for the whole curriculum are accepted, it will be important to ask whether these values will, in fact, need to be different from the values which inform personal and social development for learners in the mainstream of education. Buck and Inman (1995), in establishing a framework for the personal development of pupils in mainstream schools, identify a set of 'core democratic values' by which all people should live. With acknowledgements to *Caring for the Earth* (1991), these include:

- respect for reasoning and respect for truth;
- fairness, co-operation and acceptance of diversity;
- justice, freedom and equality;
- concern for the welfare of others;
- peaceful resolution of conflict.

Having identified the core values which may inform the kind of society we may wish to see in the future, Buck and Inman (1995) call upon their extensive work with teachers in moving on to delineate a set of 'outcomes' for the processes of personal and social development in education. These outcomes are described in terms of the 'attributes' which teachers may wish their learners to have as adults in this society. Buck and Inman's 'personal development outcomes' are:

- to have high self esteem;
- to be confident and assertive;
- to be self-aware; knowledgeable about themselves;
- to be able to take responsibility for own actions and the effects of these actions upon others;
- to be able to maintain effective interpersonal relationships within a moral framework;
- to be able to understand and, where appropriate, be sensitive to and respect the beliefs, values, and ways of life of others;
- to be critically informed about the human and physical world;
- to be able to question taken for granted assumptions and beliefs;
- to be able to think critically;
- to be concerned about promoting fairness, justice and equality on an interpersonal, societal and global level;
- to be able to promote a concern for all forms of life, now and in the future;
- to be skilled in how to work collaboratively and autonomously;
- to be able to reflect on their learning and plan for future developments.

(pp.7 and 10)

While many of these attributes may represent familiar concerns for staff working among pupils and students with learning difficulties (such as, for example, 'maintain effective personal relationships'), other issues may demand further thought and debate (how do we enable a young person with communication difficulties to be truly 'assertive'?) while some may represent new challenges (to what extent, as teachers, do we strive to ensure that young people with learning difficulties are 'critically informed'?).

Teaching staff may be encouraged to debate and agree inclusive sets of core values and personal development outcomes like these, creating a shared understanding of the principles upon which their practice is founded. A real commitment to the promotion of all learners' personal and social development, however, will dictate that the ambit of this debate should extend beyond educationally qualified professionals and include other professionals from the multidisciplinary team, support and ancillary staff; parents and governors, and the pupils and students themselves. According to many commentators, learners should also have a role, as members of the school community, in debating and deciding points of principle and philosophy. As Nieto (1994) argues, 'one way to begin the process of changing school policies is to listen to students' views about them'. This would indicate a need to promote participation and active involvement for pupils in the structures and practices of the school community through initiatives like school councils (Winup, 1994), advocacy groups (Mittler, 1996) and focused consultation which is actively used to drive policy making forward (Skill and FEFC, 1996). The extent to which all pupils and students, including those with learning difficulties and disabilities, are involved at these levels may thus provide one indicator of the extent to which the ethos of any school is truly inclusive (see Chapter 2 by Lani Florian and Chapter 7 by Richard Rose).

Rules, routines and rituals, relationships and respect

Systems of community interresponsibility, discipline and social control will have a profound impact upon learners' personal and social development. As with the discussion about values and ethos above, there are searching questions to be asked here about access for pupils and students to decision-making bodies through committees and advocacy groups so that pupil and student charters, drawn up in consultation with learners themselves, can become an explicit and valued part of the schools' social fabric.

Rights and responsibilities in the community

Rules exist in order to ensure that the school community operates in an orderly yet fair way. Rules may be best expressed through formal codes of conduct and agreed systems for applying discipline, rewards and sanctions. A commitment to learners' personal and social development would suggest that the use of praise and disapproval, rewards and sanctions should be ethically sound and age appropriate. Schools might review the ethics of using tangible, symbolic, occupational and social rewards in inclusive pupil groupings at different age stages and debate the implementation of hierarchies of universally applied sanctions which are negotiated and agreed with all pupils and students.

In formulating a discipline policy, schools might also consider interdependent sets of rights and responsibilities for pupils, parents and staff in creating and maintaining a safe, orderly and supportive climate for learning. Clarke and Murray (1996) provide evidence of this approach to policy making being successful in mainstream schools. They also note that rules can be couched in positive language, emphasising what learners should 'do', rather than lists of things that should not happen. If we assume that rules, systems of discipline and formal codes of conduct within the community reveal values, then it is perhaps appropriate that policy and practice should focus upon appropriate behaviour. This process of involving all participants in the school community in building a 'positive classroom climate' is something that Rogers (1991) describes and which has become a strong characteristic of many mainstream classrooms. These approaches, which are characterised by negotiation, consultation and agreement rather than prescription, dictate and imposition, contrast, in terms of philosophy and practice, with the more specialist methods of changing and maintaining patterns of behaviour which have traditionally been used with pupils and students with learning difficulties (Zarkowska and Clements, 1994; Harris *et al.*, 1996). Thus the challenge of seeing whether contrasting approaches to discipline can work in harmony alongside one another in inclusive settings, or whether one system should eventually apply for all learners, remains for future exploration and resolution.

Routines and rituals

Staff who work among pupils and students with learning difficulties are frequently heard to extol the virtues of consistency. Advocates of a more extreme point of view will suggest that there is an absolute link between learning and routine. This section does not set out to argue for chaos or total unpredictability, but it does suggest that staff need to review the social climate of the learning environment in order to guard against the self-fulfilling and self-perpetuating myth of the value of ritual.

It is undoubtedly true that repetitive patterns of activity can help to create a sense of familiarity and security. The provision of support and guidance, praise and disapproval according to consistent criteria and patterns of expectation can help pupils, and perhaps particularly young pupils, with learning difficulties to understand their roles within the classroom and to succeed in finding their way through what can seem a complex matrix of adult requirements (Ouvry, 1987; Ware, 1996). However, the true value of a carefully fostered sense of consistency can often only be judged when familiar patterns are interrupted (Goldbart, 1988). A rigid adherence to ritual and routine, to doing things in a certain way simply because they are always done thus, can also lead to diminished expectation and achievement. In the same way, the routine provision of help, support and guidance can lead to dependence and the denial of autonomy (Sebba *et al.*, 1993). It is for these reasons that the balance between support and challenge, help and independence, protection and autonomy, and safe practice and risk taking in the social climate of the learning environment should be maintained under constant review.

Relationships and interactions

Staff working closely with pupils and students with learning difficulties also need to consider the impact that interactions between teaching staff and other professionals, staff and parents, staff and pupils, and pupils and their peers will have upon learners' personal and social development. Staff attitudes towards one another, towards parents and towards pupils can create powerful role models for pupils. Relationships that are characterised by mutual respect, dignity, rights of privacy and confidentiality, and the conferral of adult status in appropriate age groups will be most likely to help young people to develop in terms of their self-confidence, self-image and self-esteem. Nind and Hewett (1994) discuss interactions with learners which are characterised by shared power and negotiation and by an unequivocal acknowledgement of the learners' right actively to shape their own learning opportunities.

Not all the interactions within school that have a bearing upon learners' personal and social development are, however, directly educational. Staff will also inevitably find themselves managing the special responsibilities of entering into relationships where therapy, guidance or relaxation are prime concerns for particular learners. In making these pastoral contacts, pupils may not always choose to place their trust in the school's trained therapist or counsellor. All members of staff who work with pupils and students with learning difficulties will need to develop attitudes, skills, knowledge and understanding in preparation for these privileged relationships (McLaughlin et al., 1996).

Curriculum policy and schemes of work

Much of the recent guidance on curriculum planning has inevitably focused upon the implementation of the National Curriculum (DfEE, 1995). Work in schools, and many comments made in the light of Ofsted inspections in specialist contexts, would indicate that the curriculum for personal and social education should be developed using precisely the same planning frameworks. This will mean schools developing policy, guidelines for implementation, and schemes of work for accepted areas of content in the curriculum for personal and social education. Many schools working with pupils and students with learning difficulties will also want to bring other parts of the learning day which may have an important contribution to make to pupils' personal and social development, such as mealtimes and break times, into the formal curriculum planning process. This process will be characterised by three phases of planning.

Long-term planning

At this strategic level, decisions will need to be made about the time which is to be allocated to formal schemes of work in personal and social education in each key stage. The resulting profiles will reveal the balance between, for example, National Curriculum subjects and other aspects of the whole curriculum for pupils and students with learning difficulties. Many schools who make provision for such learners find, in looking at the figures on time allocation that are provided for guidance in mainstream contexts (Dearing, 1993), that they wish to devote comparatively less time to the foundation subjects of the National Curriculum (DfEE, 1995), for example, while extending the teaching day to encompass additional work on key skills and aspects of learners' personal and social development. These decisions, which ensure the relevance of the curriculum for these learners, are acceptable provided that planning, recording and assessment procedures are operating in relation to the time which is allocated to personal and social education and provided an overarching sense of balance and proportionality in the curriculum is assured.

The curriculum map, which is drawn up for each key stage to show the results of these strategic decisions and the ways in which the curriculum is intended to address aims and content in relation to various programmes of study, should reveal the many useful links which can be made between the curriculum for personal and social education and units of work and modules in other subjects (see Chapter 3 by Richard Rose), such as science, geography, history or religious education. It will also draw distinctions between blocked and continuing work (SCAA, 1995; 1996).

Medium-term planning

Implementing a programme for personal and social education will entail developing more detailed medium-term plans for both kinds of work. On the one hand, the curriculum for personal and social education will encompass certain skills, experiences and processes which will need to be addressed continuously as ongoing regular concerns for all learners. These may include:

- teaching and learning at meal and break times;
- dressing, undressing and changing clothes;
- personal hygiene and self-care routines;
- domestic skills in home care and survival cookery;
- skills in using community facilities;
- options for leisure and relaxation.

Similarly, medium-term plans will need to be drawn up for blocked units of work or modules, covering specified areas of content, knowledge and understanding which will be taught in discrete time frames to pupils and students in particular age groups. These blocked units of work may cover, for example:

- careers education and guidance, including work experience;
- education for environmental awareness and a sustainable future;
- education for citizenship, from the personal to the political;
- education for sexuality; drug and substance abuse and misuse, and other aspects of health education;
- cultural, spiritual and moral education;
- education for economic and industrial understanding;
- education for community participation.

Formats for such planning documentation are discussed elsewhere (SCAA, 1996; Byers and Rose, 1996) but this level of planning should show, in relation to learners' personal and social development:

- intended outcomes, or objectives, referenced back to programmes of study or long-term plans;
- progression through sequences of exemplified activity;
- opportunities to record and assess the progress that pupils and students make in terms of personal and social development.

Short-term planning

Short-term plans for class or group activities will show how long- and medium-term curriculum plans can be developed and extended in order to address the needs, interests, prior achievements and aptitudes of individual pupils in particular teaching groups. Planning for implementation at this level within particular lessons and activities will therefore be concerned with:

- the details of differentiation;
- appropriate teaching methods and pupil groupings;
- the deployment of resources and staff.

In lessons which effectively promote personal and social development for pupils and students with learning difficulties, it will also be important to ensure that priority targets for individual learners are addressed in the context of group activities drawn from schemes of work for any area of the whole curriculum.

Meeting individual needs

The procedures laid down by the Code of Practice (DfEE and Welsh Office, 1994; Ramjhun, 1995; Warin, 1995) are, in contrast with curriculum planning structures, designed to ensure that teaching addresses the specific and personal needs of individual learners.

Long-term planning

Long-term planning for individual pupils and students with learning difficulties will often be accomplished, under the Code of Practice, through statements and the Annual Review process. This process may be used to ensure that progress over the past year, difficulties in priority areas, and aims for the year ahead are identified in partnerships between all the professionals in the multidisciplinary team, parents and pupils themselves. The Annual Review process may also secure relevance to individual needs by focusing heavily on issues in personal and social development.

The Code of Practice stresses the need for all pupils to experience 'the greatest possible access to a broad and balanced education' which will include the National Curriculum. However, individual education plans drawn up under the guidance of the code are not required to focus upon curriculum subjects. It is assumed that well-differentiated objectives for learning in these areas are established in schemes of work. Individual education plans, in contrast, will focus on areas of learning in the whole curriculum which are a priority for particular pupils. An emphasis, for example, upon 'pastoral care or medical requirements' may help to 'ensure a co-ordinated and inter-disciplinary approach' (DfEE and Welsh Office, 1994) and, significantly, to promote personal and social development.

Medium-term planning

Medium-term planning will ensure that priority objectives, drawn from the annual aims, are addressed on a termly basis. Opportunities to make progress towards these objectives may be identified in a range of contexts across the whole curriculum thus ensuring continuity, in terms of personal and social development, from subject to subject and from activity to activity.

Core priorities in learning for individual pupils may be set in terms of attitudes, behaviour and key cross-curricular skills (NCC, 1990; Dearing, 1996) which include:

- communication and literacy skills;
- applied numeracy skills;
- use of information technology capability;
- personal and social skills;

- study skills;
- problem-solving skills, thinking skills, cognitive skills;
- skills in co-operation, collaboration, working in groups;
- the development or maintenance of physical capability, including fine and gross motor skills and skills in positioning;
- perceptual skills and skills in sensory awareness and exploration, including use of the senses and strategies in overcoming sensory impairment;
- skills in the positive self-management of behavioural difficulties.

Short-term planning

Short-term planning will ensure that there are opportunities for each pupil to work towards his or her priority targets, which may relate to aspects of personal and social development, within group tasks set in relation to curriculum plans and schemes of work. These short-term priority targets will be:

- few in number;
- specific to the individual;
- relevant to the pupil's priority needs;
- achievable and teachable within a short-term time scale measured in weeks.

As has been noted above, teaching which most effectively addresses pupils' and students' personal and social development will integrate, within multi-faceted but holistic activities, intended learning which relates to both the schemes of work for various areas of the curriculum and learners' individual educational priorities.

Teaching approaches and learning styles

Inevitably a great deal of the debate about the curriculum and about individual needs focuses on knowledge, understanding and skills: upon the subjects of the National Curriculum (DfEE, 1995), for instance, as well as upon key cross-curricular skills (NCC, 1990; Dearing, 1996) which secure some relevance to the curriculum for personal and social education. However, the whole curriculum is about more than content and it is most appropriate that we create opportunities to debate and analyse the how of teaching as well as the what. Many authors (see e.g. Freire, 1972; Ryder and Campbell, 1988) comment upon the crucial role, in empowering and liberating learners, of pedagogy. The inspection criteria (Ofsted, 1995) also propose that planning should ensure the use of a balanced range of organisational strategies and teaching approaches, including one-to-one tuition, small-group and whole class exposition, demonstration, discussion, practical activity, investigation, testing and problem solving. These approaches to teaching will, it is suggested (Mulligan, 1992; Gardner, 1993), promote a balanced range of learning styles which will involve pupils in:

- being willing participants;
- self-organisation, self-awareness and self-responsibility;
- listening, watching, attending, focusing;
- sensing, feeling and remembering;
- the use of perception and intuition;
- making choices and decisions about the direction of their own learning;
- communication and interaction;
- thinking, reasoning and imagining;
- movement, problem solving and practical activity;
- independent, shared and co-operative activity;
- turn taking, acknowledging the contributions of others;
- taking a variety of roles and responsibilities;
- exploration and investigation;
- observation, recording and interpretation;
- review and evaluation of their own learning.

Becoming skilled and experienced in these processes will, as an integral part of engaging with the content of the curriculum, promote personal and social growth and development in learners. Byers (1994) suggests that learning opportunities which are most effective in terms of pupils' personal and social development will be those which:

- are relevant to pupils' day-to-day reality and have a clear meaning and purpose for them;
- involve learners from the outset through shared objectives and negotiated targets;
- take account of pupils' prior skills, interests, achievements and experiences and engage the whole learner;
- are interactive, encouraging exploration and problem solving through partnership, dialogue and collaboration between peers and between staff and learners;
- are intrinsically motivating, promoting pupil initiation and facilitating pupil self-evaluation through shared success criteria.

In this sense, classroom processes (Byers, 1996) constitute part of the whole curriculum along with policies, plans and projected outcomes (see Chapter 10 by Claire Marvin).

Observation, recording, assessment, reporting and accreditation

Record keeping, assessment and reporting that is accurate, fair, honest and likely to promote learners' personal and social development will have many of the characteristics of the Records of Achievement process (DES, 1990; Lawson, 1992; Hardwick and Rushton, 1994) and:

- be focused on an ongoing recognition and celebration of positive achievements;
- entail negotiation and dialogue between teacher and learner;
- recognise a wide range of experiences in the context of the whole curriculum;
- entail pupil/student ownership.

According to the Code of Practice (DfEE and Welsh Office, 1994), learners should:

- be involved in decision-making processes at all stages;
- be active participants in assessment and intervention;
- be enabled to make their views known in identifying difficulties, setting goals, agreeing a development strategy, monitoring and reviewing progress;
- be involved in implementing Individual Education Plans;
- be actively involved in the review process, including all or part of the review meeting;
- be encouraged to give their views of their progress, discuss difficulties, share their hopes and aspirations.

Strategies for the involvement of learners in record keeping, assessment and reporting will include the use of a range of modes – verbal, pictorial, symbol supported, real object, tactile, photographic, audio tape, video, for example – and will require skills in counselling and guidance on the part of teachers and skills in advocacy on the part of learners if the involvement is to be meaningful in terms of pupils' and students' personal and social development.

It is perhaps accepted that reporting and accreditation should recognise 'a continuous spectrum of talent, tastes and experiences' (Dearing, 1996). Although the Annual Report to parents will focus on progress in relation to the National Curriculum (DfEE, 1995) as well as other areas of the curriculum, and therefore units of work and modules in personal and social education, there is a continuing debate about whether National Curriculum assessment and reporting procedures are truly inclusive of pupils with special educational needs. However, Dearing's (1996) work on accreditation beyond 16 argues that 'entry level qualifications should be available to young people with learning difficulties' focusing on 'key skills' and skills for 'independent adult life'. The Annual Review process, addressing the individual needs of the individual learner under the Code of Practice (DfEE and Welsh Office, 1994), and the ongoing preparation of learners' progress files, will also afford opportunities, at whatever age, to focus on the significance of these skills and processes for lifelong learning and thus upon pupils' and students' personal and social development.

Monitoring and evaluation

Most commentators (see e.g. Rogers and Badham, 1992) describe monitoring and evaluation as elements within a cyclical process whereby information about certain focused priority areas of practice is systematically collected and presented: monitoring – value judgements are made on the basis of an analysis of that information; evaluation – in order to inform review, which entails reflection on progress so that decisions can be made about future planning and revised targets established for future development. The purpose of this cycle of monitoring, evaluation and review is to improve outcomes for learners – as far as this chapter is concerned, specifically in terms of their personal and social development. In this sense, all the aspects of the whole curriculum model which we have so far discussed are subject to review, including ethos, social climate, curriculum, individual priorities, teaching and learning, assessment, recording, reporting and accreditation. The tangible outcome of the monitoring and evaluation process may therefore be, for instance, a revised whole school policy on time allocation, ensuring that adequate opportunities for addressing personal and social education are provided within the timetable. Equally, schemes of work themselves may be revised in order to ensure that the full breadth of the curriculum for personal and social education is addressed and that there are curricular options, for instance, for learners in Key Stage 4 and beyond. Inevitably, review will also focus upon provision for individual pupils and lead to revised sets of aims and priorities modifying the details of practice for particular learners under specific circumstances.

To a large extent, schools will define their priorities for improvement in line with the agreed school development plan and their own aims and policies (DES, 1989; Wilcox, 1992), which may reflect a commitment to pupils' personal and social development. However, if the process of monitoring, evaluation and review is to be truly effective in relation to pupils' and students' personal and social development, then learners themselves should be involved in the process. Among the many approaches to monitoring and evaluation (West and Ainscow, 1991), those which may most effectively involve pupils and students include:

- interviews with pupils, in small groups or individually, in order to take account of their views, perspectives and perceptions;
- involving learners in audits based on pupil shadowing, pupil chronologies and pupil diaries;
- shared scrutiny of progress files and pupil portfolios;
- collaborative collation of subject portfolios and samples of work supporting moderation processes;
- the review of photographs, audio tape and video;
- peer tutoring and peer assessment.

Through processes such as these, pupils, students, and those ex-pupils and students who have moved on into adult life, should be enabled to contribute their perceptions to the process of monitoring, evaluation and review. As Shostak and Logan (1984) assert, 'those on the receiving end of adult educative acts have the right to comment critically or appreciatively otherwise it is undemocratic and ineducative'.

SUMMARY

This final section will draw together some of the key issues raised in this chapter and pose a series of questions which can be used to audit and review the whole curriculum in terms of its effectiveness in providing for pupils' and students' personal and social development.

Ethos, spirit and atmosphere

These dimensions of the whole curriculum should be made explicit through debate about the aims and values of the school community. A distinction should be drawn, in policy and practice, between courses in personal and social education, which may be taught by particular members of staff, and the broader, whole curriculum issue of promoting learners' personal and social development, which should be seen as the responsibility of all members of the school community. Schools may, in this way, create clarity about and ownership of the educational philosophy upon which the school is founded and ask a series of questions:

- What sort of society do we imagine school leavers will join?
- What sort of people will they need to be?
- Are mainstream aims and values appropriate for pupils with learning difficulties?
- How do schools find out about the kinds of futures leavers face?

- Are current pupils, ex-pupils and adults with disabilities involved in staff development activities and in working with parents and with pupils?
- Does the school have:
  - pupil/student councils and committees;
  - access for learners to setting targets in the school development plan;
  - representation for service users and/or advocacy groups on the governing body?

Rules, routines and rituals, relationships and respect

The social climate of the school should again be seen as a whole school responsibility and, again, a key question will be the extent to which pupils and students have access to decision-making bodies. Pupils and students with learning difficulties may sit on committees and attend advocacy groups, for example, in order to contribute to school development planning, to rule making or to the preparation of student charters. At a less formal level, learners should be involved in ensuring that the social climate is founded upon positive approaches:

- Does the school provide for opportunities such as circle time and advocacy groups?
- How are pupils involved in consultative and decision-making processes at individual, classroom and whole school levels?
- How is 'adult status' for pupils with learning difficulties expressed?
- What staff development needs are implied?

Curriculum policy and schemes of work

The school should allocate time to taught courses in personal and social education and to ongoing work to promote this by creating policy, guidelines and schemes of work for blocked units of work in aspects of the subject and in continuing aspects of pupils' personal and social development and asking:

- Does the school enable pupils/student and/or ex-pupil/student representation via co-option onto certain curriculum development working parties?
- What is the appropriate balance between work addressing pupils' personal and social development and other aspects of the whole curriculum?

- Do pupils have access to their full entitlement to whole curriculum concerns such as education and guidance about sexuality, spirituality, citizenship, morality, economic self-sufficiency or careers?
- Are there options in the curriculum, particularly at Key Stage 4 and beyond?

Meeting individual needs

Individual education plans should address issues which are priorities for particular pupils, for example key, cross-curricular skills for lifelong learning.

- Do individual education plans ensure relevance to specific pupils' needs?
- Do individual education plans ensure continuity across the curriculum?
- Does the school strive:
  - to continue to find effective strategies for meaningful pupil involvement in all phases of the individual education planning process and at Annual Review;
  - to focus individual education plans on key skills and personal and social development?
- How are individual pupils involved in the processes of identifying their own strengths and difficulties, setting their own targets, creating strategies for intervention and implementation?

Teaching and learning

Short-term planning ensures that priority targets for individual learners are addressed through participation in group activity founded in the curriculum. Approaches to teaching should be matched to curricular objectives, the individual needs of pupils and in particular their personal and social development.

- Do lesson plans imply a full range of approaches to teaching, including site visits, explorations, group work, drama, simulations and problem-solving activities, for example?
- What learning styles are implied by planned approaches to teaching?
- Do teaching approaches engage pupils in styles of learning which are relevant to their individual education plans?
- Do teaching approaches and learning styles actively promote pupils' personal and social development, through group work, negotiation, active participation, interaction, problem solving and exploration?

Observation, recording, assessment reporting and accreditation

Observation, recording, assessment, review, reporting and accreditation processes should focus on the positive, address the whole curriculum, be ongoing, facilitate pupil involvement and participation, and entail negotiation, sharing of information and pupil ownership.

- How are pupils involved in assessment, record keeping, monitoring progress, review of plans and procedures, and reporting?
- What skills and strategies do staff need to develop in order to 'listen' to pupils' views and perspectives more effectively?
- Does the school strive:

  - to continue to develop strategies for meaningful pupil self-assessment, self-evaluation and peer assessment;
  - to continue to argue for accessible assessment procedures in relation to the National Curriculum?

- How is achievement recognised, celebrated and accredited?
- Do accreditation and Records of Achievement encompass a range of nationally validated forms of accreditation, including progress files, relating to a range of whole curriculum issues?

Monitoring and evaluation

The outcomes of monitoring, evaluation and review procedures should be used to drive planning for further development in relation to:

- ownership and expression of an appropriate whole school ethos;
- an improved social climate;
- revised policy, schemes of work and curriculum plans;
- revised individual education plans;
- enriched teaching and learning;
- increased pupil participation and involvement in assessment, recording, reporting and accreditation procedures;
- so that learners' personal and social development is enhanced;
- opportunities for pupils to contribute their perceptions to the process of monitoring, evaluation and review through:

  - use of pupil interviews, pupil shadows, pupil diaries;
  - consultation with pupils through monitoring and evaluation procedures.

It is intended that these questions may be used to promote personal and social development for pupils and students with learning difficulties through an inclusive model of the whole curriculum. Arguably, this model appropriately and explicitly addresses the preparation of this group of learners for participation in a society beyond school which itself offers an increasing range of inclusive opportunities (see Part IV). It is a further responsibility of educationists, in collaboration with their fellow professionals in other disciplines and with service users themselves, to ensure that these opportunities continue to proliferate.

REFERENCES

Ainscow, M. (1991) 'Towards effective schools for all: some problems and possibilities', in M. Ainscow (ed.) *Effective Schools for All*, London: David Fulton.

Best, R., Lang, P., Lodge, C. and Watkins, C. (eds) (1995) *Pastoral Care and Personal-Social Education – Entitlement and Provision.* London: Cassell.

Buck, M. and Inman, S. (1995) 'Setting a framework for personal development', in S. Inman and M. Buck (eds) *Adding Value? Schools' Responsibility for Pupils' Personal Development*, Stoke-on-Trent: Trentham Books.

Byers, R. (1994) 'Providing opportunities for effective learning', in R. Rose, A. Fergusson, C. Coles, R. Byers and D. Banes (eds) *Implementing the Whole Curriculum for Pupils with Learning Difficulties*, London: David Fulton.

Byers, R. (1996) 'Classroom processes', in B. Carpenter, R. Ashdown and K. Bovair (eds) *Enabling Access – Effective Teaching and Learning for Pupils with Learning Difficulties*, London: David Fulton.

Byers, R. and Rose, R. (1996) *Planning the Curriculum for Pupils with Special Educational Needs – a Practical Guide*, London: David Fulton.

Caring for the Earth (1991) IUCN/UNEP/WWF: Earthscan.

Clarke, D. and Murray, A. (1996) *Developing and Implementing a Whole-School Behaviour Policy – a Practical Approach*, London: David Fulton.

Dearing, R. (1993) *The National Curriculum and its Assessment – Final Report*, London: SCAA.

Dearing, R. (1996) *Review of Qualifications for 16–19 Year Olds – Summary Report*, London: SCAA.

Department for Education and Employment (DfEE) (1995) *The National Curriculum*, London: HMSO.

Department for Education and Employment (DfEE) and Welsh Office (1994) *Code of Practice on the Identification and Assessment of Special Educational Needs*, London: HMSO.

Department of Education and Science (DES) (1989) *Planning for School Development*, London: HMSO.

Department of Education and Science (DES) (1990) Circular No. 8/90 – *Records of Achievement*, London: HMSO.

Friere, P. (1972) *Pedagogy of the Oppressed*, Harmondsworth: Penguin.

Gardner, H. (1993) *The Unschooled Mind – How Children Think and How Schools Should Teach*, London: Fontana.

Goldbart, J. (1988) 'Communication for a purpose', in J. Coupe and J. Goldbart (eds) *Communication Before Speech – Normal Development and Impaired Communication*, London: Croom Helm.

Hardwick, J. and Rushton, P. (1994) 'Pupil participation in their own Records of Achievement', in R. Rose, A. Fergusson, C. Coles, R. Byers and D. Banes (eds) *Implementing the Whole Curriculum for Pupils with Learning Difficulties*, London: David Fulton.

Harris, J., Cook, M. and Upton, G. (1996) *Pupils with Severe Learning Difficulties who Present Challenging Behaviour – a Whole School Approach to Assessment and Intervention*, Kidderminster: BILD.

Lawson, H. (1992) *Practical Record Keeping for Special Schools – Resource Material for Staff Development*, London: David Fulton.

Marland, M. (1995) 'The whole curriculum', in R. Best, P. Lang, C. Lodge and C. Watkins (eds) *Pastoral Care and Personal-Social Education – Entitlement and Provision*, London: Cassell.

McLaughlin, C., Clark, P. and Chisholm, M. (1996) *Counselling and Guidance in Schools – Developing Policy and Practice*, London: David Fulton.

Mittler, P. (1996) 'Laying the foundations for self-advocacy: the role of home and school', in J. Coupe O'Kane and J. Goldbart (eds) *Whose Choice? Contentious Issues for Those Working with People with Learning Difficulties*, London: David Fulton.

Mulligan, J. (1992) 'Internal processors in experiential learning', in J. Mulligan and C. Griffin (eds) *Empowerment through Experiential Learning – Explorations of Good Practice*, London: Kogan Page.

National Curriculum Council (NCC) (1990) *Curriculum Guidance 3: the Whole Curriculum*, York: NCC.

Nieto, S. (1994) 'Lessons from students on creating a chance to dream', *Harvard Educational Review* 64(4): 392 –426.

Nind, M. and Hewett, D. (1994) *Access to Communication – Developing the Basics of Communication with People with Severe Learning Difficulties through Intensive Interaction*, London: David Fulton.

Ofsted (1995) *Guidance on the Inspection of Special Schools*, London: HMSO.

Ouvry, C. (1987) *Educating Children with Profound Handicaps*, Kidderminster: BIMH.

Ramjhun, A. F. (1995) *Implementing the Code of Practice for Children with Special Educational Needs – a Practical Guide*, London: David Fulton.

Rogers, B. (1991) *You Know the Fair Rule: Strategies for Making the Hard Job of Discipline in Schools Easier*, Harlow: Longman.

Rogers, G. and Badham, L. (1992) *Evaluation in Schools – Getting Started on Training and Implementation*, London: Routledge.

Ryder, J. and Campbell, L. (1988) *Balancing Acts in Personal, Social and Health Education*, London: Routledge.

School Curriculum and Assessment Authority (SCAA) (1995) *Planning the Curriculum at Key Stages 1 and 2*, London: SCAA.

School Curriculum and Assessment Authority (SCAA) (1996) *Planning the Curriculum for Pupils with Profound and Multiple Learning Difficulties*, London: SCAA.

Sebba, J., Byers, R. and Rose, R. (1993) *Redefining the Whole Curriculum for Pupils with Learning Difficulties*, London: David Fulton.

Shostak, J. F. and Logan, T. (1984) 'Conclusions', in J. F. Shostak and T. Logan (eds) *Pupil Experience*, London: Croom Helm.

Skill (National Bureau for Students with Disabilities) and FEFC (Further Education Funding Council) (1996) *Student Voices – the Views of Further Education Students with Learning Difficulties and/or Disabilities* (findings from a series of student workshops commissioned by the learning difficulties and/or disabilities committee), London: Skill.

Ware, J. (1996) *Creating a Responsive Environment for People with Profound and Multiple Learning Difficulties*, London: David Fulton.

Warin, S. (1995) *Implementing the Code of Practice – Individual Education Plans*, Tamworth: NASEN.

Watkins, C. (1985) 'Does pastoral care = personal and social education?', *Pastoral Care in Education* 3(3): 179–83.

West, M. and Ainscow, M. (1991) *Managing School Development – a Practical Guide*, London: David Fulton.

Wilcox, B. (1992) *Time-Constrained Evaluation – a Practical Approach for LEAs and Schools*, London: Routledge.

Winup, K. (1994) 'The role of the student committee in promotion of independence among school leavers', in J. Coupe O'Kane and B. Smith (eds) *Taking Control – Enabling People with Learning Difficulties*, London: David Fulton.

Zarkowska, E. and Clements, J. (1994) *Problem Behaviour and People with Severe Learning Disabilities – the S.T.A.R. Approach*, 2nd edition, London: Chapman and Hall.

Chapter 5

Equal opportunities and special educational needs

Equity and inclusion

Liz Gerschel

In this chapter, Liz Gerschel examines the process of inclusion as part of a broader policy of equal opportunities, and provides guidelines for the development of equal opportunities policies in schools.

'Equal opportunities' (EO) is a phrase which has taken on various political overtones in recent years (Gipps and Murphy, 1994). The term suggests equity and fairness, and has traditionally been used in race or gender-specific contexts, such as described in the Sex Discrimination Act (SDA) and Race Relations Act (RRA) legislation intended to ensure that men and women of all ethnic backgrounds receive equitable treatment in all areas of life. It is also used more broadly to mean a concern that no group traditionally seen as oppressed, or open to oppression, should be disadvantaged, as in 'We are an equal opportunities employer'.

Increasingly, people with learning difficulties and other disabilities have been seen as a heterogeneous minority group who experience discrimination in ways similar to other minorities (Fine and Asch, 1988; Reiser and Mason, 1990). This was recognised in the Disability Discrimination Act of 1995 (DDA), which states that:

- To enable a disabled person to do their job, governing bodies and LEAs must make reasonable adjustments to their employment arrangements or premises, if these substantially disadvantage a disabled person compared to a non-disabled person;
- Governing bodies and LEAs must not unjustifiably discriminate against disabled people when providing non-educational services (e.g. when they let rooms in school for community use);
- Governing bodies, in their annual report to parents must explain their admission arrangements for disabled pupils, how they will help such pupils gain access and what they will do to make sure they are treated fairly.

(DfEE, 1997, p.1)

Clearly, the DDA has implications for the employment of people with disabilities, the use of facilities by people with disabilities and the educational opportunities offered to pupils with disabilities or special educational needs (SEN). In this way, the Act encourages inclusion of people with disabilities in the activities which typify everyday life on a broad scale. More specifically, it links SEN and EO for the first time in law. The aim of this chapter is to explore this link and to provide guidelines to schools for the development of inclusive equal opportunities policy.

HOW DO INCLUSION AND EQUAL OPPORTUNITY RELATE?

Equal opportunities in schools means treating individuals fairly, according to their needs and abilities and without discrimination, so that the opportunities to benefit from school are maximised. Inclusion recognises the right of all pupils, including those with learning difficulties, to be taught alongside their peers, while acknowledging their common and differing needs. When pupils are treated equitably, and therefore real equality of opportunity is more likely, each will have more chance to make the most of what the school has to offer, according to her or his needs. Providing equal opportunities is about planning for inclusion and equity by:

- recognising individual differences and their impact on learning;
- creating a context in which individuals are able to learn and to teach effectively;
- valuing individuals and respecting their contributions to the school and the contributions of those like them to society as a whole.

If concepts of 'equality of opportunity' and inclusion are to be effective in practice, the opportunity to participate in educational activity requires that teachers and others in authority know who the pupils in their group are and what is needed to ensure meaningful access to the curriculum.

IMPORTANCE OF ENVIRONMENT OR CONTEXT FOR LEARNING

A strong body of research (Hargreaves et al., 1975; Rutter et al., 1979; Mortimore et al.,1988; Tizard et al., 1988; Smith and Tomlinson, 1989; Sammons et al., 1995) shows that school organisation is an important factor in the achievement of pupils. (For an excellent overview of characteristics of effective schools see Sammons et al., 1995.) Rouse and Florian (1996) found that the factors that characterise effective schools are relevant to the education of all pupils, thereby helping to bring about greater equality of opportunity for pupils with learning difficulties and other special educational needs in mainstream schools.

The environment for learning is both physical and metaphysical: when it is metaphysical, it is experienced in the school's ethos and organisation (see Chapter 4 by Richard Byers), or what has been called the 'hidden curriculum'. A disability becomes a handicap when the social, physical, economic, psychological or political environment makes it so. If the environment is exclusive, focused on what is 'normal' and not accommodating of exceptions to this, then 'being different' becomes a problem. When their concept of 'normality' isolates or rejects those who are 'different', schools 'participate in the social construction of deviance' (Cooper *et al.*, 1991, p.91). Pupils who do not conform to the established norms are labelled and treated accordingly. The inequitable and punitive effect of this on some African–Caribbean pupils labelled as having behavioural difficulties has been well documented (e.g. Cooper *et al.*, 1991; Wright, 1986; 1989; 1992). When the environment and ethos are accepting and inclusive, the range of human conditions is accepted as equally valuable and difficulties are minimised.

EQUAL VALUE

The concept of equal value is essential to inclusive education. It means that schools recognise all pupils as valuable contributors to their own learning and to the school community, as well as acknowledging the contributions of others like them to the wider society.

When a school values pupils, it reflects their history, culture and language in the curriculum, not as an added extra but as an intrinsic part of the provision for all. For example, the science curriculum acknowledges the work of women and of people from ethnic minorities; the fact that many great artists and scientists have overcome disabilities is not overlooked when their work is discussed. High expectations of pupils with learning difficulties and disabilities, and respect for them and their cultures, include their right to be taught about the contribution made by people like them to society. The hidden curriculum needs to reflect this too. Displays, school meals, resources, visitors can all reflect the diversity of the population so that pupils are able to engage with a range of cultural experiences and see themselves valued in the valuing of others like them.

Inclusive schools which value individual pupils also value their parents. They recognise that parents of pupils with special needs can often feel very isolated, lacking information or support. They uphold the fundamental principle of the Code of Practice (DfEE, 1994) that parents are partners in the education of their child with special educational needs. However, research in this area has identified differences in the experience of ethnic minority and white parents. Some suggest that the shortage of teachers and other professionals with knowledge of Asian communities and languages is, in effect, depriving some members of those communities of the support and provision to which their children are entitled (Kler, 1997; Shah, 1995). This is partly because of communication difficulties. For example, Kler notes that learning difficulties and mental disabilities are difficult concepts to translate into some languages. Shah warns that lack of awareness of cultures and customs can result in behaviour on the part of professionals which is unacceptable to families and lead to suspicion or rejection. She offers advice on approaching families of Asian origin. Ahmad *et al*. (1997) mention the value of a support group for Asian parents of pupils with special educational needs. Crooks (1997) suggests that black parents are less likely to come into the mainstream classroom unless teachers specifically invite them to do so. Inclusive schools that value parents make the first move: they recognise the difficulties that parents experience because they make it their business to find out, and then they actively try to overcome problems. Where appropriate, they also reach out: some parents/carers welcome home visits.

SPECIAL EDUCATIONAL NEEDS AND ENGLISH AS AN ADDITIONAL LANGUAGE (EAL)

Many teachers are not clear about the distinctions between problems experienced by pupils because of their lack of knowledge of English, and problems attributable to learning difficulties. Research suggests that two years is the average time taken by children to acquire a working knowledge of a new language when they are in continual contact with the language. If pupils are recorded as at an early stage of learning English for more than two years of full-time education in an English school, it is time to start asking questions as to why they are not making progress. The reasons may be related to inadequacies in the EAL support they have received but the possibility of their having learning difficulties cannot be ignored. Hall (1995) offers useful advice and practical strategies for assessing bilingual pupils who may have special educational needs. It is essential that SENCOs and language support teachers work with each other in identifying and assessing pupils who may have both the need to acquire fluency in English and learning difficulties. A good starting point is to compare the SEN and EAL registers and the records of pupils' progress to ensure that misidentification is not preventing development. Daniels *et al*. (1996) make the point that resources are most equitably distributed when objective criteria are used to identify those who need special support and the school monitors the allocation of resources.

Many children who do not speak English as a first language find themselves assessed and taught as children with SEN (Troyna and Siraj-Blatchford, 1993). The Code of Practice (1994) specifically guards against misidentification of this sort (para 2.18), as did Circular 1/83, following the 1981 Education Act; however, the problem persists. Troyna and Siraj-Blatchford found that in a school where students of South Asian origin made up 58 per cent of the Year 7 cohort, no students of South Asian origin were identified as needing support for special needs, although 25 per cent of white pupils were. However, 37 per cent of the students of South Asian origin in the year were diagnosed as needing support for EAL although 31 per cent of the same group had been in English primary schools since the age of 4 and should surely have had their needs for support in learning English already met. Despite primary school assessments of their ability as average, almost all the South Asian pupils assessed as needing EAL support were placed in the lowest-ability sets. A similar pattern was revealed in Year 10. These disparities raise questions as to why so many pupils of South Asian origin, despite years in English schooling, were seen to have needs associated with their competence in English, why none were seen to have SEN and whether tests of English language competence were used as a screening device to place pupils in ability-based sets. As a consequence of the initial setting and a subsequent lack of reassessment or mobility between sets, few students of South Asian origin were able to follow GCSE courses, even in maths. Those who could have achieved GCSE success, had they been given opportunities, were disempowered. Those who genuinely needed support for special needs did not get it. In effect, the life-chances of all these students were diminished by inequitable treatment .

Assessment, attitudes and expectations

Research has shown that teacher attitudes and expectations significantly affect pupil achievement and behaviour (Mortimore *et al.*, 1988; Tizard *et al.*, 1988; Rutter *et al.*, 1979; Rosenthal and Jacobsen, 1968). Gipps and Murphy (1994) provide an excellent overview of the research on assessment and the achievement of boys and girls of different ethnic groups and explore the complexities of equity issues in these areas. Evidence suggests that some ethnic minority pupils achieve at much higher levels than others in public examinations and tests (Jones, 1993; Gillborn and Gipps, 1996). In general, students of Indian and East African Asian origin achieve better results than African–Caribbean, Pakistani, Bangladeshi or Turkish students. Gore (1997) suggests that the low expectations which teachers hold of African–Caribbean pupils influences how much emphasis they give to preparing pupils for their examinations. Troyna and Siraj-Blatchford (1993) show how misidentification of needs led to pupils of Asian origin being deprived of opportunities to take exam courses. There is every reason to believe that a change in teacher attitudes and expectations will lead to greater achievement for pupils who have previously been disadvantaged by a lack of awareness of their needs or by covert, and sometimes open, hostility.

Evidence suggests that institutional racism has an impact on understandings of SEN in several significant ways. Firstly, in identifying behavioural difficulties within certain groups of pupils, notably African–Caribbean boys, which do not necessarily exist outside the school context. Secondly, in failing to identify specific difficulties for children for whom English is a second language, or confusing SEN with EAL needs. And thirdly, in making provision for pupils from ethnic minority groups which is less useful and may impact adversely on life-chances. Gender differences in terms of who gets special education are also significant. Daniels and his colleagues (1996) investigated differences in assessment of, and provision for, the SEN of boys and girls, by 'race' and class, in four mainstream junior schools. They found that:

- schools spend more money on provision for boys who have SEN but do not have statements than they do for girls in same position;
- more than twice as many boys were getting extra help with emotional and behavioural difficulties, moderate learning difficulties and specific learning difficulties (usually reading);
- equity for girls occurred only with support for mild learning difficulties;
- the help boys received was more prestigious and expensive (e.g. literacy support, primary helper time) than the help received by girls, who got more 'cheap' or free help (e.g. from volunteers).

The researchers also found that gender disparities are strongly influenced by 'race':

- black pupils were more likely to be identified as having 'general learning difficulties', whereas their white peers would be described as having 'reading difficulties';
- black girls and black boys got almost equal help for general learning difficulties, whereas white boys got twice as much help as white girls;
- black boys were heavily overrepresented in the EBD category and black girls were also overrepresented; South Asian girls were strongly underrepresented;
- gender differences were greater in the white group than in the black group, especially among white pupils in the emotional and behavioural difficulties category.

There is an urgent need for monitoring by gender, ethnicity, identified need and provision at school, LEA and government level, of children with SEN, followed by research into patterns of identification and placement, and then by action to redress injustice and to ensure that the educational provision for all pupils is appropriate. This is an issue of equity, entitlement and human rights.

THE DEVELOPMENT OF EQUAL OPPORTUNITIES POLICIES IN RELATION TO SEN

English and Welsh schools are evaluated on how well the leadership and management of the school promote equal access by all pupils to the full range of opportunities for achievement that the school provides, as well as their effectiveness in overseeing the creation and implementation of policies to promote equality of opportunity and high achievements for all pupils (Ofsted, 1995, Section 6.1), including those with SEN or EAL.

However, not all schools have written EO policies and many who do have them do not ensure systematically that they are implemented and useful. For example, Daniels and colleagues (1996) observe that although in some mainstream schools there was 'a strong rhetoric of equal opportunities . . . no one was in charge of specifically developing it and monitoring gender issues' (p.2). Gipps and Murphy (1994) stress that the onus is on schools to 'address the issue of equal access at an actual rather than formal level' (p.276). A written policy which is not implemented is of little use to students or staff. On the other hand, there are schools whose EO practice has developed successfully in various aspects of provision over the years but is not formally recorded. Such schools need to consider the value of a written EO policy. As Cooper *et al.* (1994) point out: 'staff and pupils benefit from the security and direction provided by a consistent and coherent school-wide approach. . . . Staff derive support from clarity of purpose and a common direction' (p.7).

An EO policy is an 'underpinning policy': it provides a foundation statement of principle on which the practice of the school is built, and guidance for members of the school community. For example, an EO policy may say that all students are entitled to full access to a broad, balanced and relevant curriculum. For some pupils there may be barriers to access. Each teacher needs to assess what this means and to ensure that they plan and provide accordingly: for example, seats near the front for pupils with hearing impairments and support for those who are using lip-reading; blown-up worksheets, or work scanned into computers and enlarged, for pupils with visual impairments.

A good EO policy, in any school, will address the needs of all pupils, and will include both sexes, people from all ethnic groups and those with learning difficulties and disabilities. It will reflect the rights and responsibilities of all to have or to provide the broad, balanced, relevant and appropriate education guaranteed by the 1988 Education Reform Act. It will:

- define principles and procedures for ensuring that all adults and children receive EO to benefit from the educational services and facilities on offer;
- describe an inclusive learning environment for all pupils;
- describe an inclusive teaching and working environment for all staff;
- increase coherence within the school community by defining shared values;
- encourage better relationships between staff, pupils, governors, parents and the wider community by clarifying expectations and creating an ethos of inclusion;
- set a framework for action by individuals;
- give the individual pupil, parent, teacher or governor a defined context in which to act;
- clarify legal responsibilities of governors and staff and therefore help to ensure justice for individuals.

Effective EO policy is about raising awareness, developing trust, defining expectations, ensuring clarity of principles and procedures, defining corporate, collective and individual responsibility, creating a framework for action and building on good practice in helping pupils learn and achieve. In effect, it is a tool for managing change towards inclusion.

How can an effective policy for equality be developed?

Governors and LEAs have a responsibility under the law (SDA, 1975; RRA, 1976; DDA, 1995) for ensuring that pupils and staff (or potential staff) are not discriminated against. Governors should, therefore, be integral to the process of policy development. To begin with, an audit of the current provision for pupils, including those with special needs, can be carried out with regard to equal opportunities. This can be done by staff within the school and/or by an independent adviser who will evaluate the ethos and environment and the effect of the school's policies on different groups of pupils, in relation to their sex, ethnicity, language, culture, religion, disability or special needs. The following examples illustrate how an audit can reveal a problem which the school can then address.

When an ethnically mixed special school for pupils with SLD/PMLD had only white European dolls in primary classrooms, and few books or other resources that reflected ethnic diversity, pupils from some ethnic groups were being expected to make cultural leaps away from the familiar that white peers did not have to make and were less likely to feel comfortable to learn as a result.

An MLD school that refused to enter any pupils for GCSE exams on the grounds that most would fail, disadvantaged the small group of pupils whose ability exceeded the majority.

An audit of a grant-maintained secondary school revealed that on-site counselling services were being taken up by girls who felt they had learning or emotional and behavioural difficulties, but were being eschewed by boys. On the other hand, records of pupils who had left the school (not through permanent exclusion) revealed a disproportionately high number of boys with identified emotional and behavioural difficulties. In effect, girls with SEN were getting help on site and boys were being encouraged to leave. This difference was unwittingly supported by staff who i) took more punitive action against boys than girls and ii) encouraged girls but not boys to seek the help of a counsellor. Gender-stereotyping and teacher expectations were having a direct effect on the education and future of some pupils with learning difficulties.

By auditing and monitoring their EO provision, the schools in these examples were able to take action to address inequities, thus becoming more inclusive.

What should be in a policy for equality?

Every school will develop its own EO policy in relation to its needs and its community. The policy should be inclusive, that is it should address the wider aspects of 'race', gender, culture, social class, disability and learning difficulties. The length and language of the policy will vary. Some schools favour succinct 'overview' policies which state principles; other schools prefer extensive policy documents which cover the application of principles in a number of areas. In both cases the details of practice to ensure equity should be recorded in other relevant places. For example, the policy for physical education should make clear how the PE curriculum meets the needs of different groups of pupils by ensuring participation by children with different disabilities or medical conditions, or enabling access to a range of activities for boys and girls.

Whether the EO policy is general or specific, common elements appear in well-thought-out EO policies. Some of these can be summarised in a sentence or two, others take more definition and detail. A particular school's policy may not necessarily need to include all of the elements discussed below.

The school's aims for its pupils and staff

Such aims might be: to provide a broad, balanced and relevant education to meet the needs of all pupils; to offer EO for highest educational achievement for all pupils; to provide a safe and welcoming teaching and learning environment, free of discrimination, inclusive of and accessible to all; to show respect for all individuals and to value their individual contributions to the school; to encourage independence and responsibility in young people, etc.

A rationale for the policy

This section might include acknowledgement of the fact that equity and an inclusive ethos do not just happen. There may be a need to acknowledge the make-up of the school or local population or to recognise the ways in which discrimination affects people. It might say how the school teaches about laws regarding EO, and the reasons for, and effects of, discrimination.

Any special issues for the school and how these are addressed

Schools may want to acknowledge various minority groups including traveller, bilingual and refugee children, and say briefly how they provide for them. Many special schools will describe their provision for girls, often a minority, whereas mainstream schools may refer to on-site units or specialist provision, and residential schools in white localities may acknowledge the need to protect ethnic minority students from racism locally. Some schools include specific statements on aspects of EO.

A clear statement of what the school expects and will not accept

This section outlines the behaviour the school expects (e.g. respect for all, an inclusive ethos where everyone is equally valued, all members of the school community to help each other, etc.). It may allude to positive behaviour management and assertive discipline as a means of increasing co-operation and reducing conflict. It also says what the school will not accept (e.g. racism, sexism or any form of discrimination, bullying or harassment) and the action that the school will take if discrimination or harassment occurs. Much of the detail of this section will be found in the school's behaviour policy and staff handbook.

A broad description of what the school does actively to promote equality of opportunity for staff and pupils

This is the heart of the policy. It describes principles of equity that underline school practices. Some schools use headings, such as the example given below. Some schools make statements of principle and refer to other documents where more specific detail will be found. These other documents might include curriculum policies; staff appointment and staff development policies; policies for the welfare and care of pupils, assessment policy; documents describing the organisation of the school, teaching and social groups; admissions policies and procedures; health and safety policies; and others.

Curriculum

The EO policy might say that the curriculum will encourage pupils to recognise that communities throughout the world have different values, traditions and cultures and that pupils will be taught about languages, science, arts and other cultural forms from outside the western world. The practical expression of this principle would be seen in the content of schemes of work for different subjects and in the diversity of resources available in the school. It would also be seen in display, the range of school visits made by pupils, and the human and other resources brought into the school, such as exhibitions or theatre groups. More specifically, the EO policy might say, for example, that the range of work experience placements should cater for all pupils and that placements are checked carefully to ensure that pupils will have a safe and positive learning experience. The work experience policy would detail the range of placements and how the needs of pupils with particular learning difficulties or disabilities are met; the arrangements made to ensure that a placement is suitable for the student; what use is made of the information given by students in their debriefings, particularly if they report having experienced discrimination or prejudice.

School organisation

The EO policy might refer to principles of school organisation such as: 'Opportunities will be taken to raise the self-esteem of all pupils by giving them appropriate responsibilities for learning'. In practice, this might mean that pupils with PMLD are encouraged to make choices and express preferences, or that when paired reading programmes are set up opportunities are created for less skilled older readers to be paired with younger readers whom they can support. The school might develop the role of the school council in supporting pupils' rights to equitable treatment, and their communication skills and abilities, or deliberately structure the involvement of pupils with learning difficulties and disabilities in peer-group counselling, or community service. Details of these practices would be given in appropriate policy documents or guidance for staff.

The rights of girls and boys to equitable treatment might mean reviewing the courses available to students and addressing any issues of gender stereotyping in take-up. It might result in single-sex teaching for specific courses. A school for pupils with a wide range of learning and behavioural difficulties taught sex education to single-sex groups in Years 7–9 but also differentiated by ability, so that the two boys' groups followed the same basic programme but used different resources, worked at a different pace and addressed different levels of challenge in discussion.

A statement of the roles and responsibilities of everyone in relation to the policy

This section will say that all members of the school community are expected to promote the policy, with a sentence or two on the particular roles and responsibilities of pupils, teachers, head teacher, support staff, parents/carers, governors and visitors for making sure that equity is a feature of all aspects of school life. The details of who will do what and when will be found in codes of practice, job descriptions, staff handbook, governors' constitution, school council constitution and behaviour policies.

How and when the effectiveness of the policy will be monitored, evaluated and reviewed

The procedures for ensuring that the policy is implemented, monitored and evaluated for effectiveness should be briefly described.

1   Information gathering may include: regular audits of need and provision (how many girls are participating in extra-curricular activities?); discussions with members of the school community through parents' evenings or at annual or IEP reviews (how well have our systems worked for parents?); with pupils through school council meetings (how well does the playground meet everyone's needs?); consultations with 'experts', including inspectors; and meetings with particular groups, such as pupils with disabilities (how well are we meeting specific needs?)

2   Data, logs and records should be regularly monitored to identify any patterns which affect individuals or groups of students (including girls and boys, pupils from different ethnic groups, pupils with learning difficulties and disabilities). These may include data on attainment (SATs and exams) and progress (in literacy or numeracy), showing the 'value added' for different individuals and trends for groups; behaviour; admissions; allocation of resources; complaints; and so on. The information should be analysed, and action taken to ensure that equity for all is increased.

3   Responsibility for monitoring and evaluation will be shared by a range of people: for example, the senior management team may monitor classroom practice; the assessment co-ordinator may analyse data on attainment by 'race', gender and special needs; subject co-ordinators will ensure that the content of schemes of work and the resources reflect the

principles of the policy and are accessible and appropriate to all; the SENCO will monitor the SEN register; teachers will identify and assess need and monitor individual pupils' progress; pupils and parents/carers will inform staff of difficulties they experience with any aspect of their school experience; governors will report on the effectiveness of the SEN and EO policies in their Annual Report to parents; the head teacher will report regularly to governors on equality issues.

4   The policy should be reviewed regularly: for example, within one year of introduction, thereafter every two years.

As an EO policy draws upon and informs other school policies, it may be useful to append a list of other documents to which the policy specifically relates including policies on: SEN, admissions, behaviour and discipline, bullying and harassment, physical access, language, personal, health and social education (PHSE), curriculum, uniform, staff development, complaints procedures.

Finally, a clear summary of the policy should be included in the school's prospectus and be displayed within the building. Schools which are prepared to publish, practise and regularly evaluate their EO policies are in a better position to know whether they offer genuine equity and entitlement to all. This demands a high degree of honesty, self-criticism and determination, but the rewards are evident in the increased success of pupils and satisfaction among staff. To move towards real inclusivity, staff must be committed to recognition of the diversity within the school. Every teacher must make it their business to be aware of the effect of gender, ethnicity and social class on the experiences, abilities and disabilities of students. Pupils and staff must feel themselves valued as individuals, of equal worth to their peers. Pupils must be empowered through involvement in their own learning processes. In these ways, the school can bring together, in an inclusive environment, the different people who learn and teach in the school. As confidence, trust and security develop, so learning will increase. Only with such policy and practice can a school truly be called inclusive.

Table 5.1 Model for developing an equality policy

1   Governors and staff discuss equal opportunities, agree aims for the school and decide how to set up process
2   Governors and staff decide composition, timetable and remit of EO policy working group
3   Working group decides procedure and begins audit and consultation
4   Consultation takes place with parents/carers, pupils (if possible), staff and other interested parties
5   Working group drafts policy and reports to the whole governing body and staff
6   Contents of policy are discussed and amendments made – draft policy may be circulated for comment to parents/carers, pupils, LEA, etc.

7   Any further amendments are made and policy is ratified by whole governing body
8   Policy is made public and summarised for prospectus
9   Policy is put into practice, training is organised as appropriate and policy and practice are monitored for effectiveness over the course of a year
10 Policy is evaluated and reviewed at the end of the year and regularly thereafter

---

Table 5.2 Example of an equal opportunities policy

Our school community embraces a broad range of individuals and groups whose varied backgrounds, experiences, lifestyles, languages and cultures enrich all our lives and educational processes. We are committed to promoting the benefits of such diversity and to challenging and erasing all practices that are prejudicial and discriminatory, and which contribute to inequality on the grounds of race, gender, religion, sexual orientation, social class, ability and disability.

It is the responsibility of all members of the school community, teaching and support staff, parents/carers, pupils, governing body, to uphold this policy and to ensure that it is put into practice.

1   The curriculum:
    entitlement; whole school approaches; upper school (work experience); college links; course design; resources; curriculum delivery; language; access; assessment.
2   Organisation and administration:
    admissions; naming; pupil grouping; language; school functions; school/home; letters and information; parents'/carers' evenings.
3   School environment:
    common areas; displays; access; food; clothing.
4   School community:
    harassment; staff development and appointments; INSET.
5   Responsibility.
6   Monitoring/evaluation.

With acknowledgement to Phoenix School, London Borough of Tower Hamlets: the school offers a supported National Curriculum to pupils with a wide range of MLD.

REFERENCES

Ahmad, P., Oxley McCann, A. and Plackett, C. (1997) 'Home-school liaison in multicultural schools in Cleveland', in J. Bastiani (ed.) *Home-School Work in Multicultural Settings*, London: David Fulton.

Cooper, P., Upton, G. and Smith, C. (1991) 'Ethnic minority and gender distribution among staff and pupils in facilities for pupils with emotional and behavioural difficulties in England and Wales', *British Journal of Sociology of Education* 12(1): 77–94.

Cooper, P., Smith, C. and Upton, G. (1994) *Emotional and Behavioural Difficulties: Theory into Practice*, London: Routledge.

Crooks, B. (1997) 'Minimising obstacles, maximising opportunities: teachers and black parents', in J. Bastiani (ed.) *Home-School Work in Multicultural Settings*, London: David Fulton.

Daniels, H., Hey, V., Leonard, D. and Smith, M. (1996) 'Gender and special needs in mainstream schooling', *ESRC End of Award Report R000235059*, July 1996, University of Birmingham.

Department for Education and Employment (DfEE) (1994) *Code of Practice on the Identification and Assessment of Special Educational Needs*, London: HMSO.

Department for Education and Employment (DfEE) (1997) *Circular 3/97, What the Disability Discrimination Act (DDA) 1995 Means for Schools and LEAs*, London: HMSO.

Department of Education and Science (DES) (1983) *Circular 1/83, Assessment and Statementing of Special Educational Needs*, London: HMSO.

Fine, M. and Asch, A. (1988) 'Disability beyond stigma: social interaction, discrimination and activism', *Journal of Social Issues* 44(1): 61–74.

Gillborn, D. and Gipps, C. (1996) *Recent Research on the Achievements of Ethnic Minority Pupils,* Ofsted & Institute of Education Report, London: HMSO.

Gipps, C. and Murphy, P. (1994) *A Fair Test: Assessment, Achievement and Equity*, Buckingham: Open University Press.

Gore, C. (1997) 'Inequality, ethnicity and educational achievement', Paper and talk based on research undertaken at University of Birmingham, presented at National Children's Bureau Conference, Supporting African-Caribbean Boys in the School System, London, 16 June 1997.

Hall, D. (1995) *Assessing the Needs of Bilingual Pupils: Living in Two Languages*, London: David Fulton.

Hargreaves, D. H., Hester, S. K. and Mellor, F. J. (1975) *Deviance in Classrooms*, London: Routledge & Kegan Paul.

Jones, T. (1993) *Britain's Ethnic Minorities*, London: Policy Studies Institute.

Kler, D. (1997) 'The emotional needs of Bangladeshi families', Lecture given at Tavistock Conference, London: Tavistock Centre for Human Relations.

Mortimore, P., Sammons, P., Stoll, L., Lewis, D. and Ecob, R. (1988) *School Matters: the Junior School Years*, Wells, Somerset: Open Books.

Ofsted (1995) *The Ofsted Handbooks: Guidance on the Inspection of Primary/Secondary/Special Schools*, London: HMSO.

Reiser, R. and Mason, M. (1990) *Disability Equality in the Classroom: a Human Rights Issue*, London: Inner London Education Authority.

Rosenthal, R. and Jacobsen, L. (1968) *Pygmalion in the Classroom*, New York: Holt, Rinehart and Winston.

Rouse, M. and Florian, L. (1996) 'Effective inclusive schools: a study in two countries', *Cambridge Journal of Education* 26(1): 71–85.

Rutter, M., Maughan, B., Mortimore, P., Ouston, J. and Smith, A. (1979) *Fifteen Thousand Hours*, Wells, Somerset: Open Books.

Sammons, P., Hillman, J. and Mortimore, P. (1995) 'Key characteristics of effective schools: a review of school effectiveness research', *A Report by the Institute of Education for Ofsted*, London: Institute of Education, University of London.

Shah, R. (1995) *The Silent Minority: Children with Disability in Asian Families*, Revised edition, London: National Children's Bureau.

Smith, D. and Tomlinson, S. (1989) *The School Effect: a Study of Multi-racial Comprehensives*, London: Policy Studies Institute.

Tizard, B., Blatchford, P., Burke, J., Farquhar, C. and Plewis, I. (1988) *Young Children at School in the Inner City*, London: Lawrence Erlbaum.

Troyna, B. and Siraj-Blatchford, I. (1993) 'Providing support or denying access? The experience of students designated as ESL or SN in a multi-cultural school', *Educational Review* 45(1): 3–11.

Wright, C. (1986) 'School processes: an ethnographic study', in S. J. Eggleston, D. K. Dunn and M. Anjali (eds) *Education for Some: the Educational and Vocational Experiences of 15–18 Year-old Members of Minority Ethnic Groups*, Stoke-on-Trent: Trentham Books.

Wright, C. (1989) 'Black students – white teachers', in B. Troyna (ed.) *Racial Inequality in Education,* London: Routledge.

Wright, C. (1992) *Race Relations in the Primary School*, London: David Fulton.

Chapter 6

Managing change

Jim Wolger

This chapter considers ways in which the move towards inclusive education can be developed and effectively managed in the light of experience gained from the recent radical and rapid changes that have taken place in education in the UK. Jim Wolger makes reference to current literature and observed practice in both special and mainstream schools.

The prevailing view in special education today is that pupils with special educational needs should, wherever possible, be educated with their peers in mainstream settings (Pijl *et al.*, 1997; DfEE, 1997a). Ways in which changes can be made to the structure and organisation of schools to encourage systematic inclusion are of vital concern.

The promotion of inclusion, through school policy and practice, is seen by Stangvik (1997) in terms of change and innovation and relates to organisational developments in schools and other community agencies, and to pressures within society for the clarification of values leading to the setting of policy, and for the creation of new environments for learning. If, as Stangvik also maintains, the level of change is dictated by the nature of the required inclusion, the definition used in this book, 'the opportunity for persons with disability to participate fully in all of the educational, employment, consumer, recreational, community and domestic activities that typify everyday society', implies a higher level of commitment to, and a more comprehensive and interconnected spread of change within, education and across other social agencies (e.g. Social Services and Health) than has previously been experienced in the UK. This chapter asserts that schools and other educational institutions (individually and collectively) have a vital role to play in determining how values, attitudes and assumptions can be altered within society as a whole.

THE CONTEXT OF CHANGE

Fullan (1996) maintains that educators must learn to live proactively and productively with change in order that it can become a positive force for the initiation of good practice. It is important, therefore, to analyse the effects of changes in policy in order that their positive characteristics can be promoted and their negative ones avoided. The way in which institutional change is managed by staff in schools is affected by their ability to cope with change in the wider context. In the UK over the last two decades, staff in schools have had to deal with a wide range of national and local changes, as, since 1980, there has been more education legislation than in the previous history of state education. Whitaker (1993) maintains that this situation is a direct result of desperate attempts to respond to the confusion of rapid and accelerating changes in all spheres of life.

Bowe and Ball (1992) argue that negative aspects of recent changes in the UK stem from political ideology, especially the move to Local Management of Schools (LMS). This 'business model' approach is seen by Davie (1996) as sitting uneasily alongside attempts to value the efforts of all, even of those who are not productive in economic terms. The harsh reality of having to make a profit or 'go to the wall' (Duffy, 1990) is not in accord with a determination to care for, and educate, the most vulnerable in society. Gilbert (1990) and Fullan (1985) see this as leading to the possible loss of collaboration between the schools themselves and between schools and institutions of further and higher education; both of which are essential to the successful implementation of change in schools.

On the positive side it can be argued, however, that, out of the confusion, an adaptable teaching profession has developed which is more than capable of managing future change. Whitaker (1993) suggests that the situation indicates a change in the 'metabolism' of schools which requires an increased capacity to adapt and to modify to new circumstances and environments, and he argues that most progress will be made where there is a radical rethinking of management concepts and structures. There are, consequently, certain actions which can be taken by schools to assist in the move towards the eventual realisation of inclusive education. The first of these is to promote 'greater inclusive practice' as an 'aim' in the School's Development Plan (SDP). The effectiveness of the SDP in promoting inclusion derives from its power as a tool for the management and initiation of change.

THE SDP AS A TOOL FOR CHANGE

SDPs were introduced by the Department of Education and Science as a means of allowing schools to plan their future progress. This is a similar concept to that of the 'three- to five-year business plan' used by industry, and which encourages school management teams to respond to:

- national and local authority policies and initiatives;
- school aims and values;
- existing achievements;
- the need for development.

The SDP should identify:

- developments to be undertaken;
- those responsible for ensuring that action is taken;
- the time scale involved;
- the success criteria to be achieved, in terms of improved teaching and learning;
- those responsible for monitoring and evaluating the progress of the SDP;
- the financial implications of the required training and resources.

An example of one element (described as 'working towards inclusive practice'), taken from the SDP of an inner-city school for pupils with severe learning difficulties, includes the following details:

Action: the review of curriculum provision and delivery for SLD and PMLD pupils and the revision of the format for schemes of work to incorporate any changes made in that review; the restructuring of senior management; and a review of existing mainstream and community links.

Responsible: school staff at all levels (including governors and parents) working in partnership with Health Authority staff; staff from mainstream schools and community agencies who may provide health promotion; sex and drugs education; respite care; and leisure facilities.

Success criteria: in terms of the improved quality of teaching and learning through the full integration of the SLD and PMLD curriculum provision within a multidisciplinary framework, and including some outreach work to promote inclusive practice.

Time scale: over a 3 year period with initial reviews of school practice, the restructuring of school management and a complete review of staffing within two terms; the reformatting of schemes of work during the first year, and the reviewing of mainstream and community links during Year two. Opportunities for outreach work are provided in Year three.

Monitoring and evaluation: shared between the various governing body committees and the senior management team, with input from a multidisciplinary team (including parents) meeting at least once per term. It also includes advice from an external consultant.

Resources and training: described mainly in terms of supply cover to allow staff to undertake reviews and to write papers; 'directed time' for staff meetings, the creation of two new posts of special responsibility: 'PMLD Co-ordinator' and 'Community Liaison Co-ordinator'; and the costs involved in engaging the services of a consultant.

The example above shows the value of an SDP as a means of responding to current educational thinking, and indicates how local circumstances and the history of the school can determine distinctly individual responses: 'Development planning is the way in which each school interprets external policy requirements so that they are integrated into their own unique life and culture' (Hargreaves and Hopkins, 1993, p.7). These same authors also stress that the ability of school staff to reflect on whether their work is empowering, and allows the consolidation of good practice and future developments to be carefully planned. Consequently, the culture of the school links and interprets national policies and educational initiatives and uses them to further its own development.

Skelton *et al.* (1991) widen the argument in suggesting that the development planning process, if applied successfully, will transform what they refer to as the four 'frames' within the school:

- organisational structures;
- curriculum and instructional practices;
- the climate and culture;
- the leadership.

Gipps (1990) adds a further 'frame': teacher development, which she believes is inextricably linked to successful school development. The Department of Education (Hargreaves and Hopkins, 1991) strongly emphasised that development planning would help to track and order the various strands of development across the complex organisation of the institution by encouraging staff to ask a number of searching questions:

- Where is the school in its development?
- What changes need to be made to move forward?
- How can these changes be managed over time?
- How has that management been successful?

The questions fit into a development planning cycle of:

AUDIT ⇨ PLANNING ⇨ IMPLEMENTATION ⇨ EVALUATION

Woods and Orlik (1994) see this cycle as a method of allowing schools to establish performance indicators and effective systems of evaluation in order to monitor operations at all levels. Allan (1990) maintains that a planning cycle guarantees that the resources available in the school can be successfully identified and effectively used to increase the range of opportunities and the quality of education available for its pupils. (See Chapter 13 by Allan Day.) This concern for quality and improvement, which is the responsibility of each school, will effectively ensure the development of every pupil. Development planning, particularly the SDP, is an essential tool in the management and implementation of inclusive education.

THE CHALLENGE OF CHANGE FOR INCLUSIVE EDUCATION

Barton (1995) describes inclusive education as one of the most important and urgent issues facing all societies. Its importance to the development of education world-wide was emphasised by the UNESCO *Salamanca Statement* (1994) and recently in the UK by Wedell (1995) and Mittler (1995) and in the Government's Green Paper (DfEE, 1997a). Barton (1995), however, stresses that the policies and practice of inclusion will be complex and contentious and will demand fundamental changes to the social and economic conditions of society, especially in relation to the values involved in the prioritisation and distribution of resources:

- how society views differences;
- how schools organise themselves to cope with diversity;
- how teachers view and use teaching styles and the curriculum.

Nevertheless, schools can do something immediately to start changing the values, attitudes and assumptions held by those who influence the distribution of resources; who decide how differences are to be viewed; and how schools are organised to accommodate these differences.

It has become clear, from what has been written about 'change' and about 'inclusive education', that

- how teachers view their work in terms of inclusion,
- how they gain the knowledge and skills to enable them to deal with the differences exhibited by pupils,

and

- how they organise and deliver a curriculum capable of meeting the full range of learning needs (including how they work with other educational and non-educational agencies)

is dependent on the management and structure of individual schools. If the challenges posed by inclusive education are to be met by staff in schools, and considered within the context of their ability to deal with change, the next major development in national education policy will be more naturally inclined towards the task of ensuring that all pupils (whatever their disability) are educated together in a manner which encourages self-esteem and acknowledges the importance of self-determination and choice.

WHAT SCHOOLS CAN DO TO INFLUENCE MOVES TOWARDS INCLUSIVE EDUCATION

The first area for action relates to the perceived nature of special education and the use of terminology. Ballard (1995) is in no doubt that, as long as the word 'special' continues to be used, segregation will continue to be an accepted practice. Davie (1996), whose list of special educational needs covers the majority of pupils, calls for a review of the term in order to emphasise shared *diversity* rather than *separateness*; Norwich (1993; 1996) holds a similar view. A recent poll of opinion in the staffrooms of three schools (two special and one mainstream secondary) showed that many staff have reservations about using the word 'special' as it seems to imply 'restrictive' and 'segregated' practices rather than 'normal' provision. The use of alternative terms such as 'personal educational needs' was suggested.

If alternative terminology is to be sought to suit the 'inclusive' nature of future educational provision for pupils with special educational needs, a number of factors must be taken into account before a satisfactory descriptor can be agreed upon. Ballard (1995) points to the moral dimension, shaped by the beliefs of society, and suggests that any new terminology will be determined by innovative practice, and must relate to a definition of inclusive 'lifelong' education (such as the one promoted in this book) as the only morally justifiable system. Each and every school must be responsible for the shaping of public opinion (Tilstone, 1996).

The second area of action, useful to schools in the promotion of inclusive education, focuses on 'school effectiveness' (Reynolds, 1995; Bailey, 1995; Ainscow, 1995a; 1997), and is concerned with organisational change, involving whole school policies for the benefit of all children rather than centring on those with special educational needs.

The link between the organisational conditions required to facilitate school effectiveness and those required to carry forward inclusive education is clearly stated by Ainscow (1995a; 1997). He suggests that the same six conditions:

- leadership
- involvement
- collaborative planning
- co-ordination
- enquiry and reflection
- staff development

are helpful not only in encouraging schools to improve, but also to move schools forward in their quest to implement inclusive policy and practice. The link is symbiotic, with the quest for school improvement fostering conditions that encourage the learning of all pupils, whether or not they have special needs. The six conditions can be linked with the six 'dimensions' of inclusive education suggested by Clark *et al.* (1995), and the four 'capacities' for 'change agency' described by Fullan (1996), and have been combined in Figure 6.1.

Conditions for inclusion*	Dimensions of inclusion**	Capacities for change***	Areas of influence
Leadership	Policy	Personal vision	Personal vision and leadership
Involvement . . . Co-ordination	Organisation		Organisational co-ordination and involvement
Collaborative planning	Pedagogical and curricular . . . Resources	Collaboration	Collaboration and planning
Enquiry and reflection	Values	Enquiry	Enquiry and reflection
Staff development	Teacher development	Mastery	Staff training and development

Figure 6.1 Areas of influence for inclusive education in the context of change
Sources: *Ainscow (1995a, p.66; 1997, p.5); **Clark *et al.* (1995, p.viii); ***Fullan (1996, pp.12–17)

AREAS OF INFLUENCE FOR INCLUSION IN THE CONTEXT OF CHANGE

These 'areas of influence' can be used to lead to a more detailed examination of the kind of action that can be taken by school managers to promote inclusive education within the current and future contexts of change.

Personal vision and leadership

This area includes both the acceptance of personal vision as a driving force within the organisation and an understanding that leadership is not the sole prerogative of senior management teams. Ainscow (1997) calls for a 'transformational' leadership which is widely spread and shared throughout the school and, when combined with personal vision, becomes an irresistible force for organisational change. It leads to the adoption of group processes within a problem-solving climate, which at the same time recognises the power of individual action. Bailey (1995) lists a number of factors which influence schools in their ability to implement and/or adapt to change. Significant among these are the orientation of leadership and the amount of personal control allowed to individuals within the organisation.

Examples of good practice are evident in a number of both mainstream and special schools. In one mainstream primary school, teachers are divided into 'support groups' consisting of staff with varying degrees of expertise. The main aim of such groups is to provide all staff with the chance to develop their own levels of skill and responsibility in a supported environment. It is a system which attempts both to recognise and to nurture the power of individual action. In a special school 'subject teams' are responsible for curriculum development, and the trialling of schemes of work and teaching approaches. The aim in both schools is to improve the quality of teaching and learning within a supported framework and, most importantly, to ensure that the problems faced by teachers and support staff in meeting the needs of pupils are tackled instantly from within this framework.

It is clear from those who have described inclusive practice in other countries (Dens and Hoedemaekers, 1995; O'Hanlon, 1995; Lampropoulou and Padeliadou, 1995; Lynch, 1995; Forlin, 1995) that its success depends ultimately upon the personality and skills of the individual teacher and the close support provided within the organisational framework of the school, especially in the classroom.

Organisational co-ordination and involvement

This is described (at one end of the educational spectrum) in terms of the ability of staff to co-ordinate their responses to policy requirements through to the needs of individual pupils (at the other). Clark et al. (1995) stress that the ability to respond to pupil diversity should be at the heart of all organisational change as responses to policy, and any changes made within schools should always be measured against pupil achievement and the needs of the wider community (Ainscow, 1997). One special school has developed a multidisciplinary advisory group (consisting of members of school staff, health-team professionals and parents) which meets at least once a term to advise upon current practice within the school. Policy statements, procedures, school documents, schemes of work, educational visits are all examined to ensure that the needs of pupils are being met from as many perspectives as possible.

Fullan (1996) draws attention to the notion of schools being 'plugged into' their environment in order to survive change and to implement innovative ideas from other organisations engaged in similar and different pursuits. Ware (1995) refers to the external 'wrap-around' support provided by multidisciplinary teams, the use of community facilities, and collaboration with institutions of higher education, as being crucial to the successful practice of inclusive education. Slee (1995) extends the discussion about school co-ordination and involvement by arguing that educationists should be taking a more proactive approach to the promotion of inclusive education in order to overcome what he describes as ideological baggage firmly fixed to the structural arrangements and policy making in special education. Such ideology, he explains, has allowed a number of assumptions to be held which are barriers to the acceptance of moves by schools to promote inclusive practices. One assumption is that inclusive education is totally dependent upon the allocation of resources and, therefore, that nothing can be put into place without a major reallocation. Such a view is contrary to the one expressed in this chapter, that schools can contribute greatly by putting inclusive education firmly on the agenda through their organisational involvement.

A second assumption is that any change within special education depends upon the authority of external 'experts', thus disempowering schools. To counter this assumption, staff must see themselves as experts and rely upon local skills and experience in order to focus upon, and meet, the individual needs of their pupils. The third assumption is a negative feeling, expressed in the fear that once children with special educational needs are admitted to regular schools, the energy and time spent meeting their needs will somehow lessen the quality of education available to the rest of the pupils, an opinion that must be fiercely resisted.

One mainstream primary school has taken a firm stance on the development of inclusion by placing it as an agenda item on all staff and governor meetings. Money has been used to implement a 'programme of building accessibility' in order that full wheelchair access will be available before the year 2000. According to the Chair of Governors this small gesture has had the effect of putting the development of inclusive education firmly into the minds of staff, governors and parents. The building of ramps is now seen as a powerful statement about the determination of the school to make itself accessible and that the importance of accessibility is reflected in statements about the curriculum. In addition integration links with two local special schools have been in operation for two years and are flourishing and the development of inclusive education for some children is now regarded as a distinct possibility by many staff and parents.

Collaboration and planning

In order to promote inclusive education, what is taught in schools, how it is to be delivered and how resources, both human and material, are managed must be decided through collaborative decision making and planning (Clark et al., 1995). The task of moving towards inclusive education is one of developing the work of the school in response to pupil diversity and must include a consideration of the overall organisation of the school, the curriculum in terms of its content and style of delivery, classroom practice, support for learning and staff development (Ainscow, 1997).

Udvari-Solner and Thousand (1995) explain the supportive nature of working in teams. Leadership functions are more easily distributed and shared; teachers are able to 'model' the co-operative learning techniques that they expect students to use; teaching skills improve as teachers learn from each other; the responsibility for pupils with 'unique' learning needs is shared by the team; and human and material resources are shared or combined in order that they can be used to better effect.

Examples of mainstream integration programmes, characterised by energetic and enthusiastic co-operation between staff and pupils in mainstream and special schools, have been well recorded (Fletcher-Campbell, 1994a; 1994b). The interaction between pupils with and without disabilities, and between the staff of both types of school, is the catalyst for more intense involvement between the schools.

Enquiry and reflection

It is important that teachers are able to consider the implications of the changes required (Ware, 1995) and to develop a clear position on issues of human rights, discrimination and what is meant by 'inclusive education' and 'special educational needs' (Clark et al., 1995). To Fullan (1996) it is a matter of teachers being able to develop their 'moral purpose', which he describes as the desire 'to make a difference' because they are agents of educational change and societal improvement.

Ainscow (1995b) maintains that schools which value enquiry and reflection find it easier to sustain momentum and are better placed to monitor the extent of actual change, even in times of turbulence. Ware (1995) in reinforcing this view is concerned that qualitative research should be used to examine current classroom practice. The research agenda is transformative in its own right, but the success of inclusion depends upon the motivation of those directly involved in its implementation at classroom level and their ability to devise changes to the system through reflection and practice (see Chapter 2).

Many schools encourage teachers to undertake classroom research as part of their professional development and, since the virtual disappearance of special needs elements from initial teacher training, it is often the only method of providing special needs training. In-service training courses often require teachers to engage in classroom research. Of five special schools visited recently, one in four teachers were undertaking part-time advanced studies in SEN, and one head teacher commented that the classroom research element was proving extremely valuable for the school as a whole as the teachers were being encouraged to focus on problems and developments within the school rather than spending time on what he called 'research questions disengaged from real school life'. Topics for such in-school research were as diverse as:

- an evaluation of the use of the sensory room;
- the evaluation of a mainstream integration programme for a group of Year 10 students;
- the analysis of targets for Individual Education Plans of a group of pupils with profound learning difficulties attending a community leisure facility.

Staff training and development

The success of inclusive education depends upon the ability of teachers to respond to diversity in the classroom (Clark et al., 1995). Ainscow (1995b) maintains that if staff development is to have a significant impact upon thinking and practice it needs to be linked to school development. He argues that time should be set aside for teachers to support each other, to explore and to develop aspects of their own practice. Consequently, resources need to be redirected to support development, and the benefit of this reorientation will be a more knowledgeable staff, clearer in their purpose, more confident and empowered, and willing and able to experiment. Teachers, thus equipped, will enable the school to develop wider perspectives on curriculum development, teaching and learning, classroom organisation, and possible responses to pupils' individual needs, all of which will aid the implementation of inclusive practices.

TOWARDS THE FUTURE

The reference from Stangvik (1997), at the beginning of this chapter, suggests that the drive towards inclusive education must involve a range of interconnected changes within the main agencies (education, health, social services, employment and leisure). The implications are in line with recent government thinking which led to the White Paper *Excellence in Schools* (DfEE, 1997b), and the Green Paper *Excellence for All Children* (DfEE, 1997a). Both publications indicate the government's commitment to change in partnership with parents, teachers, governors, local education authorities and the wider community in order to change attitudes and to make special educational needs an integral part of the programme of raising standards. At the time of writing, this commitment has yet to find its way into legislation. Nevertheless, staff in schools will need to take up the challenge and be prepared for the introduction of inclusive education for the majority of pupils.

REFERENCES

Ainscow, M. (1995a) 'Education for all: making it happen', *Support for Learning* (November) 10(4): 147–55.

Ainscow, M. (1995b) 'Special needs through school improvement; school improvement through special needs', in C. Clark, A. Dyson and A. Millward (eds) *Towards Inclusive Schools?*, London: Routledge.

Ainscow, M. (1997) 'Towards inclusive schooling', *British Journal of Special Education* 24(1): 3–6.

Allan, P. (1990) 'The School Development Plan', in C. Gilbert (ed.) *Local Management of Schools: a Guide for Teachers and Governors*, London: Kogan Page.

Bailey, J. C. (1995) 'Stress, morale and acceptance of change by special educators', in C. Clark, A. Dyson and A. Millward (eds) *Towards Inclusive Schools?*, London: Routledge.

Ballard, K. (1995) 'Inclusion, paradigms, power and participation', in C. Clark, A. Dyson and A. Millward (eds) *Towards Inclusive Schools?*, London: Routledge.

Barton, L. (1995) 'The politics of education for all', *Support for Learning* (November) 10(4): 156–60.

Bowe, R. and Ball, S. (1992) 'Doing what should come naturally: an exploration of LMS in one ordinary school', in G. Wallace (ed.) *Local Management of Schools: Research and Experience* (BERA Dialogues 6), Clevedon: Multilingual Matters.

Clark, C., Dyson, A. and Millward, A. (eds) (1995) *Towards Inclusive Schools?*, London: Routledge.

Davie, R. (1996) 'Raising the achievement of pupils with special educational needs', *Support for Learning* 11(2): 51–6.

Dens, A. and Hoedemaekers, E. (1995) 'A case study. Integration through co-operation: returning pupils to mainstream school', in C. O'Hanlon (ed.) *Inclusive Education in Europe*, London: David Fulton.

DfEE (1997a) *Excellence for All Children: Meeting Special Educational Needs*, London: The Stationery Office.

DfEE (1997b) *Excellence in Schools*, London: The Stationery Office.

Duffy, M. (1990) 'Heresy and magic', *Times Educational Supplement: LMS Guide, Part 1* (16 February), London: Times Newspapers.

Fletcher-Campbell, F. (1994a) *Still Joining Forces? A Follow up Study of Links between Special and Ordinary Schools*, Slough: NFER.

Fletcher-Campbell, F. (1994b) 'Special links? Collaboration between ordinary and special schools', *British Journal of Special Education* 21(3): 118–20.

Forlin, C. (1995) 'Educators' beliefs about inclusive practices in Western Australia', *British Journal of Special Education* 22(4): 179–85.

Fullan, M. (1985) 'Change processes and strategies at the local level', *The Elementary School Journal* 85(3).

Fullan, M. (1996) *Change Forces: Probing the Depths of Educational Reform*, London: Falmer Press.

Gilbert, C. (ed.) (1990) *Local Management of Schools: a Guide for Teachers and Governors*, London: Kogan.

Gipps, C. (1990) *Assessment: a Teachers' Guide to the Issues*, London: Hodder & Stoughton.

Hargreaves, D. and Hopkins, D. (1991) *The Empowered School*, London: Cassell.

Hargreaves, D. and Hopkins, D. (1993) 'School effectiveness, school improvement and development', in M. Preedy (ed.) *Managing the Effective School*, London: Open University and Paul Chapman.

Lampropoulou, P. and Padeliadou, S. (1995) 'Inclusive education: the Greek experience', in C. O'Hanlon (ed.) *Inclusive Education in Europe*, London: David Fulton.

Lynch, P. (1995) 'Integration in Ireland: policy and practice', in C. O'Hanlon (ed.) *Inclusive Education in Europe*, London: David Fulton.

Mittler, P. (1995) 'Special needs education: an international perspective', *British Journal of Special Education* 22 (3): 105–8.

Norwich, B. (1993) 'Has special needs outlived its usefulness?', in J. Visser and G. Upton (eds) *Special Education after Warnock*, London: David Fulton.

Norwich, B. (1996) 'Special needs education or education for all: connective specialisation and ideological impurity', *British Journal of Special Education* 23(3): 100–3.

O'Hanlon, C. (1995) 'Integration practice and policy in the UK for pupils with special educational needs', in C. O'Hanlon (ed.) *Inclusive Education in Europe*, London: David Fulton.

Pijl, S. J., Meijer, C. J. W. and Hegarty, S. (eds) (1997) *Inclusive Education: a Global Agenda*, London: Routledge.

Reynolds, D. (1995) 'Using school effectiveness knowledge for children with special needs: the problems and possibilities', in C. Clark, A. Dyson and A. Millward (eds) *Towards Inclusive Schools?*, London: Routledge.

Skelton, M., Reeves, G. and Playfoot, D. (1991) *Development Planning for Primary Schools*, London: Routledge.

Slee, R. (1995) 'Inclusive education: from policy to school implementation', in C. Clark, A. Dyson and A. Millward (eds) *Towards Inclusive Schools?*, London: Routledge.

Stangvik, G. (1997) 'Beyond schooling: integration in a policy perspective', in S. P. Pijl, C. J. W. Meijer and S. Hegarty (eds) *Inclusive Education: a Global Agenda*, London: Routledge.

Tilstone, C. (1996) 'Changing public attitudes', in B. Carpenter, R. Ashdown and K. Bovair (eds) *Enabling Access*, London: David Fulton.

Udvari-Solner, A. and Thousand, J. (1995) 'Effective organisational, instructional and curricular practices in inclusive schools and classrooms', in C. Clark, A. Dyson and A. Millward (eds) *Towards Inclusive Schools?*, London: Routledge.

United Nations Educational, Scientific and Cultural Organisation (UNESCO) and the Ministry of Education and Science, Spain (1994) *The Salamanca Statement and Framework for Action on Special Needs Education*, Paris: UNESCO.

Ware, L. (1995) 'The aftermath of the articulate debate: the invention of inclusive education', in C. Clark, A. Dyson and A. Millward (eds) *Towards Inclusive Schools?*, London: Routledge.

Wedell, K. (1995) 'Making inclusive education ordinary', *British Journal of Special Education* 22(3): 100–4.

Whitaker, P. (1993) *Managing Change in Schools*, Buckingham: Open University Press.

Woods, D. and Orlik, S. (1994) *School Review and Inspection*, London: Kogan Page.

Part II

Inclusive learning

Chapter 7

Including pupils
Developing a partnership in learning

Richard Rose

The involvement of pupils in the management of their own learning can have a positive effect upon pupil self-esteem and the clarification of learning intentions. Richard Rose argues that as schools move towards improved inclusive practice, they will need to consider the means by which pupils with special educational needs are enabled to play a greater role in assessment and the planning of learning.

In considering the conditions which are necessary to promote the greater inclusion of pupils with learning difficulties in all aspects of their education, it is essential that we give some thought to the role which the pupils themselves may play in supporting moves towards the achievement of an inclusive system. Implicit in the philosophy of inclusive practice must be a commitment to provide pupils with greater opportunities both to understand and participate in the planning and management of their own learning processes. Throughout this book we have attempted to adhere to a definition of inclusion which recognises the rights of pupils to participate fully within all aspects of their education in preparation for life as independent adults. It would be a mistake to regard the terms inclusion and integration as directly interchangeable. Indeed, in our bid for good inclusive practice, we must never lose sight of the importance of providing a standard of education which sets high standards for all pupils.

The balance between a pupil's right to inclusion, and an education which fully meets his or her individual needs, is one which must be carefully addressed. It has been suggested by Lindsay (1997a; 1997b) that a rush to adopt one particular model of provision, albeit for sound philosophical reasons, may in other ways impinge upon the rights of the child to receive an education which is wholly suited to his or her needs at a particular point in time. There are many pupils with special educational needs in mainstream schools who far from being fully *included* find themselves isolated by teaching approaches which fail to give adequate consideration to their individual learning needs and thereby *exclude* them from a range of opportunities which would enhance their performance potential. Similarly, there are examples of good practice in some segregated special schools which have endeavoured to include pupils fully in many facets of the learning process which have been seen by some teachers as problematic. Witness for example the innovative approaches which have been developed to enable pupils with learning difficulties to access the National Curriculum (Ashdown *et al.*, 1991; Lewis, 1995; Rose *et al.*, 1996b; Carpenter *et al.*, 1996; Byers and Rose, 1996).

When first introduced, the National Curriculum was seen as a development most likely to exclude a substantial number of pupils with special needs, and indeed there were many teachers who initially advocated the disapplication of pupils from its framework. Many of the same teachers now recognise the increase in curriculum breadth and opportunities which the National Curriculum has brought to these pupils. However, just as these benefits have been achieved through the hard work of teachers who have a concern to raise standards and promote increased opportunities, so must further steps along the road to inclusion be taken by exploring means of promoting further involvement of pupils with special needs in all of their learning processes. This chapter will consider the role which pupils may be encouraged to play as partners in the planning and management of their own learning, and will discuss ways in which this may have benefits for both teachers and pupils.

RECOGNITION OF THE PUPIL'S RIGHT TO INVOLVEMENT

In 1989 two important pieces of legislation were published which recognised the need to give full consideration to the views of children in all aspects of their life, including education. The Children Act (1989) requires that due consideration is taken of the wishes and feelings of all children throughout any proceedings which may have a bearing upon their lives. In November of the same year the United Nations General Assembly unanimously adopted *The Convention on the Rights of the Child*. This convention was, with certain reservations, ratified by the UK government in December 1991. Ratification and implementation are not, of course, one and the same thing, and it has been suggested (Lansdown, 1996) that as a nation we exercise extreme caution when considering any legislation which may recognise the rights of children and diminish the control exerted over them by adults. As a framework for delivering fair and effective services to all children the convention is one of the most important international documents ever to have received such wide consideration, and deserves the closest attention from all who work in any capacity with children. Significant sections of the convention address issues of education, and the rights of pupils with special needs. The influence of this important document can be clearly traced through legislation, which has appeared on the statute books in subsequent years, but there is still much which needs to be achieved. For example, Article 12 of the Convention states that:

> Parties shall assure to the child who is capable of forming his or her own views the rights to express those views freely in all matters affecting the child, the views of the child being given due weight in accordance with the age and maturity of the child.
>
> (UN, 1989, Article 12)

The message from such a statement is clear: both in terms of the rights which have been given to children, and the responsibilities which those of us who are in a position to make decisions on behalf of children have to ensure that those rights are upheld. For those professionals who work with children with special educational needs, the requirements established through the Children Act, and the UN Convention have been reinforced via the *Code of Practice on the Identification and Assessment of Pupils with Special Educational Needs* (1994), in which paragraph 2:37 states that:

Schools should consider how they:

- Involve pupils in decision making processes;
- Determine the pupil's level of participation, taking into account approaches to assessment and intervention which are suitable for his or her age, ability and past experiences;
- Record pupils' views in identifying their difficulties, setting goals, agreeing a development strategy, monitoring and reviewing progress;
- Involve pupils in implementing individual education plans.

(DfEE, 1994, para. 2:37, p.15)

With the introduction of such legislation, one might expect that the rights of the child to be heard could be assured, yet the very tone of both the UN Convention and the Code of Practice could lead to exclusion of a significant minority of pupils. Who, one may ask, will sit in judgement on a pupil's capability? The convention's view that some pupils may not be capable, and to some extent the notion within the Code of Practice that teachers should make decisions about a pupil's ability to participate in processes which determine their own needs, could in themselves undermine the move towards greater pupil participation. The spirit of these documents is clear, but it requires vigilance on the part of concerned professionals and parents to ensure that the intentions are upheld. Not least, there is a heavy burden upon teachers working with pupils with special educational needs to identify ways in which pupils may access the means to voice their own opinions and influence the decisions which effect all aspects of their lives.

The passing of legislation is, of course, only one step in the process of improving practice. Without sufficient guidelines and training of staff, it is unlikely that even the most well-received legislation will have the impact which was intended. Staff in schools need clear guidance with regards to the ways in which pupils can be fully included at each stage of their learning. This in itself requires a new emphasis upon research into the ways of motivating pupils to learn, and of providing them with a greater understanding of their own strengths as learners. There is a danger that in our rush to address curriculum content and to explore new ways of providing a broader range of subjects to all pupils, we neglect the analysis of teaching and learning styles which may provide the key to access for many pupils.

A significant area of need is that of promoting teacher confidence, particularly with regards to their own classroom role. It is evident, however, that in order to promote pupil involvement, significant changes in classroom practice will be required. In a survey of 115 primary and secondary school teachers, Wade and Moore (1994) found that less than a third of these teachers took any account of the opinions of pupils, and that pupil influence upon planning or meeting their own needs was negligible. There is a tendency amongst some teachers to adopt a position of authority and control in an effort to be seen to be managing pupils with learning difficulties, who might otherwise challenge their regular classroom routines. A feeling that allowing pupils to have a say in their own assessment, or the planning of their own work, may be undermining the authority of the teacher, is pervasive in some schools (Cowie, 1994; Charlton, 1996). However, it is easy to apportion blame to teachers for a slowness in reacting to changes in their practice. At a time when schools have been deluged in enforced legislation and change it is hardly surprising that a call to shift practice in an area which may well be regarded as destabilising has been slow to gather momentum.

A similar concern relates to the difficulties which some teachers have in establishing a learning environment which is fully conducive to pupil involvement. In order to develop the skills of negotiation and communication which are required for such participation, pupils need opportunities to work in a range of situations which are based upon both formal and informal settings. If, as required by the National Curriculum, pupils are to learn to express themselves in a variety of situations and contexts, an adherence to one particular teaching style is likely to be found wanting. The pupil who is to be encouraged to take some responsibility for his or her own learning must be encouraged to develop an ability to see and respect the opinions of others. In order to achieve this goal, teachers will need to consider the provision of a diversity of situations which encourage interaction at many levels.

Certainly there is good practice in schools which have recognised the advantages of including pupils in their own learning procedures, as will be demonstrated in this chapter. A major difficulty appears to centre far more upon an understanding of what can be achieved rather than a lack of willingness to address the problem. There remains a significant number of obstacles which must be overcome before the dissemination of such practice sufficiently influences change across all schools. Rose et al. (1996a) described the findings of the QUEST project which examined the response of mainstream and special schools to pupil involvement as advocated within the Code of Practice. Their survey of local authorities in England and Wales requested the identification of centres of good practice in promoting pupil involvement. These selected schools were then questioned about the approaches which they used to involve pupils in target setting, measuring their own progress and in the writing of reports. The picture which emerged from the research was of inconsistencies in practice in all areas of pupil involvement. Measuring progress appeared to present the greatest challenge, with less than 55 per cent of mainstream and 50 per cent of special schools claiming to have addressed this issue. Remembering that these were schools identified as promoting good practice in pupil involvement, it seems likely that the broader picture would present an even greater need for development.

WHY INCLUDE PUPILS IN THE PLANNING, ASSESSMENT AND MANAGEMENT OF LEARNING?

The Code of Practice (DfEE, 1994) recognised that the promotion of pupil involvement would not be easily achieved. However, over a number of years schools have seen the value of involving pupils in the various stages of planning assessment and recording (Pollard et al., 1994; Griffiths and Davies, 1995). In some instances this practice has been extended to provide greater participation by pupils with learning difficulties (Richmond, 1994; Jones et al., 1996).

Griffiths and Davies (1995) undertook work in a Nottinghamshire primary school which involved a considered review of the teacher–pupil relationship. They describe how through encouraging pupils to play a more active role in decision-making processes they were able to improve pupil self-esteem, increase task focus, and engender a more mature attitude to school work on the part of all pupils. Their work on goal setting indicates that the greater involvement of pupils enabled them to become more proficient in reflecting upon their own practice and achievements, and to discuss learning outcomes with teachers in a way which led ultimately to improved performance. At the core of their work is the belief that listening to pupils and valuing their opinions has a substantial impact upon the quality of learning. Griffiths and Davies recognised that for some pupils the ability to express themselves with confidence would not be easily achieved. They assisted pupils through this process by providing them with learning contracts which used key questions to aid pupils in thinking about their own needs. Statements such as 'these are the things which I need to improve on when working in school' and 'the most important of these which I think I can improve is' provided starting points for discussion and encouraged pupils to become more analytical about their own learning, and supported teachers in the consideration of their planning.

The emphasis upon listening to pupils is to be found in most studies of successful pupil participation. Padeliadu (1995; 1996), emphasised that pupils with learning difficulties often articulate strong opinions about their responses not only to specific teaching approaches, but also about the locations in which they are taught, and the peers alongside whom they have to work. She concludes that students make conscious decisions about where and to whom they go when they need help in school, and that this is based upon the pupils' perception about who has time and who will listen to them. Pupils have opinions, and if these are not heard it is likely that opportunities to ensure the most effective means of accessing their special needs will be missed. The findings of Padeliadu reinforce the views of Mac An Ghaill (1992a; 1992b), who stressed that teacher–pupil dialogue which takes genuine account of the views of pupils can be a powerful tool in overcoming negative attitudes towards school and the learning process. Mac An Ghaill also believes that pupils have a clear perception of the effects which school climate and the attitudes of people who work within a school can have upon their own learning outcomes. He concludes that fuller inclusion of pupils in the curriculum process can have a radical impact upon both the respect which pupils show towards schooling, and their willingness to participate in lessons.

Bennathan (1996), in a study conducted in mainstream schools, cited improved motivation and morale, and a lessening of behaviour problems as key benefits of increased pupil participation. She also identified a positive school ethos and strong leadership as critical elements which need to be well developed before a school is likely to move towards a successful programme of increased pupil participation. In her study, changing staff attitudes, where these were not seen as supportive, were seen as the central issue upon which pupil involvement could succeed or fail. The difficulties which staff may have in adopting their personal teaching style from that of the expert/provider to a more sharing and facilitative role are understandable. For some, the change in relationship is likely to cause them concerns that they may experience increases in behaviour difficulties in class. Bennathan, in recognising this difficulty, emphasises the part which senior staff must play in both supporting and providing a role model. The insecurity felt by some teachers when faced with the need to change an approach is likely to lead to a failure of implementation unless adequate support and training is put into place. Equally important is a clear understanding of what is expected of them by all staff and all pupils at every stage of the curriculum process. Schools need to be clear about their values, and have systems in place to monitor and evaluate their effectiveness which consider the maintenance of these values with as much rigour as they may pursue standards in other areas. A failure to provide this will mean that pupils are unsure of how they should react with different teachers in different situations. A pathway of planning for pupil involvement, as discussed later in this chapter, is critical to the success of any pupil involvement project. In instances where such a climate is achieved, as Bennathan has indicated, the more likely is an outcome of increased pupil participation an improvement in standards of behaviour.

Hardwick and Rushton (1994) described an approach to action planning for young people with learning difficulties. They saw the Records of Achievement movement which has encouraged pupils to make choices about their own work, and to retain as a record those documents or examples of which they are particularly proud, as providing an opportunity to assist pupils with identifying their own learning objectives, and measuring their progress towards their achievement. In their work they overcame considerable difficulties of communication experienced by pupils with severe learning difficulties, through the use of symbols, photographs, information technology and video materials, to enable pupils to make decisions about their own learning needs. As in the work of Griffiths and Davies (1995), they devised a format for contracting pupils which identified learning targets and outcomes, and indicated the benefits which pupils would gain on achieving these. Hardwick and Rushton recognised that each individual pupil would present a different challenge to the teacher who promoted pupil involvement, and that using just one approach would not enable all pupils to develop the necessary skills for full participation. In experimenting with a range of access devices and approaches which encouraged independent decision making, they concluded that pupils were able to relate more readily to the targets which they had played a part in setting, and that they became more adept at managing their own learning time.

LeRoy and Simpson (1992; 1996), describing work undertaken in Michigan, outlined their ideas on the importance of pupil involvement in individual target setting when including pupils with learning difficulties in mainstream classes. They described how, for pupils with learning difficulties coming into a mainstream school, it was necessary to devise a three-point individual planning process based upon the following steps:

- team identification;
- team orientation to the individual student;
- individual programme development.

In each of these three phases pupils were involved in making decisions about their own learning needs and the approaches to be used in meeting these. At the team identification stage, a collaborative team was established to provide the pupil with an appropriate degree of support to enable full participation in the school. The pupil played a leading role in needs identification and planning outcomes, and had a major say in which adults would play significant roles. During team orientation the pupil was encouraged to express views about how the classroom situation was progressing and to make suggestions for any necessary changes. The development of an individual programme enabled the pupil to work collaboratively with staff to identify opportunities for working on specific targets, and to discuss success criteria and teaching approaches.

LeRoy and Simpson describe the successes of inclusion in Michigan, in terms of demonstrating that outcomes for pupils with learning difficulties can be significantly improved through careful planning, which involves the pupil in all stages of the process. At the centre of their work, a set of key beliefs provide direction:

- participation is a right, not a function of ability level;
- activities and materials should be age appropriate;
- activities should be co-operatively implemented with typical peers;
- activities should promote self-advocacy, self-determination, and healthy interdependence;
- activities should be functional and outcome oriented;
- the use of natural supports should be promoted wherever possible.

The place of the pupil as a self-determining individual who also has the ability to function interdependently as part of a team is at the heart of the successful outcomes described by LeRoy and Simpson. They recognise that a key element in effective inclusion is the ability of the pupil to participate through the expression of opinions and the self-determination of goals. They equally acknowledge that this will not be achieved unless all members of the team working with the individual promote a climate which is conducive to the encouragement of full pupil involvement. Similarly, they recognise that many of the skills which a pupil will need to succeed in such an environment will need to be taught, and will not come about without considered planning and careful management.

The suggestion that pupil involvement may be a critical factor in the characteristics of effective inclusive schools is consistent with the views of many who have researched this area. Stoll (1991) cites student involvement and responsibility as a key element of creating an effective school ethos which enables successful inclusion to take place. This is a theme further developed by Rouse and Florian (1996). They elaborate on how other, more specific, variables associated with school effectiveness such as self-monitoring of behaviour, accepting responsibility for each other, involvement in formulation of rules and regulations, and giving all pupils a stake in the school, are important elements in creating an inclusive climate which is conducive to learning for all. In their study of schools in Utah, USA, and Newham, England, they found that some schools have already undertaken measures to involve pupils in their own assessment, and that staff interviewed about this component of promoting inclusion saw it as an important factor.

Evidence from these and others writing about this subject seems to suggest that involving pupils more fully in their own assessment and learning procedures has a number of direct benefits which may be listed as:

- increased self-esteem;
- greater focus upon personal learning needs and outcomes;
- improved behaviour;
- improved communication skills;
- improved teacher–pupil relationships.

These are outcomes which would clearly be desirable from any approach to teaching, but we should not assume that greater involvement of pupils with learning difficulties, even if recognised as advantageous, will be achieved without a structured path which is both developed and implemented by all staff in a school.

The skills required for pupil participation

When promoting the involvement of pupils with learning difficulties, it is often easier to list the obstacles which exist than to identify the means to overcoming them. Teachers responding to the QUEST project research (Rose et al., 1996a) were able to cite many reasons for not involving pupils in assessment and learning procedures. These included the lack of ability on the part of the pupils:

- to make choices;
- to negotiate;
- to predict;
- to share ideas with others;
- and to communicate effectively.

Ironically, many of these skills are closely related to the very ones seen as improving through greater pupil participation. It is likely that many pupils will fail to develop the necessary skills to overcome these obstacles unless they are specifically taught. However, it is quite implausible to believe that the ability to negotiate, or predict, or indeed to develop any of these requirements, will be achieved unless they are taught within context. The process of pupil involvement should be seen as an important teaching element, which has as its aim the provision of skills which enable the pupil to become a more independent and proficient learner. Through the design of teaching programmes which incorporate opportunities for pupils to learn to negotiate, and to communicate their own learning needs or preferred approaches to working, we are moving them towards a higher degree of independence, and preparing them for greater inclusion.

In classrooms which promote inclusive practice pupils take responsibility for their own workspace, and for the management of resources. They support each other and show respect for the views of their peers (Ofsted, 1995). Such behaviours are an important requisite for the provision of an effective learning environment which is ready to support inclusion. Pupil involvement must be seen as an important step along the route to providing all pupils, including those with learning difficulties, with the ability to function independently in the classroom.

MOVING TOWARDS INCLUSION THROUGH PUPIL INVOLVEMENT

Where should the teacher who wishes to prepare pupils for inclusion begin? It is clear from the literature in this area that individual teachers working in isolation are far less likely to have an impact than those who work in schools where the ethos supports pupil participation. Schools need to begin by taking stock of the conditions which they themselves create to ensure that an inclusive environment is at the head of their agenda. Inevitably amongst any group of professionals, attitudes and opinions will differ with regards to the extent to which pupils can and should be involved in procedures which may, until now, have been seen as the exclusive domain of the teacher. The school which believes that greater pupil involvement can be achieved without recourse to a fundamental review of its philosophy is likely to encounter obstacles at each stage of development. A framework of principles which not only charts opportunities for participation, but clarifies the intended outcomes and the advantages of such a system, should be seen as an important starting point for any school.

Identifying opportunities for pupil involvement will depend upon the existing systems in school and the needs of the individual pupil. Gersch (1994) recognises that pupils are likely to be at differing levels of preparedness for involvement, and that teachers will need to identify their readiness for participation at a range of levels. However, the school that begins this process in the early years of education, by encouraging pupils to begin with simple choices, may well find the more complex skills required for involvement in assessment and planning procedures easier as pupils progress through the school. Nutbrown (1996) emphasises that even in the earliest stages of education, pupils need to know what they are doing and why, and that they are capable of developing a level of reasoning which enables them to make sensible choices and to begin to see the consequences which go with these. It would be inappropriate to suggest that all pupils on entry to school should be fully involved as independent players in the whole planning, assessment and learning process. It is more likely that a staged approach, which moves towards greater independence as pupils mature and progress through the school, will achieve results.

Schools might consider identifying the stages of assessment and planning within their existing curriculum management approach, and review their practice to see how greater pupil involvement could be achieved. Byers and Rose (1996), in their work on planning the curriculum, suggested a linear progression through the curriculum from policy to assessment and reporting, which might well form the basis for identifying opportunities for pupil involvement at each stage. Their model, which is largely in line with that adopted by most schools, consists of the following headings:

- policy making;
- long-term planning;
- medium-term planning;
- short-term planning;
- short-term target setting;
- recording responses;
- evaluation and review;
- assessment and reporting.

Each of these headings could form a starting point for discussion on the roles which may be played by pupils.

As stake-holders in their own education, pupils may well have a valuable contribution to make to *policy making*. In many schools pupils have assisted in drawing together school rules, and have then played a major part in their implementation. In some schools, the establishment of school councils, or forums for discussion, have resulted in improved behaviour and clarification of roles and responsibilities (Cooper, 1993). Some schools for pupils with learning difficulties use circle time as an opportunity for pupils to express their views on a whole range of issues which can then be used to influence changes of policy or practice around the school. However, when embarking upon these approaches, it is essential that pupils see that their opinions are respected, and that they lead to constructive action. Pupil councils which are no more than forums for discussion have little impact upon the promotion of inclusive opportunities.

The *long-, medium- and short-term planning* stages should provide opportunities for discussion with pupils about courses to be taught, and anticipation of difficulties which they may perceive. The pupil who is uncertain about the future may well demonstrate insecurity through inappropriate behaviour, or may withdraw from participation. Pupils with learning difficulties often have problems with prediction, and encouraging discussion about those activities which have been planned for them can both enable them to think ahead and put into context the individual activities which form part of a course. It is appropriate that for some activities pupils should be encouraged to make choices with regard to the groupings in which they may work. Similarly, choices with regard to materials or working practices will help in the development of independent working practices. This does not imply that pupils will be able to make such choices on all occasions. Part of becoming independent is having a realisation that there are aspects of all of our lives over which we have little choice or control. However, for the pupil who has gained some independent working skills, providing choice over factors such as the location in which activities can be completed may have benefits. For example, being allowed to finish a written task in the library, when others are working in the classroom, may well be acceptable. Similarly, some autonomy with regards to the order in which tasks may be completed – 'this morning you need to complete English, maths and computer activities, but you can decide which order you do them in' – is an approach which encourages responsibility, and enables pupils to learn to manage their time.

Short-term target setting focuses upon the individual and is therefore an obvious area for development of inclusive approaches. Action planning to involve pupils requires both time and vigilance on the part of teachers, to ensure that the value which pupils place upon targets is recognised, and their implementation monitored. Pupils need to be encouraged to make decisions about their own targets on the basis of detailed information supplied by the teacher who is likely to have a clear idea of how the pupil needs to progress within a curriculum area. Target setting is not about pupils setting the curriculum agenda, but rather about exploring the route which will be taken by the pupil in order to maximise learning opportunities. The teacher may, for example, have a detailed plan for the mathematical development of a pupil which is based upon current attainment, and a hierarchy of mathematical skills. Target setting will focus upon those skills, and enable the pupil to discuss their purpose and how they will be gained. It should also be about discussing time scales, favoured resources, and the criteria set to measure successful attainment, which will enable both pupil and teacher to recognise and celebrate success. Some schools have begun to use target management sheets such as that illustrated in Figure 7.1. These sheets, prepared in consultation with the pupil, give an indication of what is to be achieved, the desirable outcomes of target-related activity, and performance indicators whereby both teacher and pupil may measure success.

In the example given, the school has linked the targets negotiated for an

What will the pupil do?	How will this be achieved?
Lloyd (pupil) will discuss his own needs with Sue (teacher) during action planning sessions, and identify his targets for the coming half term. He will type these on to his planning sheet ready to bring to his Annual Review meeting (7 Feb) using 'Writing with Symbols'.	Sue will organise action planning sessions for Lloyd and will help him to keep a diary of these sessions, which is confidential to Lloyd and herself.
Lloyd will attend his Annual Review, bringing with him his own report, and his own targets for the next half term. He will join in the target-setting discussion.	She will ensure that word processing facilities, including 'Writing with Symbols', are made readily available for each action planning session.
Lloyd will keep a record sheet each week which indicates work and progress on his targets. He will discuss these with Sue every Monday morning.	Sue will help Lloyd to prepare for his Annual Review, assisting him with report writing, and through role play and showing him a video of a previous Annual Review.
During the last three weeks of the half term he will work with Sue in tutorial time to revise his targets.	Sue will ensure that Lloyd is given adequate tutorial time each week to discuss his targets.
	Kate (head teacher) will ensure that Lloyd is able to have his full say at his Annual Review, and will monitor the language used by others at the meeting.
What are the desired outcomes?	**How will we measure success?**
Lloyd taking more responsibility for managing his own time and learning resources.	Lloyd being more willing to assist in preparation and tidying up of classroom after lessons.
Lloyd developing greater confidence in expressing his own opinions.	Lloyd being able to identify his own successes in working towards his targets.
Lloyd's parents being able to recognise and accept opportunities to support him in decision making and expressing his own opinions.	Lloyd having the confidence to share his targets with others in the Annual Review.

Figure 7.1 Target management

individual pupil to preparation for an annual review. Responsibilities have been identified for both the pupil and the teacher, and criteria have been set for measuring the success of the approach. Figure 7.2 illustrates three of the targets set by Lloyd during the implementation of the target management plan illustrated.

When negotiating targets with a pupil, it is essential to remember that many are suggestible, and will be eager to please. Negotiation of targets should be undertaken by someone who knows the pupil well, and in whom the pupil has total confidence. It also requires an understanding of the most appropriate forms of communication, and the development of a consistency of approach to planning sessions which enables the pupil to become familiar and comfortable with routines. Target-planning sessions should have a well-defined agenda which is discussed with the pupil, and it may be necessary to discuss the purpose and intended outcomes at the start of each session.

Schools have been imaginative in their approach to *recording responses*. Self-evaluation sheets and recording formats are to be found in most schools and examples have been well documented (Lawson, 1992; Sebba, 1995; Hardwick and Rushton, 1994). However, these often provide little more than a summative response, or an evaluation of whether or not a pupil enjoyed an activity. This may well be a useful introduction to self-evaluation, but should not be regarded as an end in itself. Successful evaluation requires that the focus is shifted from the activity to the outcome, enabling a pupil to comment on what has been learned as well as what has been experienced. Accessing recording through use of concept keyboards or other IT devices, audio or video recording, or use of augmented forms of communication, has been a real source of success for many schools.

The process *of evaluation and review* is an area which many more schools

Figure 7.2 Lloyd's target sheet

have begun to consider since the arrival of the Code of Practice (DfEE, 1994). The annual review procedure, and the formality which surrounds it, can be a threatening forum for many pupils. Some success has been achieved in developing a staged format to pupil involvement beginning with pupils in the early years of their education. Some schools encourage pupils to attend for a few minutes, bringing with them a piece of work, or a certificate of achievement which they can show and talk about. This can lead on to a later stage where pupils prepare a report beforehand, and talk about this and their intended targets. In a number of schools, opportunities are provided for pupils to make tape recordings to be played in review, or to be video recorded presenting their own report. This avoids the necessity of attendance for pupils who find such occasions intimidating. The use of role play and drama sessions which act out annual review procedures can be useful in preparing pupils, and some schools have made recordings of actual reviews to use with pupils prior to attendance at their own.

In order to achieve success, schools must work closely with parents when involving pupils in review procedures. Some parents find difficulties accepting the presence of their child at review, even during the later years of schooling. Clarifying purpose and having a clear school policy in this area are essential if conflict is to be avoided. All parties involved need to understand the role which they are expected to play, and they need to have the confidence that their views will be fully considered and valued. Inevitably, in any meeting which discusses the future of an individual, there is the potential for conflict. Schools where attendance of pupils at reviews has become the norm establish a pattern with which, over time, parents become familiar. An understanding of rights and responsibilities will not eliminate conflict, but can help the school in both anticipating and resolving difficulties as they arise.

In many mainstream secondary schools the contributions of pupils to their Annual Reports have become the norm. *Assessment and reporting* on progress are key elements to which the pupil can make a valuable contribution. By encouraging pupils to revisit their individual targets and to measure progress against set criteria, teachers are promoting responsibility in pupils for an important aspect of their learning. As schools improve in the setting of targets with pupils which are measurable and attainable, so they find it easier to assist pupils in making judgements about their own progress.

Assessment must be an integral part of the teaching process, and as such should provide opportunities for a celebration of achievement and experience. It must also form the basis for discussion about further targets, and the means of addressing these. Consultation with pupils about their achievements and experiences should be a constant factor of good classroom practice, and teachers need to note those accomplishments which mean most to the individual pupil. These may not always equate to the achievements upon which adults place highest credit. Both parties have a legitimate interest in establishing priorities, and the provision of a framework for negotiation which ensures that opinions are properly considered before reaching final decisions can assist in the prevention of conflict. The Records of Achievement movement has done much to enable pupils to recognise their own worth and achievement. It must be remembered that these documents are the property of the pupil, and it is they who should make decisions with regards to content.

Pupil involvement is only one aspect of the many and complex issues which challenge the move towards inclusive education. However, it is an area in which all teachers can have an immediate impact, and one which needs to be fully addressed if we are to prepare pupils for an included education. Pupil involvement depends upon teachers and schools taking the initiative, and challenging practices which exclude pupils from important areas of their learning. For many schools it will require a significant change of practice, but unless these changes are made, we will continue to have a society in which the ability of a significant number of people to play a full part will be denied.

REFERENCES

Ashdown, R., Carpenter, B. and Bovair, K. (1991) *The Curriculum Challenge*, London: Falmer Press.

Bennathan, M. (1996) 'Listening to children in schools, an empirical study', in R. Davie and D. Galloway (eds) *Listening to Children in Education*, London: David Fulton.

Byers, R. and Rose, R. (1996) *Planning the Curriculum for Pupils with Special Educational Needs*, London: David Fulton.

Carpenter, B., Ashdown, R. and Bovair, K. (1996) *Enabling Access*, London: David Fulton.

Charlton, T. (1996) 'Where is control located?', in K. Jones and T. Charlton (eds) *Overcoming Learning and Behaviour Difficulties*, London: Routledge.

Children Act (1989) London: HMSO.

Cooper, P. (1993) *Effective Schools for Disaffected Students*, London: Routledge.

Cowie, H. (1994) 'Ways of involving pupils in decision making', in P. Blatchford and S. Sharp (eds) *Breaktime and the School*, London: Routledge.

DfEE (1994) *Code of Practice on the Identification and Assessment of Special Educational Needs*, London: HMSO.

Gersch, I. (1994) *Working together for Children and Young People: the Student Report*, London Borough of Waltham Forest Department of Educational Psychology.

Griffiths, M. and Davies, C. (1995) *In Fairness to Children*, London: David Fulton.

Hardwick, J. and Rushton, P. (1994) 'Pupil participation in their own Records of Achievement', in R. Rose, A. Fergusson, C. Coles, R. Byers and D. Banes (eds) *Implementing the Whole Curriculum for Pupils with Learning Difficulties*, London: David Fulton.

Jones, K., Charlton, T. and Whittern, R. (1996) 'Enhancing and auditing partnership with pupils', in K. Jones and T. Charlton (eds) *Overcoming Learning and Behaviour Difficulties*, London: Routledge.

Lansdown, G. (1996) 'The United Nations Convention on the Rights of the Child – Progress in the United Kingdom', in C. Nutbrown (ed.) *Children's Rights and Early Education*, London: Paul Chapman.

Lawson, H. (1992) *Practical Record Keeping for Special Schools*, London: David Fulton.

LeRoy, B. and Simpson, C. (1992) *Inclusive Education Implementation Evaluation: Rochester Community Schools*, Wayne State University, Developmental Disabilities Institute.

LeRoy, B. and Simpson, C. (1996) 'Improving student outcomes through inclusive education', *Support for Learning* 11(1): 32–6.

Lewis, A. (1995) *Primary Special Needs in the National Curriculum*, London: Routledge.

Lindsay, G. (1997a) 'Are we ready for inclusion?', in G. Lindsay and D. Thompson (eds) *Values into Practice in Special Education*, London: David Fulton.

Lindsay, G. (1997b) 'Values, rights, and dilemmas', *British Journal of Special Education* 24(2): 55–9.

Mac An Ghaill, M. (1992a) 'Student perspectives on curriculum innovation and change in an English secondary school', *British Educational Research Journal* 18(3): 221–3.

Mac An Ghaill, M. (1992b) 'Teachers work: curriculum restructuring, culture, power and comprehensive schooling', *British Journal of the Sociology of Education* 13(2): 177–99.

Nutbrown, C. (1996) *Children's Rights and Early Education*, London: Paul Chapman.

Office for Standards in Education (1995) *Guidance on the Inspection of Nursery and Primary Schools*, London: HMSO.

Padeliadu, S. (1995) 'Preferences of students with learning disabilities for alternative service delivery modes', *European Journal of Special Needs Education* 10(3): 210–26.

Padeliadu, S. (1996) 'What can student preferences tell us about educational programming? A response to Kusuma-Powell', *European Journal of Special Needs Education* 11(2): 217–19.

Pollard, A., Broadfoot, P., Croll, P., Osborn, M. and Abbott, D. (1994) *Changing English Primary Schools?*, London: Cassell.

Richmond, R. (1994) 'The Code of Practice in schools: learning from recording of achievement', *British Journal of Special Education* 21(4): 157–60.

Rose, R., Fergusson, A., Coles, C., Byers, R. and Banes, D. (1996a) *Implementing the Whole Curriculum for Pupils with Learning Difficulties*, 2nd edition, London: David Fulton.

Rose, R., McNamara, S. and O'Neil, J. (1996b) 'Promoting the greater involvement of pupils with special needs in the management of their own assessment and learning processes', *British Journal of Special Education* 23(4): 166–71.

Rouse, M. and Florian, L. (1996) 'Becoming effective and inclusive: cross cultural perspectives', in L. Florian and M. Rouse (eds) *School Reform and Special Educational Needs: Anglo-American Perspectives*, Cambridge: University of Cambridge Institute of Education.

Sebba, J. (1995) *Geography for All*, London: David Fulton.

Stoll, L. (1991) 'School effectiveness in action: supporting growth in schools and classrooms', in M. Ainscow (ed.) *Effective Schools for All*, London: David Fulton.

United Nations (1989) *The Convention on the Rights of the Child*, Brussels: United Nations General Assembly.

Wade, B. and Moore, M. (1994) 'Good for a change?', *Pastoral Care in Education* 12(2): 23–7.

Chapter 8

Understanding challenging behaviour

Prerequisites to inclusion

Ted Cole

In this chapter Ted Cole focuses on ways in which teaching and organisation strategies can be used effectively to enable more children with learning difficulties, who challenge the system, to be included in the mainstream.

Why in the mid 1990s did so many special schools for pupils with moderate learning difficulties (MLD) remain open, some with waiting lists, in many parts of the country (Male, 1996)? The most likely reasons (apart from a difficult-to-change status quo) were: the 'upward percolation' of pupils with severe learning difficulties (SLD) (Male, 1996); the intractable family and social reasons for pupils boarding in residential schools (Cole, 1986); and challenging behaviour beyond the resources of many mainstream schools. Male (1996) also recorded the increasing number of exclusions from MLD schools, all for behavioural reasons.

And yet there were local education authorities, with few or no special schools for pupils with MLD, in which mainstream schools coped with the challenging behaviour of many pupils with MLD and often SLD. Cooper *et al.* (1994) recounted the slow absorption and ultimate abolition of an on-site MLD unit into the main body of a comprehensive school over a five-year period by the new head, in the face of initial staff resistance. Clearly, greater inclusion can be achieved for more pupils with MLD if staff were more confident in their ability to manage challenging behaviour. A worthwhile step in the process of teacher empowerment is to increase their understanding of the aetiology of behaviour and how theory can be related to practice. The aims of this chapter, therefore, are to consider research over the last three decades on teaching and organisation, relating to greater inclusion, before discussing theories of behaviour, in particular the ecosystemic perspective (Cooper *et al.*, 1994) which has evolved from, and draws together, strands from other schools of thought. Comments are also made in the light of my own research as the writer of a team examining good practice in relation to pupils with EBD (Emotional and Behavioural Difficulties) in both special (Cole *et al.*, 1998) and mainstream settings. Many pupils deemed EBD have quite pronounced learning difficulties and some of our findings would seem to apply with equal strength to pupils deemed to have MLD and indeed SLD.

DEVELOPING TEACHERS; CREATING INCLUSIVE SCHOOLS

One factor which may well have a negative impact upon the promotion of inclusion of pupils with challenging behaviours is the unappealing nature of parts of the curricular content which at times seems a catalyst for difficult behaviour. The demands of the National Curriculum can require the presentation of materials which pupils with behavioural and learning difficulties find difficult or threatening (e.g. creative writing) or irrelevant (some aspects of modern foreign languages) (Cole *et al.*, 1998). While expert teaching will find ways round these pupil perceptions, difficulties are likely to remain in many classrooms, where perhaps teachers are underconfident in dealing with pupils with special educational needs.

Without-child causes clearly relate to skills in basic classroom management as the Elton Committee (DES, 1989) reported. Sometimes the practical aspects of how to manage behaviour and motivate pupils have been insufficiently developed in initial teacher training or as part of in-service development (Hanko, 1995). Predictably, children with EBD (sometimes also with learning difficulties) are less tolerant of teacher shortcomings. Much of children's difficult behaviour is *situation specific*, even when there are deep psychological scars. Nearly every child, whether he or she has special educational needs or not, can behave differently for different adults or for the same teacher at different times or in different places. Often his or her actions will be sparked off by identifiable *triggers* in particular environmental *settings*. The majority of pupils, including most of those with MLD and behavioural difficulties, do not have a behavioural *disease* which requires specialist medical or psychiatric *treatment*. In most subject areas they are responsive to proficient pedagogy – and good teaching is good teaching wherever it happens and usually fosters good behaviour (Ofsted, 1993; DfEE, 1994a; 1994b). Factors making for teacher effectiveness in the SLD schools (Harris *et al.*, 1996) seem close to those required in the EBD sector or in mainstream (Cooper *et al.*, 1994; Cole *et al.*, 1998). Personal qualities of commitment, empathy and organisational skills are required of staff in abundance but not mysterious and exclusive methods to teach and motivate pupils.

Some teachers, unwittingly and from the best of intentions, tend to upset classes, precipitating challenging behaviour, while other colleagues may have styles which defuse, amuse and motivate the most difficult. My research supports this conclusion and suggests that a lack of training opportunities, to assist teacher style and performance, protracts and increases the need to move children with MLD/EBD into less inclusive settings. Self- or peer appraisal, mentoring and supervision schemes and other forms of staff development, which should be used to analyse and then address shortcomings in performance, can be patchy and sometimes non-existent (Hanko, 1995). Teacher style and classroom management, which would aid the cause of inclusion for pupils with MLD, are dealt with in depth in Gray and Richer (1988), Montgomery (1989), Stone (1990), Kyriacou (1991) and Smith (1996). Neill and Caswell (1993) have undertaken useful research on 'body language' and the teacher.

'Without-child causes' also relate to shortcomings in the organisation and ethos of school communities which, under pressure to obtain better examination results, can neglect the needs of the less able, thereby precipitating alienation and difficult behaviour from those who feel they have little stake in the school. Pupils with MLD often fall within this latter group, as reported in Male (1996) and earlier in Galloway and Goodwin (1987). The latter presaged the message of the Elton Report (DES, 1989) and much subsequent literature on school effectiveness (Hargreaves et al., 1975; Rutter et al., 1979; Mortimore et al., 1988; Smith and Laslett, 1993; DfEE, 1994a; 1994b; Power, 1996) that school organisational style and resulting ethos can contribute to the creation of behaviour problems leading to segregation for the less academic by persevering with fragmented, unsympathetic and rigid approaches. The whole school practices and inclusive policies that are found in some schools (DES, 1989; Galloway, 1990; Cooper et al., 1994; DfEE, 1994b; Clarke and Murray, 1996) are beneficial to all children but particularly those with learning and behavioural difficulties. These policies include the framing of behaviour strategies which, as well as outlining clear codes of behaviour, rewards and sanctions, also cover practicalities such as the movement of pupils through buildings and arrangements for dinner breaks.

Effective schools also allow for the voices and opinions of their pupils and for personal, social and *individual* educational needs, not only the delivery of the National Curriculum. Such a climate creates inclusive school practices and children with MLD are less likely to rebel through challenging behaviour: even in Years 10 and 11, they will believe that their school has something to offer to them.

THEORETICAL PERSPECTIVES ON BEHAVIOUR

School and individual teacher improvement, which aids the inclusion of pupils with MLD presenting challenging behaviour, can be brought about and will be further aided by teachers reflecting on the major theories of positive and negative behaviour development, to which the rest of this chapter is devoted.

Biological/medical explanations

Barrett and Jones (1996) use 'familial retardates' as a term for some children viewed as having MLD, reminding us that however much we may hope that learning difficulties are attributable more to delayed development than inherent defects, it is hard to deny that inherited characteristics play a part not only in cognitive potential but may also predispose children to behavioural attributes. As we inherit blue eyes and red hair from our fore-bears, why not a *short fuse*?

We remain unsure about the mix of nature and nurture which determines the chemical balances, and sometimes imbalances, in our brains or the efficiency of our synapses (the junctions between neurons: the pathways of our brains). Our emotions and externalised behaviour, however, may be determined by such factors. As medical and psychological research develops, more links are being discovered between mental and physical actions. Pattison (1993) asks whether *mental* actions (thoughts and feelings) are actually *physical* actions occasioned by chemical 'transmitters' such as dopamine, serotonin or noradrenalin acting on our neurons. Links have been established between brain dysfunction and phenylkytenuria, Tourette's syndrome, epilepsy and Parkinson's disease. What other discoveries await us which will aid our understanding of difficult behaviour in the classroom? It seems likely that, in time, researchers will provide clearer guidance on the nature and extent of attention-deficit and hyperactivity disorder (ADHD) (Cooper and Ideus, 1995) and which drugs may ethically and safely be used for a number of conditions primarily to assist the children, but also to make life easier for their parents and teachers.

Pattison (1993) posits the idea that balances in neural transmitters, and therefore behaviour, can relate to the food ingested. Extreme malnutrition is thought to hamper cognitive development but what of the child who usually has a full stomach? While much of the evidence for food affecting how children act in class remains unconvincing, it seems plausible that an unbalanced diet can affect behaviour (Kelly, 1988; Swinson, 1988).

The psychodynamic perspective/attachment theory

The persuasive idea, popularised by Freud (cited, for example, in Trieschman *et al.*, 1969), is that much externalised behaviour is governed by impulses shaped by our subconscious. Crucial to a child's healthy development is the development of his or her *ego*, the mechanism by which he or she makes sense of the world. Also important is the *superego*, roughly analogous to one's conscience, which helps to keep in check the instinctual and sometimes powerful sexual or aggressive urges of the id. The ego has been described as a psychological gatekeeper (Ayers *et al.*, 1995). Whether it grows healthily will have been determined by experiences in very early life.

This view was reflected in the seminal work of Bowlby (1953) which, while criticising the Freudian emphasis on the child's phantasy life, stressed the cruciality of the baby developing a healthy attachment to his or her mother. Bowlby argues that maternal deprivation inflicts severe and lasting damage. Rutter (1972) suggested that the all-important bonding did not have to be with the birth-mother; another permanent primary caregiver would suffice. However, children who do not form firm attachments at an early stage will not develop the secure emotional base on which many aspects of their development are likely to be founded.

The externalised challenging behaviour, which educators encounter, may be an 'acting out' of inner, deep-seated trauma, although the view of many psychotherapists in the 1950s (Ministry of Education, 1955) was that it was a necessary part of therapy for children then called 'maladjusted'. Subsequently, the argument that if a child indulged in an orgy of window breaking, it was to be tolerated, convinced fewer and fewer professionals (Wilson and Evans, 1980). However, even if the acceptance of acting out is unnecessary, at times teachers will be aided by trying to understand some of a child's subconscious drives and motivations, and psychological defence mechanisms as Greenhalgh (1994) advises. Teachers must seize even the fleeting moments which occur in the school day to listen and talk to children (Cooper *et al.*, 1994), perhaps gaining some insight into the emotional turmoil which may give rise to challenging behaviour. While they have neither the training nor the time to delve deeply into the recesses of a child's mind, looking beneath the surface should engender empathy in teachers. This approach is likely to produce a better response from pupils with MLD, as well as from those deemed EBD, mitigating challenging behaviour and thereby lessening the need for segregation.

The behaviourist perspective

The reliance of the psychodynamic approach on intuition and insight was increasingly viewed as suspect and perhaps wasteful of time and energy (Wilson and Evans, 1980). Behaviourists argued that what mattered was the here and now of observable behaviour not the swirling mists of a child's early life. What the child actually does and the immediate environment of his or her actions should be accurately observed and recorded. Only then should hypotheses be generated and clear targets set. The basic premise is that behaviour is maintained and strengthened when it is reinforced. The knack is to find easily delivered and appropriate rewards for desired behaviours which strengthen their occurrence until the child internalises them and then generalises them to everyday life (McMaster, 1982; Cooper *et al.*, 1994). The hope is that the initial reliance on the delivery of external reinforcers, such as sweets or tokens, will be replaced first by non-tangible reinforcers, such as the giving of praise, and later by the child experiencing intrinsic satisfaction with the newly acquired, pro-social behaviours. Therein lies the enduring problem: how to generalise behaviours when the (perhaps) unnatural and contrived system of extrinsic rewards is removed. Despite this problem, aspects of behaviourism are commonly observed operating in special and mainstream schools. Points systems, physical rewards (such as 'smily' stickers, extra pocket money and meals at McDonald's) have been found to be prevalent by the present writer in special schools for children with EBD (Cole *et al.*, 1998) while government inspectors (Ofsted, 1993) recommend merit systems and special privileges as useful adjuncts to achieving good behaviour in all school settings. My experience over many years suggests that these are equally effective with pupils with MLD and challenging behaviour. In the best practice, the giving of rewards is clearly linked to the clear setting of targets by the teacher, in consultation with the pupil. Behaviourism notes that punishment can be used to suppress, but hardly ever to extinguish, unwanted behaviour, and some approaches such as aversion therapy (e.g. the use of electric shocks) are of dubious ethical nature. In place of punishment, experimenters came to realise that ignoring undesirable behaviours was sometimes sufficient if enough stress was laid on the development of positive alternatives (Montgomery, 1989); or a child might be given 'time out': the act of removal from the place and from those who generally provide the positive reinforcement for the child. These approaches can be useful to teachers of children with MLD in both main-stream and special school settings. Also central to behaviourism or 'learning theory', as some prefer to describe it, is the notion that children learn from the behaviour they see around them, be it good or bad. They will copy the actions of people who have become 'significant others' to them. It is there-fore crucial that educators set the right example for pupils with MLD, and that they model the behaviours they wish children to adopt. Perhaps the most memorable maxim for educators (and members of the child's family) is the need to pay attention to the so-called 'ABC' of behaviour (Ayers *et al.*, 1995). While not delving into distant aetiology, attention has to be paid to the setting in which the behaviour occurs and the triggers which often precipitated it.

A   antecedents;
B   the behaviour;
C   the consequences.

This ABC should be used to analyse problematic behaviour as a matter of course and should be applied factually and accurately: teachers should not infer or generalise or include descriptions of past occurrences or possible consequences. Stone (1990) calls this process 'ORA': *o*bserving, *r*ecording and *a*nalysing in order to establish a reliable baseline for interventions.

There have been numerous accounts of the development and refinement of behaviour modification/learning theory as it applies to children in educational settings. Good short summaries are available in Ayers *et al.* (1995) and Cooper *et al.* (1994), while Jones (1983) describes a structured application in a highly specialist school for children with SLD. Conducting rigorous behaviourist approaches in mainstream settings is not easy although it is possible to target specific behaviours, particularly if the teacher has the assistance of a learning support assistant (LSA). As Cooper *et al.* (1994) note, application of the theory can be a useful part of a teacher's repertoire and can aid the inclusion process.

The humanist and cognitive/behaviourist perspectives

Modern sympathisers for a behaviourist approach would wish to distance themselves from any practice which might be seen as unethical (e.g. involving severe and repeated punishment) or mechanistic and difficult to apply in educational (particularly mainstream) settings for pupils with MLD. My present research into special and mainstream provision for pupils with EBD suggests widespread use of, and support for, behaviourist schemes, but these are operated by staff who believe firmly in the centrality of relationships in any successful interventions with challenging pupils, including those with MLD. Staff in good-practice schools (both special and mainstream) might not articulate the details (Cole *et al.*, 1998) or even the names, but are clearly applying the principles advanced by Abraham Maslow and Carl Rogers.

First published in the 1940s (Maslow, 1943), the Triangle of Needs (Figure 8.1) has appeared virtually unaltered in many child care and educational texts, particularly when troubled and troublesome children are the subject (Galloway, 1990; Harris and Hewett, 1996; Roffey and O'Reirdan, 1997). The Triangle was first described as a theory of motivation and neglecting it seemed likely to promote difficult behaviour in pupils. Maslow proposed different levels of need from basic satisfaction of physical wants ('bodily comfort speaketh the loudest' recalled Maier, 1981, p.37) to providing the goals and life-challenges which constitute 'self-actualisation'.

The original notion was that needs had to be satisfied at a lower level before he or she would be concerned about needs at a higher level. Only when children's physiological needs had been met and when they felt safe, and had people to care for them, would they be concerned about self-esteem and then self-actualisation. This process now seems untenable: busy, playing children will forget their hunger for a time while juvenile car thieves will

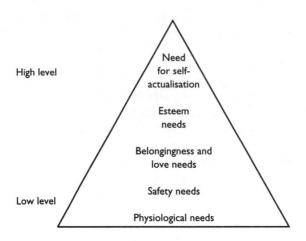

Figure 8.1 Maslow's Triangle of Needs

put self-actualisation ahead of safety needs. However, in general, Maslow's theory still convinces and many schools would benefit from considering its implications for practice. For example, the Victorian 'feeding schools' of the 1880s, where former truants were offered three meals a day, were an early recognition that hungry children make reluctant learners (Cole, 1989). Following the example set in some schools for pupils with EBD (Cole *et al.*, 1998) perhaps more pre-school breakfast clubs for pupils with MLD and challenging behaviours could be offered. Maslow's perspective on the world through the eyes of the 'client' echoes the beliefs of Carl Rogers that it is often counter-productive to force change on feelings or behaviours. Often individuals have to be helped to find their own solutions by non-directive means: they have to discover for themselves the sense of alternative ways of acting; they have to own possible solutions to problems. The adults working with them should actively listen, gently question and generally help the young people along the road to finding their own answers. The application of Rogerian approaches in special school settings is entertainingly intro-duced by Mallon (1987). Davie and Galloway (1996) also consider the approach as part of a wider personal and social education (PSE) framework to inclusive practice in mainstream settings. However, in the cut-and-thrust and breathless activity of real school life, there are clear limits to a non-directive approach. Sometimes situations require flexibility, leeway and significant pupil input in arriving at solutions; at other times pupils want swift, clear guidance. Pupils might misinterpret a non-directive approach as weakness or a lack of care on the part of the teacher.

The central concern of humanists for the quality of interaction between adult and child remains at the heart of inclusive practice. Children with learning and behavioural difficulties are far more likely to do as requested by a teacher if a good relationship exists between them. Maier (1981) emphasises that: 'children learn most readily from those who have vital meaning for them'. Central to Maslow's and Rogers' thinking is a concern for young person's views of themselves and ways in which these can be enhanced. Thus the humanist is linked to what, in recent years, has come to be called the cognitive-behaviourist or simply the cognitive approach (Ayers *et al.*, 1995). Pupils who present problems, particularly those who have endured years of limited success in the classroom in front of their 'brighter' peers (Staines, 1958) or who have suffered the chronic indignity (as some of them will see it) of being placed in what they term the 'divvy' or 'dimbo' school, will often have a negative view of themselves.

The most important determinants of self-image are children's relationships with their families followed by their experiences at school (Coopersmith, 1967; Thomas, 1980). Many with learning difficulties come from dysfunctional homes which are unlikely to have fostered self-worth. They then embark on what often prove to be unrewarding school careers where friendship might be hard to make owing to deficits in their social skills (Barrett and Jones, 1996) and where, sadly, they may be labelled as failures by unsympathetic peers and some staff. Minor rule infraction may have been handled insensitively, giving rise to more serious 'secondary deviance' (Hargreaves *et al.*, 1975) leading to chronic emotional and behavioural difficulties. In time, these children internalise the views of those around them and act according to the negative labels and low expectations bestowed upon them, including the display of behaviours which may result in their being moved to less inclusive settings. Self-respect is preserved by rebellion, but this is likely to hide inner self-doubts.

Poor self-concept may influence their view of the world as conceptualised in their 'locus of control'. Confident, successful people tend to believe that they can influence and direct events. Children who lack self-belief are apt to adopt a pessimistic view of life in which things are 'done to them' and, if plans go awry, the blame is shifted to others. 'A loser believes in "fate" . . . a winner believes we make our fate by what we fail to do' (Harris cited in Rogers, 1990, p.1). Rogers (1994), reflecting the views of the psychodynamic and humanist schools, wrote:

> The fundamental maxim behind cognitive-behavioural theories is that thinking, emotion and behaviour are inextricably involved with each other. Self-defeating behaviour is related to self-defeating thinking which in turn is related to feeling 'down'.

Cognitive theorists stress the need to counteract unduly pessimistic views of the world held by many children. The aim of intervention according to Ayers *et al.* (1995), particularly for teachers striving to increase the inclusion of challenging pupils with MLD, is to 'identify and challenge the distorted or irrational thinking that leads to emotional and behavioural difficulties' (p.41). The child needs freeing from a fatalistic 'learned helplessness' in which the acting out of destructive or annoying behaviour seems to be the best way to fight back against a world perceived as unjust.

Finding time in the special school setting to address such pessimistic attitudes is not easy, and even more difficult in the mainstream, unless a learning support assistant is available. To alter a child's self-perception, however, it is necessary to construct, where possible with the child, learning tasks which are matched to a pupil's interests or in areas which he or she knows are valuable. These must be broken down into small steps which increase the likelihood of repeated success and, allied to frequent listening and talking between teacher and child, can be an effective antidote to challenging behaviour and are likely to enhance prospects for inclusion. Pro-social achievement becomes ego boosting and a better motivator than disruption.

The ecosystemic perspective

Breaking into negative cycles of distorted thinking which can often lead to undesirable behaviour is also a major part of the ecosystemic approach. According to this perspective the child is part of a web of interconnecting systems: the internal physical and mental systems of the child which interact with the classroom system; the school system; the neighbourhood system; and, importantly, the family system. *The within child* factors in a young person are in recurring dialogue with *without-child* factors in one or more of these systems or with subsystems within them.

Too often for the child with learning difficulties some of the constituents in any one of these systems may exacerbate his or her difficulties, making worse the self-defeating negative cycle in which he or she may be locked. A pupil's reading difficulties may precipitate common low-level disruption such as 'talking out of turn' or 'out of seat' behaviour (DES, 1989) which may annoy classmates. It may also anger the teacher who feels less able to offer assistance in a caring, understanding frame of mind. The reading problem worsens, the child's disruption increases, his or her unpopularity grows and the relationship with the teacher becomes more confrontational and hostile. In the staffroom the teacher tells colleagues of the difficulties and a *label* precedes the pupil into other classrooms, where relationships and learning may also suffer. Meanwhile, in the playground, children seek revenge for the annoyance caused by the child in class. Poor behaviour may be communicated to his or her family, who become angry, and within time the child perceives most aspects of the ecosystem as hostile.

Cooper *et al.* (1994) and Ayers *et al.* (1995) proffer useful advice to aid the process of inclusion for children with MLD as well as those with EBD. They discuss the possibilities of breaking into the negative cycles which exist in the interlinking systems of the child in class, around the school and in his or her family. The teacher should look at practical, daily issues which impinge on his or her relationship with the pupil, while the staff as a whole should examine school structures and routines. How a teacher greets a child before a lesson starts, what tone of voice he or she uses, what assumptions are made about challenging behaviour and where a pupil sits are all worthy of re-examination, while what the school requires and offers at breaks and lunch-times should also be scrutinised. A basic premise is that it does not matter in which part, or parts, of the established negative cycles you sow and nurture the seeds of beneficial change. Also, that improvement in one part of a system can have positive effects in other parts: the first ever good letter home praising Karen for classwork well done, may come as a pleasant surprise to her mother and precipitate the creation of a more virtuous cycle at home as well as at school.

Home visits by the school's EWO (Educational Welfare Officer) or by members of the teaching staff can build on these situations. The ecosystemic approach emphasises the desirability of working with the family to alter perceptions, to try to win its support for the child and for the school; a difficult task, but one which is achieved in some special (Cole *et al.*, 1998) and mainstream schools. While teachers are not social workers the way to communicate with the pupil with MLD and challenging behaviour, thereby lessening the tendency to segregate and exclude, is to adopt a holistic approach.

Key elements in the ecosystemic approach are the need for those involved in the child's various systems to dispense with instinctive assumptions leading to negative labelling. Secondly, time needs to be found to think about the style of staff approaches to the pupil and teachers need to work with pupils in non-confrontational, often non-directive, yet clear and assertive ways.

Reduced to a few paragraphs, this perspective may at times sound a rose-tinted view of children who, in real life, may be unpleasant and knowingly provocative. Nevertheless, confident, well-organised class teachers who adopt this positive, reflective and holistic view are more open to self-analysis, seeing in the child an essential goodness and capacity for positive development, thus enabling the child to attain maximum degrees of inclusion.

APPLYING THEORY TO INCREASE INCLUSION

Growing awareness of biological/medical explanations for behaviour will perhaps ease the process of inclusion for pupils with learning difficulties and challenging behaviour. The popularity of the work of Greenhalgh (1994) suggests that the major messages for teachers from the psychodynamic perspective remain influential in understanding and helping children with MLD/EBD.

Similarly the stress of behaviourists on the need for specificity in measurement, target setting and assessment should aid the construction of individual educational and behaviour plans, helping to create learning and management programmes which address the needs of the pupil with MLD more efficiently, thereby lessening his or her challenging behaviour which might lead to placement in less inclusive settings. The ABC of behaviour and its variants help to keep a teacher focused on a child's priority needs. Aspects of behaviourism, particularly the potential of positive reinforcement, have proved useful at individual, class and whole school levels, as attested by the star charts, the 'smilies', the points and token systems operating for children with learning difficulties in EBD schools (Cole et al., 1998). The modelling of desirable behaviour by staff through their own punctuality, their use of language, and their values and beliefs, for example, is also very important.

To be effective, behaviourism has to have a heart. Cold, mechanistic systems, half-heartedly applied, unsupported by warm, positive relationships between staff and pupils, can be more of a hindrance than a help and may sometimes precipitate exclusion. To promote the inclusion of pupils with MLD, teachers should allow for the emotional as well as the cognitive needs of the child. Personal and social education, as Galloway (1990) advocates, has to permeate school life (see Chapter 4 by Richard Byers).

Cole et al. (1998) re-emphasise the usefulness of 'needs theory'. To feel safe and to belong children with behavioural and learning difficulties appreciate order and predictable structures in their lives. The American pioneer Fritz Redl wrote of 'the great ego-supportive power of traditionalised routine' (Cole, 1986). Proficient staff, clearly in control, operating within a regular timetable and established patterns for breaks (Blatchford and Sharp, 1994), are essential. To boost self-esteem disturbing pupils need supportive relationships with trustworthy teachers. Only then will they be willing to commit themselves in class, or to risk new challenges with their attendant possibilities of failure in preference to 'opting out' through disruptive behaviour.

The vital relationships which are the key to coping with challenging behaviour will not be achieved through regularly confrontational, autocratic and didactic approaches which relay the message 'Do as I say because I know best because I am the teacher!' In inclusive settings, pupils feel the adult's interest and empathy and see the sacrifices made on their behalf, for example clubs offered by the staff after school. Relationship formation is aided by the teacher involving the pupil to a greater extent in the planning of his or her educational and social development (Charlton and David, 1993; DfEE, 1994c) (see Chapter 7 by Richard Rose). Greater rapport is established where staff find time to listen to children and to reflect back their feelings, becoming respected, trusted and frequently liked. Meaningful relationships cannot be built in a neutral emotional state which relies solely on the teacher's classroom technique and subject knowledge, crucial though these are in the era of the National Curriculum.

If more teachers could become the reflective practitioners that Gray and Richer (1988) suggest, and consider the background factors which impede and encourage classroom learning, the challenging behaviours of children with learning difficulties would be lessened, more children with MLD would thrive in mainstream settings, and fewer would need to be excluded.

REFERENCES

Ayers, H., Clarke, D. and Murray, A. (1995) *Perspectives on Behaviour: a Practical Guide to Effective Interventions for Teachers*, London: David Fulton.

Barrett, H. and Jones, D. (1996) 'The inner life of children with moderate learning difficulties', in V. Varma (ed.) *The Inner Life of Children with Special Needs*, London: Whurr.

Blatchford, P. and Sharp, S. (1994) *Breaktime and the School: Understanding and Changing Playground Behaviour*, London: Routledge.

Bowlby, J. (1953) *Child Care and the Growth of Love*, Harmondsworth: Pelican.

Charlton, T. and David, K. (eds) (1993) *Managing Misbehaviour in Schools*, 2nd edition, London: Routledge.

Clarke, D. and Murray, A. (1996) *Developing and Implementing a Whole-School Behaviour Policy*, London: David Fulton.

Cole, T. (1986) *Residential Special Education: Living and Learning in a Special School*, Milton Keynes: Open University Press.

Cole, T. (1989) *Apart or A Part? Integration and the Growth of British Special Education*, Milton Keynes: Open University Press.

Cole, T., Visser, J. and Upton, G. (1998) *Effective Schooling for Pupils with Emotional and Behavioural Difficulties*, London: David Fulton.

Cooper, P. and Ideus, K. (1995) *Attention Deficit/Hyperactivity Disorder*, Maidstone: AWCEBD.

Cooper, P., Smith, C. and Upton, G. (1994) *Emotional and Behavioural Difficulties: from Theory to Practice*, London: Routledge.

Coopersmith, S. (1967) *The Antecedents of Self-Esteem*, San Francisco: Freeman.

Davie, R. and Galloway, D. (eds) (1996) *Listening to Children in Education*, London: David Fulton.

DES (1989) *Discipline in Schools: Report of the Committee of Inquiry (The Elton Report)*, London: HMSO.

DfEE (1994a) *Pupils' Behaviour and Discipline* (Circular 8/94), London: HMSO.

DfEE (1994b) *The Education of Children with Emotional and Behavioural Problems* (Circular 9/94), London: HMSO.

DfEE (1994c) *Code of Practice on the Identification and Assessment of Special Educational Needs*, London: HMSO.

Galloway, D. (1990) *Pupil Welfare and Counselling*, London: Longman.

Galloway, D. and Goodwin, C. (1987) *The Education of Disturbing Children: Pupils with Learning and Adjustment Difficulties*, London: Longman.

Gray, J. and Richer, J. (1988) *Classroom Responses to Disruptive Behaviour*, London: Routledge.

Greenhalgh, P. (1994) *Emotional Growth and Learning*, London: Routledge.

Hanko, G. (1995) *Special Needs in Ordinary Classrooms: from Staff Support to Staff Development*, 3rd edition, London: David Fulton.

Hargreaves, D., Hester, S. K. and Mellor, F. J. (1975) *Deviance in Classrooms*, London: Routledge & Kegan Paul.

Harris, J., Cook, M. and Upton, G. (1996) *Pupils with Severe Learning Disabilities who Present Challenging Behaviour: a Whole School Approach to Assessment and Intervention*, Kidderminster: British Institute of Learning Disabilities.

Harris, J. and Hewett, D. (1996) *Positive Approaches to Challenging Behaviours*, Kidderminster: British Institute of Learning Disabilities.

Jones, M. (1983) *Behaviour Problems in Handicapped Children*, London: Souvenir Press.

Kelly, B. (1988) 'Bad food; worse behaviour', *Special Children* 17 January: 22–3.

Kyriacou, C. (1991) *Essential Teaching Skills*, Hemel Hempstead: Simon & Schuster.

Maier, H. (1981) 'Essential components in treatment environments for children', in F. Ainsworth and C. Fulcher (eds) *Group Care for Children*, London: Tavistock Press.

Male, D. (1996) 'Who goes to MLD schools?', *British Journal of Special Education* 23(1): 35–41.

Mallon, B. (1987) *An Introduction to Counselling Skills for Special Educational Needs*, Manchester: Manchester University Press.

Maslow, A. (1943) 'A theory of human motivation', *Psychological Review* 50: 370–96.

McMaster, J. (ed.) (1982) *Methods in Social and Educational Caring*, Aldershot: Gower.

Ministry of Education (1955) *Report of the Committee on Maladjusted Children* (The Underwood Report), London: HMSO.

Montgomery, D. (1989) *Managing Behaviour Problems*, London: Hodder & Stoughton.

Mortimore, P., Sammons, P., Stoll, L., Lewis, D. and Ecob, R. (1988) *School Matters*, Wells: Open Books.

Neill, S. and Caswell, C. (1993) *Body Language for Competent Teachers*, London: Routledge.

Ofsted (1993) *Achieving Good Behaviour in Schools*, London: HMSO.

Pattison, N. (1993) *Process of Growth: Biological Bases of Behaviour (Unit 2, Module One: The Developmental Psychology of Childhood and Adolescence)*, EBD Distance Education Course, University of Birmingham.

Power, S. (1996) *The Pastoral and the Academic: Conflict and Contradiction in the Curriculum*, London: Cassell.

Roffey, S. and O'Reirdan, T. (1997) *Infant Classroom Behaviour*, London: David Fulton.

Rogers, W. (1990) *You Know the Fair Rule*, London: Longman.

Rogers, W. (1994) *Behaviour Recovery*, Melbourne: Acer.

Rutter, M. (1972) *Maternal Deprivation Reassessed*, Harmondsworth: Penguin.

Rutter, M., Maughan, B., Mortimore, P. and Oyston, J. (1979) *Fifteen Thousand Hours*, London: Open Books.

Smith, C. J. (1996) 'The management of children with problems in mainstream and special schools', in V. Varma (ed.) *Managing Children with Problems*, London: Cassell.

Smith, C. J. and Laslett, R. (1993) *Effective Classroom Management: a Teacher's Guide*, London: Routledge.

Staines, J. W. (1958) 'The self picture as a factor in the classroom', *British Journal of Educational Psychology* 28.

Stone, L. (1990) *Managing Difficult Children in School*, Hemel Hempstead: Simon & Schuster.

Swinson, J. (1988) 'In praise of chemical food', *Special Children* 18 February: 6–7.

Thomas, J. B. (1980) *The Self in Education*, Slough: NFER.

Trieschman, A., Whittaker, J. and Brendtro, L. (1969) *The Other Twenty Three Hours*, Chicago: Aldine.

Wilson, M. and Evans, M. (1980) *Education of Disturbed Pupils*, London: Methuen.

Chapter 9

Promoting inclusion through learning styles

Geoff Read

A greater understanding of the different learning styles of pupils, and the ability to adapt teaching approaches to address these differences, are essential if pupils with learning difficulties are to be fully included in mainstream schools. Geoff Read suggests that any review of the ways in which pupils learn and which leads to more effective teaching should be welcomed.

INTRODUCTION

Understanding teaching and learning styles remains a major key in the development of inclusive learning, and it is essential for teachers to move beyond a general acceptance of this principle and consider its practical applications. Cognitive style analysis is one way in which teachers can start to gain a greater understanding of approaches to teaching and learning styles. Most teachers acknowledge that they have a particular teaching style which they find most natural and comfortable, although the best teachers develop skills in the use of other styles. A greater understanding of learning styles can allow teachers to profile whole groups of pupils, although many secondary schools profile and group according to ability and pay less attention to styles.

COGNITIVE STYLE ANALYSIS

Riding and Cheema (1991) likened the learning styles of individuals to a computer working on two continua: information being processed in the brain and being represented during thinking. They have suggested that the ways in which the brain takes in stimuli and processes vary from individual to individual: on the one hand, those who tend to process information as a *whole* (the 'Wholists'); on the other, those who process information in *parts* (the 'Analysists'). There is also a similar continuum (when information is represented within the brain during the thinking process) between those who are inclined to verbalise (the 'Verbalists') and those who tend to use mental images or pictures (the 'Imagers'). Other terms used in the research are: 'field dependent', 'field independent' or 'global', 'articulated', which refer to attentional and perceptual elements (Witkin *et al.*, 1977); and 'impulsive/reflective' (Kogan, 1976), concerned with cognitive styles.

Wholists, when viewing situations or materials, will tend to take in the whole picture and see each part within the wider context, quickly gaining an overview of a situation and an understanding of how individual parts or actions relate to the whole. Wholists would, for example, grasp how the complex interrelationships of subsidiary, associated and amalgamated companies work as part of a conglomerate, or understand the mechanics of celestial movements. Their strength is in identifying patterns within overall pictures; in contrast, they are less likely to focus on details and on the individual parts of a whole.

Analysists are at the other end of this continuum and they tend to focus on the parts or details of a situation. To use the company analogy, they would be able to tell you about each company and would seek to gain an overall understanding by first exploring the details of each unit. They work from the detail upwards, whereas Wholists work from the wide picture towards the detail.

The processing continua reflect each individual's preferred representing style, and are characteristic of the way that he or she prefers to learn. It is possible for most individuals to use learning strategies that do not match their style, but a greater conscious effort is needed and the process will inevitably take longer.

Verbalists represent ideas and thoughts in words and through language, and they are most likely to 'see' words when thinking. Imagers, by contrast, tend to present ideas through images or pictures. Figure 9.1 identifies the characteristics of groups of learning styles.

LEARNING STYLE CHARACTERISTICS

Cognitive research findings are often presented in ways that are not readily accessible, or of immediate use, to classroom practitioners. Figure 9.2, by showing the characteristics of each style group, identifies the range of learning strengths and weaknesses that may exist across a group of learners.

The preferred learning characteristics of each group are presented as the extremes on the continuum, and most individuals will find themselves somewhere between the two extremes on each bipolar continuum. The central point on the continua is known as 'Bimodal', which has both the strengths and weaknesses of each type of learning style.

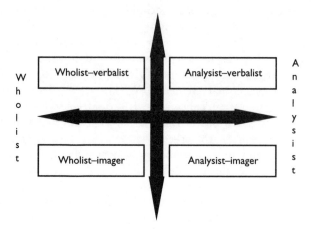

Figure 9.1 Learning style groups

By combining the Wholist–Analysist characteristics of individuals with their Verbalist–Imager characteristics, a clear picture of the learning styles becomes apparent. Analysist–Imagers are clear-thinking, organised people who are also socially less outgoing, restrained and perhaps passive in learning situations. Wholist–Verbalists tend to be much broader in their outlook, more able to weigh things up, but less organised people who find language and reading easier than most. This probably reinforces their tendency to be gregarious and outspoken extroverts.

The characteristic learning styles of pupils can be used by teachers to profile class groups as a means towards the preparation of learning materials that complement and promote effective learning for pupils with special educational needs. The use of pictures and diagrams will help Imagers to learn more effectively; similarly sections of text will be more effective for Analysists. Teachers can use this information about learning styles to form balanced class groups when planning co-operative group learning when pairing pupils for activities (see Chapter 10 by Claire Marvin). The purpose behind an exploration of an individual's learning style characteristics is to help develop those strategies that lead to a more effective learning performance.

THE SCHOOL LEARNING ENVIRONMENT

In considering an appropriate learning environment for pupils with special needs, a number of questions need to be asked. How does the school learning environment relate to the innate, learning style characteristics of

Verbalist

↑

Wholist–realist

Socially: informal, spontaneous, extrovert, mixes easily.
Organisationally: organised, independent, likes to work with others, can exaggerate and domineer.
Learning: good verbal memory, retains facts, articulate, likes structured materials.
Thinking: overall perspective, realistic, able to adjust, willing to be directed, not discerning/critical, impulsive.
Most able reader.

Better with text
Prefers 'text plus text' materials
Good recall on complex and unfamiliar text
Good early reader – marked advantage exists to 11 years
Unconscious generation of verbal images as representation
Conscious generation of pictorial images as representation
Verbal images less stable/permanent
Pictorial images more stable/permanent
Preference for verbal representation increases with ability
Socially outgoing
Tendency to be extrovert
Likes groups/pairs work
Confident use of language

Analysist–verbalist

Socially: outgoing but restrained, moderately formal, socially aware, likes group activity.
Organisationally: self-organising, prefers small groups, prefers clear role/tasks.
Learning: prefers structure & facts, likes tables, good verbal memory, retains facts, fairly articulate.
Thinking: strength in analysing situations, clear views, weighs pros and cons, idealistic, contributes/leads groups.

Wholist

← Focuses on whole, not parts. Likes overview. Prefers to discover principles to fact learning. Balanced and moderate views. Keeps things in proportion. Less organised. Less consistent. Pragmatic/realistic. Vague. Flexible. Gregarious. Prefers group/pairs work. Dependent.

Analysist

Focuses on whole, not parts. Likes detail, fact learning comes easily. Tendency to exaggerate and gets things out of proportion. Organised. Consistent. Idealistic. Self-reliant. Tolerant of individual work. Independent. →

Wholist–imager

Socially: informal, relaxed, looks to others for lead, private person, hides feelings, reasonably outgoing, restrained, polite, withdrawn.
Organisationally: willing to be organised, diligent, takes instructions, likes informality, tendency to exaggerate.
Learning: likes structured materials, prefers diagrams/pictures, concise in writing and speech, verbally hesitant.
Thinking: good at summing up, realistic, flexible, sees other points of view, flexible, not critical, open to persuasion. Prefers closed tasks.
Weakest reader.

Better with images
Prefers 'text plus pictures/diagrams' materials
Better recall on highly descriptive and emotive text
Weakest early reader – marked advantage exists to 11 years
Unconscious generation of pictorial images as representation
Conscious generation of verbal images as representation
Pictorial images less stable/permanent
Verbal images more stable/permanent
Preference for pictorial/diagrammatic representation increases with ability
Socially less outgoing
Tendency to be introvert
More tolerant of individual work
Less confident use of language
More passive and inward looking
Polite and restrained
Tendency to divert thinking

Analysist–imager

Socially: restrained, formal, cold/distant, socially unaware, introverted, reluctant to speak out, inhibited.
Organisationally: prefers to organise self, likes clear-cut tasks, isolationist within large groups.
Learning: structured in approach, prefers facts, likes use of clear headings & paragraphs, pictures & diagrams most effective, hesitant to speak out, concise in speech.
Thinking: good at analysing situations, obtains clear view, reflective, good at generating new ideas, weighs pros & cons, idealistic, socially unrealistic, logically correct.

↓

Imager

Figure 9.2 Learning style characteristics

students? To what extent do teachers take the learning style of individuals into account in their planning? Is it possible and realistic for teachers to differentiate according to the learning style of students? Differentiation is the matching of what is taught to pupils relative to ability and aptitude (DES, 1985).

There has been considerable evidence over the years of mainstream schools' inability to deploy successfully the elements of differentiation identified by *Better Schools* (DES, 1985). The Oracle Project's (Galton *et al.*, 1980) classroom-focused research in primary schools, the extensive work of Bennett *et al.* (1984), and the *Primary Education in Leeds Report* (Alexander, 1991) all point to the difficulties teachers face in balancing the effective learning equation. Although less work has been undertaken in the secondary schools, the extensive survey data from HMI and the findings of statutory school inspections continue to confirm that they too have similar problems (DES, 1978; 1989; 1990; Ofsted, 1995). Schools appear to find most difficulties during Key Stage 3, with more than one-third of lessons being identified in some subjects as 'poor' (DES, 1989) and, using the current Ofsted criteria, 19 per cent as 'unsatisfactory'.

A range of factors have been identified as leading to the difficulties of schools in matching learning to individual abilities and aptitudes, amongst which 'effective teaching practice' has been identified by Ofsted as the single most important factor in poor performance (Ofsted, 1995). Effective teaching was the subject of an Ofsted survey (1994) which sought to identify those practices within the classroom leading to improved pupil performance. The factors listed confirmed that effective teaching depends on: skilled questioning; the use of varied teaching styles; a balance between different grouping strategies; and the matching of learning tasks.

A survey sponsored by TVEI (Technical, Vocational and Educational Initiative), within Nottinghamshire secondary schools (Read, 1992), sought to identify teachers' self-reported 'effective practice'. Using a structured interview questionnaire, teachers were asked to report on a single effective lesson using a series of prompts, designed to explore a range of variables within the classroom learning environment. The results gave a clear picture of the characteristics of teachers' perceived 'effective practice'. 'Whole class teaching' predominated, followed by 'individual' and some 'paired work'. Teaching styles were usually didactic, with lessons starting with a presentation. Pupils were mainly required to learn through listening and the completion of follow-up worksheet or textbook-based activities. Teachers used 'coped well' or 'completed task' as their main indicators of pupil task evaluation. The majority of pupils, except those 'with special educational needs', were given the same unmodified tasks, and textbooks and worksheets featured strongly in the majority of lessons.

LEARNING CHARACTERISTICS OF LESS ABLE STUDENTS AND THE SCHOOL ENVIROMENT

Less able students often appear to form the majority of poor performers particularly in secondary schools, and teachers find them the most challenging. Nevertheless, small adaptations such as subtitles within the text or an abstract or overview at the beginning of a text can radically improve their performance. Picture cues accompanying a text help Imagists; Verbalists tend to have less difficulty in coping with complex and unfamiliar texts.

Many teachers in special schools have successfully developed a range of learning strategies to provide access to the curriculum, often based on the experience of working with challenging pupils. Not all such practices, however, are easily transferable to the mainstream (Ainscow, 1997) and individual programming has not been as successful as most integrationists and inclusionists had expected. Riding and Read (1996) discovered that a number of 'good practices' used within secondary schools hindered rather than helped less able pupils. More able pupils were adept at controlling learning situations by reshaping tasks to match their preferred learning strategies. The less able, in marked contrast, appeared less flexible in their use of different strategies or in their ability to reshape tasks in order to maximise performance. Consequently the performance of the less able, regardless of cognitive style, was much more sensitive both to 'subject format dominance' and to 'teacher format preference'.

Effective teachers offer pupils with learning difficulties opportunities to learn by using a range of strategies, including those commensurate with their preferred cognitive styles. The best equipped teachers, therefore, are skilled at differentiating the learning environment of their class in order that activities, learning materials and pupil groupings are appropriate to individuals and to clusters of pupils. Inclusive practice, however, is not restricted to differentiation according to ability, but has to take account of *how* individual pupils learn most effectively. Pupils with learning difficulties are often those who are most vulnerable to mismatched learning situations, making them the most open to failure. An awareness of learning styles helps teachers to adjust their presentation and to select relevant activity materials without compromising subject content. In addition, an awareness of pupil learning style characteristics; the reformatting of texts and diagrams; the grouping of Analysts with Wholists; a focus on group or individual work; allowing oral or written (pictorial or text) presentations to be the focus of task completions, are all possible variations used by sensitive teachers.

Pupil preferences indicated that all, regardless of cognitive learning styles, preferred to work in groups or pairs and that none expressed a preference for working alone on individual tasks (Riding and Read, 1996). A preference for working alone correlated with ability, and the most able were least averse, although Analysist–Verbalisers showed a slight preference. The least able, however, showed a universal dislike of working alone, even though it might have been expected that Analysist–Verbalisers (of all abilities) would have been the *most* tolerant of this mode of working. This data is in marked contrast to the predominant learning organisation adopted by most secondary schools and the TVEI survey (Read, 1992) found that the most effective lessons were predominately 'whole class' followed by 'working alone on individual tasks'.

It is not clear why less able students prefer to work in small groups. Nevertheless, it would appear that individual working can accentuate differences and that the required seating arrangements tend to isolate pupils from their peers. Group working, however, may provide welcome support and may allow individuals to mask their weaknesses. (See Chapter 10 by Claire Marvin.)

An analysis of learning tasks has often been a starting point for the development of differentiation. Teachers have sought to break down learning into small steps (Ainscow and Tweddle, 1988; Brennan, 1985) in the belief that less able students will be able to cope with smaller units of learning, a practice that may have been adapted more for the convenience of measuring progress, than for identifying those learning components suited to an individual's learning characteristics (Norwich, 1994).

From my own research, it would appear that pupils with special educational needs do not like differentiated assignments and expressed a clear preference for 'open' as opposed to 'closed' tasks. Both terms are taken from the National Curriculum subject non-statutory guidance (i.e. Mathematics, NCC, 1989) and are used to indicate the breadth of acceptable answers. 'Open' tasks allow for a range of possible, correct answers, whereas 'closed' indicates that there is only one acceptable answer. This preference is in direct contrast to most special needs practices where modified tasks have often limited the scope for responses.

Students with learning difficulties also expressed a preference for 'process'- rather than 'product'-based tasks. 'Process' tasks are those that relate to completing a series of steps in an activity. An example might be where pupils are required to discuss a topic and come to a group decision. 'Product'-based tasks require the production of an actual piece of work which can be assessed. Again it might be said that less able students see 'process', or 'doing', tasks as easier to complete, possibly because they often involve working collaboratively with peers. A 'product' may have similar connotations to 'closed' tasks, restricting choice and clearly identifying failure. In contrast, many individually prepared tasks for students with learning difficulties are by their nature 'product' orientated, allowing teachers to make easier assessments of progress and narrowing the focus of the task to clear concrete outcomes. Nevertheless, assumptions about how pupils learn most effectively do not always correlate with student preference.

COGNITIVE RESEARCH AND INCLUSIVE PRACTICE

The ways in which we think and learn are inextricably linked, and this chapter has explored these processes. If inclusion reflects the right of individuals to participate in learning, it must also be concerned with the development of thinking skills and learning strategies, particularly for pupils with special educational needs. It is known that individuals learn in many different ways, and that the identification of appropriate teaching and learning styles is essential in order to raise standards of performance to meet individual needs.

The use of cognitive style analysis should not be confused with developing 'thinking skills' (Nisbet, 1991). An understanding of how individuals learn most effectively can be the basis for the development of targeted, complementary learning materials. Thinking skills programmes are concerned with the development of pupils' skills which can lead to improvements in their thinking processes. Advocates of the teaching of thinking skills are generally agreed on their importance, but tend to disagree over ways in which they can be taught. On the one hand, it is claimed that thinking skills are most effectively taught in isolation and then applied to particular subject areas (Feuerstein et al., 1980; de Bono, 1976; Blagg et al., 1988); on the other hand, it is believed that skills must be taught within a subject context in order to be meaningful (Lipman et al., 1980; Nisbet and Shucksmith, 1986). Those who believe that the correct place of thinking skills development is within and across the curriculum point to the importance of the teachers' role in the development of learning (Nisbet, 1991). Schmeck (1988) identifies two basic approaches to learning: surface and deep. Teachers who encourage knowledge-led learning which focuses on information and facts (as opposed to meaning, understanding and interpretation) develop a surface approach to learning in pupils. He points to the insidious links between how we are taught and how we approach learning. Those who become accustomed to surface learning take on the characteristics of this approach and do not look for meaning or feel compelled to be able to understand and synthesise ideas. They do not develop inner resources for problem solving. Deep learning approaches, however, place greater emphasis on understanding and interpreting ideas. They are a naturally more reflective approach to learning which often relies on discussion and collaborative working. The use of language, both internally and within the learning group, becomes central to the thinking process, as highlighted by Vygotsky (1987). Daniels (1996) has pointed to the need for a 'responsive pedagogy' which emphasises the type of 'teaching and thinking' proposed by Vygotsky.

The use and development of effective language skills is central to inclusive learning. Those interested in thinking skills (Quicke, 1992; Schmeck, 1988; Lipman et al., 1980) have highlighted the importance of how teachers use language within the classroom and the use of quality whole class questioning is an important element in developing deep approaches to learning. Quicke (1992) sees the use of story telling as a powerful vehicle for promoting reflective and critical thinking. The 'Aristotelian' discourse, which places the learner in a contrary position, forcing him or her to think through responses in a reflective manner, is essentially a deep and interpretative approach to learning.

CONCLUSION

Inclusion is more than welcoming the 'hard to teach' into a classroom, and an understanding of how each of us learns can lead to a more accurate use of learning styles to maximise performance. 'Targeting learning' and 'individualising learning' can take on new meanings, not as separate and isolationist approaches, but as part of a cognitive pedagogy. How we encourage pupils to learn and how they then develop their own thinking are intrinsically linked. If pupils are disadvantaged by inappropriate teaching and learning styles, by a failure to develop an understanding of how individuals learn most effectively, they become the recipients of a 'compound deficit model' of learning and disadvantage.

REFERENCES

Ainscow, M. (1997) 'Towards inclusive schooling', *British Journal of Special Education* 24(1): 3–6.

Ainscow, M. and Tweddle, D. A. (1988) *Encouraging Classroom Success*, London: David Fulton.

Alexander, R. (1991) *Primary Education in Leeds*, Leeds: University of Leeds.

Bennet, N., Desforges, C., Cockburn, A. and Wilkinson, B. (1984) *The Quality of Pupil Learning Experiences*, New Jersey: LEA Publishers.

Blagg, N., Ballinger, M. and Gardner, R. (1988) *Somerset Thinking Skills Course*, Oxford: Blackwell.

de Bono, E. (1976) *Teaching Thinking*, London: Temple Smith.

Brennan, W. K. (1985) *Curriculum for Special Needs*, Milton Keynes: Open University Press.

Daniels, H. (1996) 'Back to basics: three "R's" for special needs', *British Journal of Special Education* 23(4): 155–61.

Department of Education and Science (1978) *Mixed Ability Work in Comprehensive Schools*, London: HMSO.

Department of Education and Science (1985) *Better Schools*, London: HMSO.

Department of Education and Science (1989) *Standards in Education 1987/88: the Annual Report of HM Senior Chief Inspector of Schools*, London: HMSO.

Department of Education and Science (1990) *Standards in Education 1988/89: the Annual Report of HM Senior Chief Inspector of Schools*, London: HMSO.

Feuerstein, R., Rand, Y., Hoffman, M. B. and Miller, R. (1980) *Instrumental Enrichment: an Intervention for Cognitive Modifiability*, Baltimore: University Park Press.

Galton, M. (1989) *Teaching in the Primary School*, London: Routledge & Kegan Paul.

Galton, M., Simon, B. and Croll, P. (1980) *Inside the Primary School*, London: Routledge & Kegan Paul.

HMI (1991) *Aspects of Primary Education in France*, London: DES.

Kogan, N. (1976) *Cognitive Styles in Infancy and Early Childhood*, New Jersey: Lawrence Erlbaum.

Lipman, M., Sharp, A. M and Oscanyon, F. S. (1980) *Philosophy in the Classroom*, Philadelphia: Temple University Press.

National Curriculum Council (1989) *Mathematics: Non-statutory Guidance*, York: NCC.

Nisbet, J. (1991) 'Methods and approaches', in S. Maclure and P. Davies (eds) *Learning to Think: Thinking to Learn*, Oxford: Pergamon Press.

Nisbet, J. and Shucksmith, J. (1986) *Learning Strategies*, London: Routledge & Kegan Paul.

Norwich, B. (1994) *Individual Education Plans (IEPs)* (Discussion Paper II), London: University of London Institute of Education.

Ofsted (1993) *The Integration of Pupils with Moderate Learning Difficulties into Secondary Schools*, London: Ofsted.

Ofsted (1994) *Primary Matters: a Discussion of Teaching and Learning in Primary Schools*, London: Ofsted.

Ofsted, (1995) *The Annual Report of Her Majesty's Chief Inspector of Schools, Part 1: Standards and Quality in Education*, London: HMSO.

Quicke, J. (1992) 'Clear thinking about thinking skills', *Support for Learning* 7(4): 171–6.

Read, G. (1992) *A Survey of Effective Practice* (unpublished), Nottingham: TVEI(E), Teaching and Learning Styles Group.

Riding, R. J. and Cheema, I. (1991) 'Cognitive styles: an overview and integration', *Educational Psychology* 11(3) and (4): 193–215.

Riding, R. J. and Read, G. (1996) 'Cognitive style and pupil learning preferences', *Educational Psychology* 16(1): 81–106.

Schmeck, R. R. (1988) 'Strategies and styles of learning', in R. R. Schmeck (ed.) *Learning Strategies and Learning Styles*, New York: Plenum Press.

Vygotsky, L. S. (1987) 'Thinking and speech', in R. Rieber and A. Carton (eds) *The Collected Works of L.S. Vygotsky, Vol.1*, New York: Plenum Press.

Witkin, H. A., Moore, C. A., Goodenough, D. R. and Cox, P. W. (1997) 'Field-dependent, and field-independent cognitive styles and their educational implications', *Review of Educational Research* 1(64).

Chapter 10

Individual and whole class teaching

Claire Marvin

The teaching styles and approaches adopted by teachers can have a major influence upon the promotion of inclusion in schools. In this chapter, Claire Marvin argues that achieving a balance between a range of individual, group and whole class teaching approaches is critical to meeting the needs of all pupils.

An analysis of teaching approaches and learning styles is an essential process for the teacher who wishes to develop an inclusive classroom. However, the development of an analytical approach is a complex area and one which has recently been the subject of both research and controversy. The effective use of all resources, human and material, requires arrangements which take full account of the needs of the pupil, the teaching environment, and the learning activities planned. Inevitably this will mean adopting different forms of organisation for different situations and occasions. Within this chapter, whole class, small-group, paired and individual teaching will be examined. The relevance and relative merits of each will be explored and strategies for their use with pupils with learning difficulties described. Any move towards inclusion will require that teachers are fully conversant with an appropriate range of teaching strategies and learning styles, and that they will have the ability to apply these in order to ensure effective access for all pupils.

INDIVIDUAL TEACHING

The use of individual teaching sessions has been a commonly used strategy in the education of pupils with learning difficulties. It has been argued that, for children who experience difficulties, there is a need to provide moments of intense concentration with an adult if they are to learn effectively (Hammond and Read, 1992). The relatively small numbers in classes in special schools has led to the popularisation of this approach, but classes which may have thirty or more pupils in a mainstream school make this difficult to organise, and in some instances to justify (Alexander, 1992; Moyles, 1992). As emphasised by Florian in Chapter 2, the environmental conditions of the mainstream classroom may not always be appropriate for all pupils at all times, and therefore the place of individual teaching as a part of inclusive practice needs to be examined. This will be followed by an exploration of the organisational implications of teaching one learner at a time.

What good individual teaching looks like

Working with individual pupils should enable teachers to match their teaching as accurately as possible to each pupil's needs. Perceiving a very close relationship between teaching and learning is instrumental to ensuring that the match is good. Vygotsky (1978) suggests that young children learn primarily through social interaction, through being with and interacting with adults. He proposes that if this interaction occurs in what he calls 'the Zone of Proximal Development' (ZPD), children will progress in their thinking and learning. This zone is described as the distance between what a child already understands and what he or she can understand with adult support. In Vygotskian terms, the support the adult provides is based upon what is received from the child. Thus the relationship is interdependent. This approach continues to be used in special schools, and when pupils are taught in withdrawn situations in the mainstream.

Individual teaching sessions are opportunities to appreciate how this relationship can be achieved. Finding the child's ZPD becomes a realistic possibility when relating to one pupil at a time, but will only be achieved if individual teaching sessions are carefully structured. Vygotsky recommends assessing the child, not only on what he or she can achieve alone but also on what the child can achieve when receiving support from a more experienced learner. It is by analysing the difference between what is accomplished independently and with help that the teacher knows what to teach. It is expected that teachers should 'baseline' pupils in order to establish what pupils know, understand or can do, and to define a starting point from which teaching can begin (Gardner et al., 1983). Commonly, such assessments are related to closely defined curriculum plans with the intention of finding the right place within the context of that curriculum to begin teaching. Finding the child's ZPD is a similar process but is broader in that it does not directly relate to a written curriculum but will embrace both the knowledge base and the learning strategies used by the pupil (Dockrell and McShane, 1993). The pupil's learning is examined with an open mind, though not, of course, in a vacuum and the teacher takes his or her lead from what he or she observes. Individual teaching and learning can then proceed from this point.

When working with individual pupils, teachers not only want to find the exact point at which to begin the teaching but also to promote an effective match between the styles of both teaching and learning which are to be deployed. Learning style has been extensively examined and it can be said with confidence that individuals learn in different ways (Banner and Rayner, 1997). Pollard and Tann (1993) summarise some of this research and suggest that there are two main aspects to take into consideration, these being cognition and personality. For example, from the cognitive aspect, some learners are wholists (who like to grasp the whole) whilst others are serialists (who like to piece their learning together bit by bit); some learners are naturally divergent (and use inspirational flair) whilst others are convergent (and prefer closed situations and right answers). From the personality aspect, some learners are extroverts and others are introverts; some are competitive and some collaborative (see Chapter 9 by Geoff Read). When working with a whole class or even a group of pupils, it is extremely difficult for teachers to match every task to every learner's learning style, but in individual teaching sessions, this is not only possible but also highly desirable. This is the opportunity for teachers to spend time discovering the way in which the child learns most effectively

---

Example

Mary is working with her teacher on developing her writing skills. Mary responds best if she has an overview of the task and the outcomes she is expected to achieve. She then likes to get all her ideas down on paper without worrying about the spelling and writing. Sometimes she uses symbols or a tape recorder to help her because then she can work more quickly before she loses the thread of her ideas. After this stage, Mary can be persuaded to work on parts of her writing to practise the mechanics. Often the finished product will consist of a combination of symbols, writing by the teacher and writing by Mary herself.

Not only can learning style be carefully matched but activities and materials can be appropriately targeted in terms of interest and person needs and preferences. The learning experience can be genuinely student led, something which Wells (1986) found so important in his research into the development of young children's language. He suggested that those children whose parents listened well and joined them in talking about topics initiated by the children were more advanced and capable in their language than those whose parents were didactic or directive. In school, this does not mean that teachers cannot plan and must wait for the lead to come from the child, but it implies an open mind and careful assessment of individual interests to use as motivators and initiators of activities. Based on taking the lead from the child, teaching can be very effective when the teacher works alongside, giving ideas by example rather than by directive teaching.

Example

Rani is developing her ability to make things using a variety of materials. Her teacher worked alongside her on the floor, firstly making his own construction and then encouraging Rani to join with him in a joint venture. He asked her to watch him on occasions but most of the time was spent with him watching and imitating her. He gave a running commentary sometimes focusing on Rani's construction and sometimes on his own. Following the session, the teacher was able to write a full assessment of Rani's construction skills and understanding from which he could plan their next joint effort.

When working with an individual learner, quality adult–child interaction is possible. There is less pressure to keep the pace moving and juggle the needs of a whole class, so the pace can suit the individual and time can be used in an optimum manner. In summary, individual teaching is an opportunity to utilise all the factors relating to good teaching which are so difficult to achieve when faced with a whole class. It is likely to be used most frequently for incremental learning (the introduction of new skills) or for problem solving in new situations rather than for practice of skills already learned (Ainscow and Muncey, 1989). For some learners, particularly those with the most severe or profound learning difficulties, interaction with and support from an adult may be necessary for a large proportion of their learning, including that which involves practising the familiar.

Individual Education Plans

Although there is still debate concerning the appropriate content and presentation of Individual Education Plans (IEPs) there is agreement that these should relate specifically to individual needs (Ramjhun, 1995). It can be argued that the IEP should focus on the most fundamental needs of the pupil, beginning with those aspects of need which will increase access to a wider range of learning opportunities. For example, for most children with learning difficulties, basic communication, literacy, numeracy, study skills and personal and social education will be areas which are likely to form the bedrock for access to the rest of the curriculum. IEPs written in these five areas could then be placed within a whole variety of different subjects and topics. Indeed, the importance of ensuring a fusion between targets identified on an IEP and the activities planned for curriculum delivery is a key issue in terms of meeting the entitlement of pupils with special educational needs. Individual teaching sessions are excellent opportunities to concentrate on the programmes which arise from the five IEP areas, although they will not be the only openings as much fundamental learning benefits from being placed in a variety of curriculum areas rather than in isolation.

Example

John's IEP contains the following target:

To use a junior dictionary to look up the spelling of words during writing activities

An adult spends ten minutes individually with him two or three times a week. The first few minutes are spent on a mechanical exercise aimed at increasing his speed at finding letters in the alphabet and the rest of the time on a piece of writing (or typing) which is related to either football or the television, both of which are motivating topics for John. Sometimes they will just talk about the words, looking them up but not writing them.

John also uses this method of supporting his writing in whole class activities which relate to different subjects on the curriculum. There are, however, other times when he is not expected to look up words, nor even to write, recognising the need for pupils who experience difficulties in writing to have access to the curriculum through channels with which they have more success.

Managing individual teaching sessions

Teaching learners individually usually means exactly what it says: one teacher and one learner. However, there are times when it is possible to teach individually but in a small group. At its worst, this can become a juggling act while the teacher attempts to split him- or herself into two or three parts, and does not interact satisfactorily with anyone, but there are advantages as well as disadvantages, especially if the individual programmes overlap or if one student is able to act as a model for others (see 'pair work' below). It can also be effective if the tasks are alternated between high and low support or naturally contain moments when the pupil does not need attention, thus freeing the adult to work in turn with each learner.

Organising the classroom to facilitate individual teaching usually involves more than one adult, although it can be managed very successfully in mainstream classes where pupils have been taught to work independently, supporting each other when the teacher is engaged with individuals (Ainscow and Tweddle, 1988; Westwood, 1997). If there is more than one adult, one can have the role of teaching individuals or a small group while the other teaches the rest of the class (Wolfendale, 1992). This can be very effective if well planned in advance. It is less effective when the adults become fixed in one role. For example, if a learning support assistant is always expected to work individually with pupils with learning difficulties, it is possible for those pupils to be rarely taught by the teacher (Thomas, 1992). Overdependence upon a support assistant, or the use of withdrawal teaching, can in some circumstances become a major obstacle to inclusion. In schools where withdrawal teaching is used excessively, pupils can miss significant parts of their entitlement to the subjects from which they are removed. When well managed, individual teaching develops the skills and esteem of pupils with learning difficulties, and enables them to be included more fully and with greater confidence in group and whole class situations.

GROUP WORK

As stated previously earlier developments in the teaching of pupils with learning difficulties tended to concentrate on individual instruction to the exclusion of other approaches. More recently, working in small groups has been not only more widely explored, but recognised as beneficial to learning and a highly effective way of promoting inclusive classrooms (Ainscow, 1995).

Galton and Williamson (1992) classify the range of small groups commonly developed in classrooms as follows:

- seating groups, where pupils sit together but are engaged in separate tasks and produce separate and often quite different outcomes;
- working groups, where pupils tackle similar tasks resulting in similar outcomes but their work is independent;
- co-operative groups, where pupils have separate but related tasks resulting in a joint outcome;
- collaborative groups, where pupils have the same task and work together towards a joint outcome.

Each grouping has its strengths and weaknesses and can be used for different purposes. Mounting evidence from research, both in the UK (Bennett and Cass, 1988; DES, 1989; Lewis, 1991; 1995a) and the USA (Johnson and Johnson, 1982; Slavin, 1983; Thousand and Villa, 1991), has led writers to conclude that where opportunities to work together are provided all pupils can and do effectively learn as members of a group. The research suggests that well-organised group work has benefits for all pupils, and can be a powerful tool for the development of inclusive practice. To achieve success this type of group work demands considerable thought and preparation. For the remainder of this section attention will be paid to the benefits of co-operative and collaborative groups and how best to organise them.

Why should pupils work in groups?

There are a number of significant arguments for the use of co-operative learning strategies, and these need to be considered in all schools which have increased inclusion as an aim. Social exchanges encouraged through group work can be a powerful learning tool. As stated previously, psychologists such as Bruner (1972) and Vygotsky (1978) believed that a pupil's potential for learning is revealed and often realised in interactions with more knowledgeable others, such as a teacher or peer group. Thus, co-operatively achieved success lies at the foundation of learning and development. Group work creates opportunities for pupils to formulate and share their ideas through talk and it encourages mutual support in a safe environment which, in turn, can lead to personal success and raised self-esteem (Johnson et al., 1990). In addition, as Hart (1992) suggests, the support process which develops within successful groups can become self-sustaining thus allowing the teacher more time to address the needs of individual pupils. Well-managed group work also provides essential opportunities for pupils to develop, practise and generalise their social skills. If much of their experience at school is restricted to a one-to-one teacher–pupil relationship they may be denied this chance. Sebba et al. (1995, p.42) suggest that 'the achievement of sociability may often be the most demanding requirement placed upon pupils and teachers alike' but it is one that must not be overlooked. The acquisition of basic social skills may lead to collaboration and successful interaction, and is certainly an important factor in the development of inclusive classrooms. This, in turn, suggests a need to develop the skills of negotiation. At one level this will be between pupils, at another it will involve pupil and teacher sharing in the responsibility for managing the child's learning. (See Chapter 7 by Richard Rose.)

Example

Richard and William are at the early stages of negotiation. Supported by an adult they are making a simple plan concerning the construction of a model aeroplane out of junk materials. Each is encouraged to listen to the other's ideas and to negotiate their role. Richard decides to find the junk, William the glue, sticky tape and scissors. During the construction of the aeroplane materials are shared, turns are taken and questions modelled by the adult. For example, 'I wonder what will happen if . . . ?' At this early stage the adult's role as a facilitator is critical to success. Together the pupils are supported in achieving the joint goal.

Given the strengths of the arguments for co-operative learning it would be reasonable to assume that the use of such approaches would be common in schools. Both Rose (1991) and Ware (1994) are of the opinion that group work is becoming more widespread in many special schools. Yet there is a significant body of evidence from research in mainstream settings to suggest that co-operative learning is in fact rare (Mortimore *et al.*, 1988; Alexander, 1992; Bennett and Dunne, 1992; Galton and Williamson, 1992). For the most part it remains a neglected art. There are several factors which influence the lack of structured group work in some schools and it is certainly recognised that the management of group work makes great demands upon the teachers involved in terms of the motivation, organisation, management and monitoring of the groups (Alexander, 1992; Pollard and Tann, 1993; McNamara, 1994; Farrell, 1997). The concept of co-operative learning is recognised as important, but very few teachers have received any specific training in this area (Merrett and Wheldall, 1993). The fact that collaborative learning is seen as integral to the delivery of the National Curriculum and an essential aspect of some of the programmes of study puts the onus on teachers to adapt their teaching styles to encourage the active involvement of pupils (Sebba *et al.*, 1995). Groupings must not simply be chosen to manage learners but to manage learning. This requires a radical shift in thinking and initially the untidy, uncomfortable and difficult to control learning which may ensue appears threatening to some (Biott and Easen, 1994). Teachers who are adequately supported and secure in their grasp of appropriate group work management skills will be ready to take the risks, and will see that it encourages far greater inclusion for pupils with learning difficulties.

Planning group work

Collaborative group work should not be regarded as a single specific form of classroom organisation. There are many different ways of organising groups depending on the kind of task demand and the social ability of the pupils involved. For any group work to prove effective an understanding of the needs of individual pupils must combine with a clear analysis of lesson content, possible learning opportunities, intended outcomes and group dynamics. Consideration should also be given to creating favourable class-room conditions where pupils learn to value working together and have opportunities to give and experience help, support and challenge in their relationships with others (Ainscow and Muncey, 1989; Galton and Williamson, 1992; Sebba et al., 1995). The size and composition of the group can be crucial to its success or failure. In recognition of its importance group structure has been the focus of much research (see reviews in McCall, 1983; Lewis, 1995b; Smith and Urquhart, 1996).There is evidence to suggest that groups of four are most effective for developing co-operation (Bennett and Dunne, 1992) although younger or less experienced pupils may need to work initially in friendship pairs (National Oracy Project, 1990). Larger groups can split into dyads or trios or may allow individuals to opt out.

Most teachers need to manage groups of pupils of widely differing abilities, which can be highly challenging and require careful organisation. Findings from research show that most pupils make the greatest progress both academically and socially when working in mixed-ability groups (Swing and Peterson, 1982; Johnson and Johnson, 1982; Bennett and Cass, 1988) and that groups which include pupils of lower ability are often highly successful. One exception may be pupils with profound and multiple learning difficulties. Westling et al. (1982) report that individual teaching is more effective than small groups for these pupils but Ware (1994) cautions that this should not preclude them from group work. She suggests that other benefits may be derived from taking part, for example it may increase pupils' awareness of group identity and sense of belonging. Moreover Collis and Lacey (1996) suggest that their needs are of a level where almost any activity can prove relevant providing that time is allowed for their response – a tolerance that other pupils in the group will have to learn. When planning classroom groupings, specific pupil characteristics, friendships, interests and learning styles will all have a direct effect on group interaction and will need to be considered at the planning stage.

Following their extensive research on collaborative group work in schools, Bennett and Dunne (1992) concluded that the most important contributory factor to its success is the nature of the task itself. For each pupil teacher's need to be able to make clear and appropriate decisions about the intended outcome of the activity before making decisions regarding the type of task to be used and the most suitable group structure to be employed. Small-group work can be used for all types of learning task: for example, incremental, restructuring (which often involves problem solving), or enrichment (generalisation tasks). Within the activity each pupil will learn different skills at their own level.

Example

A group of Amy's friends were making a large cake for her birthday. Kieran and Jasmin learned that by measuring, mixing and heating familiar products using pre-existing skills a complete change took place and a cake was produced. Ryan and Ann learned that while margarine, eggs and flour taste disgusting on their own, when mixed together they taste rather good. Samantha learned about simple measures, David practised skills in cutting, stirring and spreading (the icing), Razia learned to stir.

Galton and Williamson (1992) conclude that it is best to begin with small practical activities where there is a specific and achievable solution. Such tasks might involve simple problem solving where completion of the task is within the joint capabilities of the group. 'Tight' or closed tasks have been found to generate the most talk.

Example

Kirk, Pervas and Leanne have been asked to arrange the classroom furniture for a drama session. They know how many chairs are needed and that they are to be placed in a circle. This week they have been asked to put a large table, stored in the hall, in the middle. They must work together to locate the chairs, lift the table and complete the task to their joint satisfaction.

Over time, the tasks could become much more complex and provide valuable opportunities for discussion and debate: for example, building a hutch for a rabbit, producing a school newspaper or planning a class outing. These kinds of tasks which are lacking a correct answer are described as abstract, 'loose' or open ended and have been found to generate higher-quality exchanges.

Meeting individual needs

Attention needs to be paid to group aims as well as individual needs. Initially co-operation with other members of the group may well be the only teaching aim. It cannot be assumed that placing pupils in groups will enable them to work effectively together. Meaningful interactions do not occur automatically. Findings from research show that they must be planned for and the relevant skills explicitly taught (Hundert and Houghton, 1992; Hardman and Beverton, 1993; Gregory, 1996). Skills can be developed and practised using a variety of methods at a variety of levels from the intensive interaction techniques advocated by Nind and Hewett (1994) involving basic pupil and adult interaction to work in pairs such as that promoted by Veronica Sherborne (1990) often utilising an older and younger pupil pairing to small-group or whole class, mixed-ability Circle Time activities (Ballard, 1982; Mosley, 1991; 1993; Curry and Bromfield, 1994). Where pupils have gained more experience of group work more specific individual cognitive skills can be promoted. Sebba et al. (1995) give an example of how, with the help of the teacher as facilitator, it was possible for two pupils to share in drawing and labelling a picture as a record of their visit to an agricultural college. The task enabled them to practise both their individual skills in writing and drawing and the collaborative skills necessary in order to achieve a joint outcome. The teacher's role was crucial in offering the 'scaffolding' necessary for success. Encouraging effective co-operation often requires flexibility from the teacher – knowing when to stand back and allow mistakes to be made and when to step in with direction and support (Johnson et al., 1990; Bennett and Dunne, 1992; Galton and Williamson, 1992). The task described above was split into several stages. At the end of each one the teacher helped to plan the next by facilitating the necessary negotiation and discussion. The pupils were then able to continue unsupported, knowing their role and what it was they were expected to achieve.

Types of co-operative group work

Working in pairs

Working pupils together in pairs can provide an initial step towards the successful development of group work. There are several ways in which paired work can be organised and much will depend on the nature of the task in hand and the needs of the pupils. The teaming of skilled pupils with those whose needs are greater is one method which affords teachers the opportunity to utilise the benefits of difference: for example, different ability, different knowledge, different age (McNamara and Moreton, 1997). Much partner work can be organised within one class (see, for example, PE groupings, Sugden and Wright, 1996) but pairings can take place between parallel classes, year groups or separate schools. A perceived problem associated with organising mixed-ability pairwork is the tendency for the more able pupil to dominate the task, which in turn reinforces the learned helplessness of less able pupils and does very little to promote interactive learning. Research on pairs and groups has shown that in order to encourage positive attitudes, to raise self-esteem and create effective learning, all pupils should at some stage be encouraged to take on the role of 'instructor' or 'organiser' (McConkey and McCormack, 1984; Wade and Moore, 1994). For pupils with profound and multiple learning difficulties this might mean being given the opportunity to take control by, for example, 'signalling' when to roll a car down a slope during an activity exploring friction. For more able pupils it could mean being invited to 'tutor' a mainstream partner in Makaton sign language or teaching the use of a microswitch. Explorations in the area of paired work have been extensive (Topping, 1988; Hornby et al., 1997) and provide clear evidence of success when promoting interaction between pupils of all abilities and need.

Larger groups

It is possible to organise a variety of co-operative groups with a bewildering array of names such as buzz, snowball, carousel, rainbow, and envoying (Cowie and Rudduck, 1988; Byers and Rose, 1996; McNamara and Moreton, 1997). The most appropriate group method to use will depend on the intended outcome of the lesson, the needs of the individuals involved and the available resources, particularly in terms of adult support. To ensure success the teacher must ensure that:

- every pupil is actively involved;
- their work is valued as an important part of the whole;
- they are aware of the purpose of the activity and the intended outcome.

One method that has been used successfully with a wide range of pupils with learning difficulties is jigsawing. First designed by Aronson (1978) and modified by Johnson and Johnson (1987a; 1987b) in the USA, it was adapted for use in the UK by Rose (1991). A somewhat similar approach is the use of scripted groups modified from the work of Brown et al. (1980)

and exemplified in Ware (1994). Byers and Rose (1996) suggest that jigsawing may be used to:

- promote the development of new skills, concepts, knowledge and understanding;
- encourage the maintenance, consolidation, demonstration in new contexts and generalisation of existing skills, concepts, knowledge and understanding.

(p.62)

In the jigsawing approach a group activity is broken down into smaller interdependent parts which can be achieved by individual or subgroups of pupils who, in turn, need to co-operate in order to achieve the whole. In this way pupils are assigned (or encouraged to select) a task appropriate to their individual needs and abilities while, at the same time, developing their skills of interaction and sociability by working co-operatively (Byers, 1996; Mount and Ackerman, 1991; Sebba, 1994; 1995; Byers and Rose, 1996). This approach has been successfully used to encourage the participation in group situations of pupils with a wide range of abilities, including those with profound and multiple learning difficulties.

Organising the classroom to facilitate the subgroups created within co-operative group work usually involves more than one adult. The identification of different levels of learning tasks, which is possible in jigsawing for example, allows for effective differentiation, helps to ensure efficient use of staff time and encourages purposeful class groups. This type of organisation is exemplified by Byers (1996) in his description of a lesson designed as part of an integrated scheme of work on 'Living and growing'. One task is adult intensive and involves the practising of new skills; the second is a semi-structured problem-solving activity planned to make use of pupils' existing skills and knowledge. This requires an adult to introduce it and then withdraw. The third engages pupils in the solution of their own problems with support from other members of their group with a member of staff overseeing this and intervening only when essential.

WHOLE CLASS TEACHING

Most pupils with learning difficulties can be enabled to learn through whole class teaching, especially if it reinforces and builds upon the skills and knowledge addressed in the individual sessions. There may be a few pupils with the most profound disabilities or with severe autism, for example, who will find it difficult to cope in a whole class situation. For these pupils it will be necessary to plan a staged approach to eventual participation. Retaining a focus upon the individual needs of everyone in a special school class of twelve to fifteen pupils invariably proves to be challenging for one adult. In mainstream schools, whole class teaching that takes into account the special needs of a few of its pupils is possible but underlines the necessity for keeping individual targets few in number.

Whole class teaching can be used in a variety of different ways. There are times when it is used for drill and rote learning or for story time, choral singing or for introducing a new topic (Moyles, 1992; Pollard and Tann, 1993). It can range from purely teacher directed to interactive and dialogic. All techniques are effective at different times and for different purposes. In this section, it is whole class interactive teaching that will be examined, offering some ideas for ensuring that, in mainstream classrooms, pupils with special needs are included and, in special schools, that pupils have a chance to get the most from this form of teaching and learning.

All teachers make considerable use of questioning pupils as a teaching tool. These questions are sometimes intended to find out what pupils know but more effectively questioning is engineered to encourage thinking and sharing of information across the class. Perrott (1982) suggests that teachers have to work hard at learning how to use questioning to provoke thinking. Research has shown that the majority of questions only require learners to recall data. Where questioning does offer the opportunity to explain, explore and reflect on knowledge teachers do not always wait long enough for a reply. Valuable contributions are lost as the teacher moves on (Watson, 1996). Kerry (1982) provides some guidance to help teachers build up skills in sequencing questioning: moving from demanding recall of data, naming and showing comprehension towards requiring learners to hypothesise, analyse, evaluate and problem-solve. Many pupils with learning difficulties find questions difficult to answer and even harder to pose themselves. Work by the teacher on question and answer routines in individual learning sessions can help whole class interactive teaching to be more effective for all pupils. Targeting specific questions at individual pupils, whilst being sensitive to issues of pupil confidence, is another way of ensuring everyone feels included in the session. This may involve teaching the whole class to respect the opinions of classmates and providing rules to prevent the interruption or derision of contributors. The creation of a climate of trust is essential if learning is to take place in a large forum.

The use of brainstorming where pupils are encouraged to take turns to call out their ideas on a subject is commonly used in schools. This can be useful at the beginning of a new teaching theme so that the teacher find the class ZPD before embarking on a course of teaching. Pupils can be directed to each other for exchanging information and support. Children with learning difficulties will need to be included by being given more thinking space or by being supported by an adult who might provide part of an idea. Encouraging discussion can be difficult but rewarding when achieved. Circle Time as advocated by Mosley (1991; 1993), has been developed to encourage pupils to listen to each other and develop the ability to express ideas. Although specifically designed to help regulate behaviour and foster a caring atmosphere, this can have beneficial repercussions in other areas of learning. Forming a student council can also encourage the formation and expression of opinions, leading to the development of self-esteem and eventual self-advocacy (Winup, 1994). Pupils with learning difficulties will often need to be taught very specifically how to take part in such activities.

Within the general area of discussion, teachers have opportunities to develop the skills of evaluation in whole class interactive teaching (Watson, 1996). Many subjects in the National Curriculum refer to developing pupils' abilities to evaluate what they do, see and hear. Pupils with learning difficulties can be specifically taught how to evaluate. They need to learn the vocabulary of appreciation and be given opportunities to use this in relevant contexts. Arts subjects can provide an effective vehicle for developing such skills (Peter, 1994; 1996). One approach to developing evaluation skills is through the High/Scope Curriculum where the plan–do–review sequence is used. Pupils plan their work, carry it out and subsequently review the activity (Hohmann et al., 1979; Mitchell, 1994). At the end of the session they are encouraged to talk about what they have been doing, what they have achieved, what was significant and how they feel about it. If this technique is introduced early in pupils' schooling they grow up through the school expecting to be involved in regular sessions of reflection and self-review. Such expectations may prove to be critical as we endeavour to promote greater inclusion in classrooms.

There are times when teachers can allow children to take the lead in whole class interactive teaching. They will not be using a questioning technique but one of commenting. Although there will be a framework for the session, the exact path will not be mapped out and the teacher will have to judge the right moment for making a comment which might push thinking on. This can be a somewhat unnerving way to teach as the destination is not always clear. Good teachers can capitalise on the flow of what is happening and draw all children into it, whatever their needs.

CONCLUSION

This chapter has been concerned with examining issues of classroom organisation in order to give greater involvement and responsibility to pupils and to foster inclusive practice in schools. Research has shown that no one method is a panacea for pupils' social and cognitive development (Galton and Williamson, 1992; Bennett and Dunne, 1992; Hastings and Schwieso, 1995). Each kind of classroom grouping has a different purpose and specific potential. Professional judgement is needed to select from what may be viewed as a 'continuum of grouping' in order to achieve an appropriate balance and to satisfy pupil needs. The critical notion is one of 'fitness for purpose' (Alexander *et al.*, 1992). In collaboration with the pupils where possible, it is the teacher's responsibility to decide the purpose of an activity and the most appropriate method of fulfilment to enable them to take a more active part in managing their own learning. Through the promotion of such practice we move ever nearer to inclusion.

REFERENCES

Ainscow, M. (1995) 'Special needs through school improvement; school improvement through special needs', in C. Clark, A. Dyson and A. Millward (eds) *Towards Inclusive Schools?*, London: David Fulton.

Ainscow, M. and Muncey, J. (1989) *Meeting Individual Needs*, London: David Fulton.

Ainscow, M. and Tweddle, D. (1988) *Encouraging Classroom Success*, London: David Fulton.

Alexander, R. (1992) *Policy and Practice in Primary Education*, London: Routledge.

Alexander, R., Rose, J. and Woodhead, C. (1992) *Curriculum Organisation and Classroom Practice in Primary Schools: a Discussion Paper*, London: DES.

Aronson, E. (1978) *The Jigsaw Classroom*, Beverley Hills, CA: Sage.

Ballard, J. (1982) *Circlebook*, New York: Irvington.

Banner, G. and Rayner, S. (1997) 'Teaching in style: are you making the difference in the classroom?', *Support for Learning* 12(1): 15–18.

Bennett, N. and Cass, A. (1988) 'The effects of group composition on group interactive processes and pupil understanding', *British Educational Research Journal* 15(1): 19–32.

Bennett, N. and Dunne, E. (1992) *Managing Classroom Groups*, London: Simon & Schuster.

Biott, C. and Easen, P. (1994) *Collaborative Learning in Staffrooms and Classrooms*, London: David Fulton.

Brown, F., Holvoet, J., Guess, D. and Mulligan, M. (1980) 'The individualised curriculum sequencing model III: small group instruction', *Journal of the Association of the Severely Handicapped* 5: 352–67.

Bruner, J. (1972) *The Relevance of Education*, London: Allen & Unwin.

Byers, R. (1996) 'Providing opportunities for effective learning', in R. Rose, A. Fergusson, C. Coles, R. Byers and D. Banes (eds) *Implementing the Whole Curriculum for Pupils with Learning Difficulties*, London: David Fulton.

Byers, R. and Rose, R. (1996) *Planning the Curriculum for Pupils with Special Educational Needs*, London: David Fulton.

Collis, M. and Lacey, P. (1996) *Interactive Approaches to Learning: a Framework for INSET*, London: David Fulton.

Cowie, H. and Ruddock, J. (1988) *Cooperative Groupwork: an Overview*, London: BP Education Service.

Curry, M. and Bromfield, C. (1994) *Circle Time*, Tamworth: NASEN.

Department of Education and Science (DES) (1989) *Discipline in Schools* (The Elton Report), London: HMSO.

Dockrell, J. and McShane, J. (1993) *Childrens' Learning Difficulties: a Cognitive Approach*, Oxford: Blackwell.

Farrell, P. (1997) *Teaching Pupils with Learning Difficulties. Strategies and Solutions*, London: Cassell.

Galton, M. and Williamson, J. (1992) *Groupwork in the Primary Classroom*, London: Routledge.

Gardner, J., Murphy, J. and Crawford, N. (1983) *The Skills Analysis Model*, Kidderminster: BIMH.

Gregory, S. P. (1996) 'Inclusive education for pre-school children with disabilities', *Support for Learning* 11(2): 77–82.

Hammond, C. and Read, G. (1992) 'Individual v individualised: into the 1990s', in K. Bovair, B. Carpenter and G. Upton (eds) *Special Curricula Needs*, London: David Fulton.

Hardman, F. and Beverton, S. (1993) 'Cooperative group work and the development of metadiscoursal skills', *Support for Learning* 8(4): 146–50.

Hart, S. (1992) 'Differentiation – way forward or defeat?', *British Journal of Special Education* 19(1): 10–12.

Hastings, N. and Schwieso, J. (1995) 'Tasks and tables, the effects of seating arrangements on task engagement in primary schools', *Educational Research* 37(3).

Hohmann, M., Banet, B. and Weikart, D. P. (1979) *Young Children in Action*, Michigan: High Scope Press.

Hornby, G., Atkinson, M. and Howard, J. (1997) *Controversial Issues in Special Education*, London: David Fulton.

Hundert, J. and Houghton, A. (1992) 'Promoting social interactions of children with disabilities in integrated pre-schools: a failure to generalise', *Exceptional Children* 58: 311–19.

Johnson, D. W. and Johnson, R. T. (1982) 'The effects of cooperative and individualistic instruction on handicapped and non-handicapped students', *Journal of Social Psychology* 118: 257–68.

Johnson, D. W. and Johnson, R. T. (1987a) *Learning Together and Alone*, Englewood Cliffs, NJ: Prentice Hall.

Johnson, D. W. and Johnson, R. T. (1987b) *Joining Together. Group Theory and Group Skills*, 3rd edition, Minnesota: Interaction Book Company.

Johnson, D. W., Johnson, R. T. and Johnson-Holubec, E. J. (1990) *Circles of Learning*, 3rd edition, Minnesota: Interaction Book Company.

Kerry, T. (1982) *Effective Questioning*, London: Macmillan.

Lewis, A. (1991) 'Entitled to learn together?', in R. Ashdown, B. Carpenter and K. Bovair (eds) *The Curriculum Challenge*, London: Falmer Press.

Lewis, A. (1995a) *Childrens' Understanding of Disability*, London: Routledge.

Lewis, A. (1995b) *Primary Special Needs and the National Curriculum*, 2nd edition, London: Routledge.

McCall, C. (1983) *Classroom Grouping for Special Needs*, Stratford-upon-Avon: National Council for Special Education.

McConkey, R. and McCormack, B. (1984) 'Changing attitudes to people who are disabled', *Mental Handicap* 12: 112–14.

McNamara, D. (1994) *Classroom Pedagogy and Primary Practice*, London: Routledge.

McNamara, S. and Moreton, G. (1997) *Understanding Differentiation*, London: David Fulton.

Merrett, F. and Wheldall, K. (1993) 'How do teachers learn to manage classroom behaviour? A study of teachers' opinions about their initial training with special reference to classroom behaviour management', *Educational Studies* 19: 91–106.

Mitchell, S. (1994) 'Some implications of the High Scope curriculum and the education of children with learning difficulties', in J. Coupe O'Kane and B. Smith (eds) *Taking Control. Enabling Pupils with Learning Difficulties*, London: David Fulton.

Mortimore, P., Sammons, P., Stoll, L., Lewis, D. and Ecob, R. (1988) *School Matters: The Junior Years*, Wells: Open Books.

Mosley, J. (1991) *All Round Success*, Trowbridge: Wiltshire County Council.

Mosley, J. (1993) *Turn Round Your School*, Wisbech: LDA.

Mount, H. and Ackerman, D. (1991) *Technology for All*, London: David Fulton.

Moyles, J. R. (1992) *Organisation for Learning in the Primary School*, Buckingham: Open University Press.

National Oracy Project (1990) *Teaching, Talking and Learning in Key Stage One*, York: National Curriculum Council.

Nind, M. and Hewett, D. (1994) *Access to Communication*, London: David Fulton.

Perrott, E. (1982) *Effective Teaching*, Harlow: Longman.

Peter, M. (1994) *Drama for All*, London: David Fulton.

Peter, M. (1996) *Art for All*, London: David Fulton.

Pollard, A. and Tann, S. (1993) *Reflective Teaching in the Primary School*, 2nd edition, London: Cassell.

Ramjhun, A. F. (1995) *Implementing the Code of Practice for Pupils with Special Educational Needs*, London: David Fulton.

Rose, R. (1991) 'A jigsaw approach to group work', *British Journal of Special Education* 18(2): 54–8.

Sebba, J. (1994) *History for All*, London: David Fulton.

Sebba, J. (1995) *Geography for All*, London: David Fulton.

Sebba, J., Byers, R. and Rose, R. (1995) *Redefining the Whole Curriculum for Pupils with Learning Difficulties*, London: David Fulton.

Sherborne, V. (1990) *Developmental Movement for Children*, Cambridge: Cambridge University Press.

Slavin, R. (1983) *Cooperative Learning*, New York: Longman.

Smith, R. and Urquhart, I. (1996) 'Science and special educational needs', in E. Bearne (ed.) *Differentiation and Diversity in the Primary School*, London: Routledge.

Sugden, D. and Wright, H. (1996) 'Physical education', in B. Carpenter, R. Ashdown and K. Bovair (eds) *Enabling Access*, London: David Fulton.

Swing, S. and Peterson, P. (1982) 'The relationship of student ability and small group interaction to student achievement', *American Educational Research Journal* 19(2): 259–74.

Thomas, G. (1992) *Effective Classroom Teamwork. Support or Intrusion?*, London: Routledge.

Thousand, J. and Villa, R. A. (1991) 'Accommodating for greater student variance', in M. Ainscow (ed.) *Effective Schools for All*, London: David Fulton.

Topping, K. (1988) *The Peer Tutoring Handbook*, London: Croom Helm.

Vygotsky, L. (1978) *Mind in Society: The Development of Higher Psychological Processes*, Cambridge, MA: Harvard University Press.

Wade, B. and Moore, M. (1994) 'Feeling different: viewpoints of students with special educational needs', *British Journal of Special Education* 21(4): 161–5.

Ware, J. (1994) 'Classroom organisation', in J. Ware (ed.) *Educating Children with Profound and Multiple Learning Difficulties*, London: David Fulton.

Watson, J. (1996) *Reflection through Interaction*, London: Falmer Press.

Wells, G. (1986) *The Meaning Makers. Children Learning Language, and Using Language to Learn*, London: Hodder & Stoughton.

Westling, D. L., Ferrell, K. and Swenson, K. (1982) 'Intraclassroom comparison of two arrangements for teaching profoundly mentally retarded children', *American Journal of Mental Deficiency* 86(6): 601–8.

Westwood, P. (1997) *Commonsense Methods for Children with Special Needs*, 3rd edition, London: Routledge.

Winup, K. (1994) 'The role of a student committee in promotion of independence among school leavers', in J. Coupe O'Kane and B. Smith (eds) *Taking Control. Enabling People with Learning Difficulties*, London: David Fulton.

Wolfendale, S. (1992) *Primary Schools and Special Needs. Policy, Planning, Provision*, 2nd edition, London: Cassell.

Part III

A reconfigured role for special schools

Chapter 11

Moving towards the mainstream

Vision and reality

Christina Tilstone

Special and mainstream schools have attempted to work together, over a number of years, in different and innovative ways. In this chapter, Christina Tilstone examines some of the links made which have benefited children with severe learning difficulties and their mainstream peers. She recognises that although it is important to pursue new ways of ensuring inclusive practices, it is equally important to build on those already in existence.

Inclusion has been the main focus of educational debate in the UK for the last ten years, indicating a natural progression from the controversy of the last twenty-five years surrounding the processes and practices of *integration*. The three traditional provisions of integration identified by the Warnock Committee (DES, 1978) – locational, social and functional – have, with some minor variations, been the main methods of bringing children with special educational needs and their ordinary peers together. This consortium of provision does not in itself determine the quality of the education received by children with special educational needs, and the limited number of evaluative studies which have provided clear evidence of integration contain mixed messages (Beasley and Upton, 1989). The outcomes depend on the criteria used for evaluation and are not always fully articulated in the limited research available.

The terms 'integration', 'mainstreaming' and 'inclusion' are sometimes used synonymously in the literature to indicate the participation of children with special education needs in mainstream education. The first two, however, although requiring access to buildings, do not necessarily demand changes in curricular provision (Sebba, with Sachdev, 1997). The definition of inclusion as:

the opportunity for persons with a disability to participate fully in all of the educational, employment, consumer, recreational, community and domestic activities that typify society

(Inclusion International, 1996)

which underpins the theory and practice in this book, ultimately requires the restructuring and reorganisation of each mainstream school and its curriculum in order that the *differences* between children are recognised, celebrated, and provided for in a non-restrictive environment. As one teacher colleague stated: '*integration* is about the child fitting around the school, *inclusion* is about the school fitting around the child!'

THE VISION AND THE REALITY

This concept of total inclusion is of course a goal, an aim towards which all endeavours are directed. Rather like a bright star, it provides an ideological vision which guides the long-term legislation, policies, planning and the resourcing of educational provision. The realisation of such a goal is influenced by past events and the principles and values held by professional groups or individuals which have, in turn, been shaped by what has gone before.

Historically, the children who are the focus of this book have only recently been welcome in some mainstream schools, and many (those with severe and profound multiple learning difficulties) were completely excluded from the education system until 1971. Not only have they experienced a *life apart* from education, but when education did become available it was, with very few exceptions, offered in segregated provision.

The radical perspective on inclusion is that it is a fundamental human right, and that to deny a child a place in a mainstream school is to segregate him or her in a way in which criminals are, through prison sentences, removed from normal society (Lewis, 1995). Documents from the Centre for Studies on Inclusive Education, for example, articulate the

struggle to abolish segregated education which denies children with disabilities the right to be part of mainstream schooling and reinforces society's prejudice and discrimination against them.

(CSIE, 1997a, p.5)

It is often overlooked that segregated provision has developed owing to the difficulties facing schools in incorporating the different abilities of all pupils (Dessent, 1987). It can also be argued that a basic human right is the right to *choose*, and that having the opportunity to make an informed choice on a particular educational provision (e.g. between special and mainstream schooling) is preferable to having a situation where mainstreaming is imposed (Lindsay, 1989; Hornby *et al.*, 1997). Such a view raises the fundamental issue of 'who should choose?' Are parents given enough information to make informed choices or are the crucial decisions made by professionals who, supposedly, *know best*? Even if they are provided with relevant information, are parents really in the best position to make a decision anyway, as it is argued that they, in the main, are the able-bodied speaking on behalf of those with disabilities (Lindsay, 1997)? Increasingly, adults who have been educated in segregated provisions are questioning the decisions surrounding their placement (Swain *et al.*, 1993; Reiser, 1994). Should the views of children with special educational needs be sought on where they want to be educated and, if so, what information is available to them? When should they be consulted? How? And by whom? Chapter 7 by Richard Rose addresses these issues in more depth, but it is important to reflect on what strategies, if any, schools are using to ensure that pupils with special educational needs have a say in all aspects of their education, including the nature of provision itself.

Another important perspective, which includes the right of children to be consulted, and is often overlooked in the enthusiasm for a speedy closure of special schools, stems from the innovations and initiatives in Denmark on the quality of life for people with severe and profound and multiple learning disabilities. Holm *et al.* (1994) identified three essential conditions for an acceptable quality of life in any situation, including schooling. Firstly, that any individual should be involved in the social network; secondly, that the pupil should have control over any situations in which he or she is involved; and thirdly, that the relationships within the learning environment should lead to positive experiences. They stress that it is important not to intervene in the lives of others on the basis of undefined, or merely implied, ideas of what is *good* for them and it is, therefore, of vital importance to set up systems which enable pupils with special educational needs to be actively involved in the decision-making process. This will not be easy for those pupils who are developmentally young, or whose language development may be at an early stage, although strides have been made to identify the necessary components (Tilstone and Barry, 1998). However, as highlighted in Chapter 7, practices must be developed which encourage choice and decision making, and the recognition that pupils can be partners too.

It can be argued, of course, that the *special needs industry* is seeking to perpetuate the vested interests of the professionals working within it (Tomlinson, 1982; Barton, 1988; Norwich, 1990), and whilst special schooling remains, resources (both human and financial) will be diverted away from the mainstream. Special schools do not have the *right* to exist, but the professionals within them are doing a great deal more than they are given credit for in aiding inclusion. They have been responsible for developing a wide range of additional provision, including placements in mainstream schools, and have continued to explore the possibility of greater participation in the community for all their pupils. The recent Green Paper (DfEE, 1997), concerned with meeting special educational needs sees an extended role for special schools in working even more closely with mainstream schools in order to increase inclusion. It states that:

> If we are to move successfully to greater inclusion, it is essential that pupils with complex SEN in mainstream schools receive specialist support. The role of special schools should reflect this changing context. In principle teachers in special schools are uniquely equipped to help colleagues in mainstream schools to meet complex needs. But currently there are no requirements for special and mainstream schools to co-operate together. Arrangements do exist, but their incidence is patchy and there is little co-ordination.
>
> (p.49)

The Green Paper has called upon staff in both mainstream and special schools to develop new ways of working on behalf of children. The fundamental change in thinking required by the concept of inclusive education will lead to the development of new methods. However, the good practice developed in the name of integration must not be undervalued.

PROFILES OF TWO CHILDREN

'J' and 'S' both have complex needs and epitomise the real challenges to the restructuring and reorganisation of mainstream curricula in order that they are able to progress academically. They are typical of many children who experience forms of integration and ultimately help to change attitudes towards the greater inclusion of people with complex needs in society.

'J'

'J' is almost 5 years old. She understands simple commands including the prepositions 'in' or 'on', and can point to a number of body parts, including shoulders, eyebrows, fingers and thumbs. She can name simple objects, and label pictures of single objects, but her spontaneous speech is a babble containing few clear, single words. When playing alone with an adult she will repeat familiar words and attempt to sing a number of nursery rhymes and simple songs.

She walks unsteadily with feet wide apart, and climbs stairs by bringing her feet together on each step; she descends in a sitting position. She can kick a ball without falling over and throw it inaccurately. She is predominantly right-handed and uses a palmer grip to control a pencil. She can copy a circle and vertical and horizontal strokes. She cannot cut with scissors and has some difficulty in building a *tower* of more than two bricks. 'J' plays alongside other children and often gets upset when invited to interact with them. She needs to be reminded to go to the toilet, and bowel control is not established. She has Down's syndrome and her large tongue makes feeding difficult.

'S'

In contrast 'S' is 10, and has physical difficulties. He is still at an early stage of development. He can sit with support, but needs to use a special chair and a standing frame to strengthen muscles and to encourage correct positioning. He receives physiotherapy twice a week, and his teacher carries out the prescribed programmes daily. When placed on the floor he can roll around the room and can also move by pushing his feet whilst lying on his back. Like 'J', eating is difficult as he has a tongue thrush, but he manages to eat mashed food when it is placed in one side of his mouth. He can control parts of the eating process by taking a loaded spoon of food to his mouth. He likes people and has a ready smile. He uses his whole body in an enthusiastic welcome routine with familiar children and adults, and will indicate that he does not want things by turning away or pushing objects from him. He shakes his head for 'no' and makes a consistent gesture for 'yes'. He can select familiar objects from a choice of two and can eye-point to two familiar and similar objects in a group of three. He does, however, find it difficult to open his hands and grasp objects, but after massage his performance improves. Although bowel and bladder control are not established, he will remain clean and dry throughout the day if toileted at regular intervals.

Unfortunately, the number of children with severe learning difficulties, like 'J' and 'S', who are fully integrated into mainstream schools is not known, as computerised school records tend to show only statemented children *with special educational needs* on their registers. Rightly or wrongly, the adoption of this global term has made it difficult to distinguish, from the data available, those children with complex learning difficulties from those with a visual or hearing impairment and mild learning difficulties. The number of those who have full-time placements in their local primary school is increasing steadily, but there is evidence that many of them return to a segregated special school when they reach secondary age (Tilstone, 1991). As has already been stated, it would be naïve to suggest that full-time integration into a mainstream school can be anything more than the placement of a child within its walls (until the factors which have been identified by Lani Florian in Chapter 2 are in place). Individual case studies often show that the integrated placement is, in fact, a microcosm of segregation (O'Hanlon, 1997).

A recent report by the Centre for Studies on Inclusive Education (1997b) states that in 1996 the special school population dropped to the lowest it has ever been (88,849 or 1.4 per cent of all 5 to 15 year olds) and that 71 out of 107 local education authorities reduced the numbers of pupils placed in special schools. Such figures should be regarded with caution as a considerable number of children with special educational needs, particularly those with challenging behaviour, or with emotional difficulties, once placed in mainstream school, are then being permanently excluded.

Nevertheless by focusing on the experiences of 'J' or 'S', it is possible to give an indication of the reality of the situation for the majority of children like them, and to challenge the all-too-often assumption that the staff of special schools have their own vested interests in keeping special schools open and are, consequently, not interested in promoting inclusion. Special schooling is often reported as a negative experience which devalues children and denies them opportunities. It is rarely recognised that there may be a need for an *enabling stage*, which helps to promote an inclusive ethos, and to lay the foundation for true inclusion.

Many children will do equally well, socially and academically, in the mainstream but others (like 'J' and 'S') are excluded, through fear and prejudice, from schools which have accepted other pupils with less complex needs. In their case, far from perpetuating educational apartheid, the special school staff have taken the initiative to break down barriers to acceptance.

'J' is attending an integrated nursery within a special school for children with severe learning difficulties. The lack of nursery facilities in her rural area prompted the special school to develop much needed nursery provision for up to twenty pre-school children between the ages of 2 and 5 years, half of whom have special educational needs. At compulsory school age, the ordinary children transfer to their local primary school, but for those with special educational needs a range of other options is available, including the opportunity to join their peers in the mainstream, or to attend a unit for children with learning difficulties within a mainstream school. Arrangements for transfer are flexible, and 'J', although she will remain on the roll of the special school in which the nursery is housed, will, when she reaches compulsory school age, attend the mainstream school along with her ordinary peers for part of each day. The nursery's teachers and support assistants are on the staff of the special school, and provide varying degrees of help when children with severe learning difficulties transfer to full or partial participation in mainstream settings. 'J' will be in a group of five children with special needs, who will be accompanied by a nursery nurse during their first term of partial integration into mainstream (a situation which is closely monitored and reviewed). The school has also employed a support teacher, whose main function is to develop extensive links across all sectors of education, not only with mainstream schools in the locality, but with others in its rural area. She is part of the senior management team and it is hoped that her role can be extended to develop links with social service departments and the health authority. The work of this special school can be identified as:

- providing an additional facility, where all children are educated together;
- encouraging the right to choose an appropriate provision at school age;
- providing evidence on which an informed choice can be made;
- giving support to children in their move between special and mainstream schools;
- encouraging the staff of the special school and mainstream schools to work together and to learn from each other;
- providing opportunities for young children with a diversity of needs to be taught together;
- promoting collaboration between schools and the appropriate services.

The experiences of 'S' are very different, as, despite his profound and multiple learning difficulties, he participates in two contrasting forms of integration. In the first, he is fully integrated into classes of more able children with severe learning difficulties within the special school – an example which appears to be typical of recent developments in integration along the continuum of special education. Farrell (1996) argues, however, that the literature on inclusive practices consistently overlooks the experiences of children with profound and multiple learning difficulties, who are often still segregated in special classes within special schools. He emphasises that an important first step along the continuum of increased inclusion is the abandonment of such special classes. This philosophical/sociological argument has influenced practice, although there is little research evidence on the educational benefits for all the children involved. O'Connell's (1994) small-scale research indicated that where a child with profound and multiple learning difficulties and a child with severe learning difficulties were paired to work together in structured activities (*special friends scheme*), higher levels of interaction were recorded than if the children had worked independently. The more able, who were paired, also showed a greater degree of tolerance to their partners with profound and multiple learning difficulties. This point is reflected in the general literature on link schemes designed to extend and deepen contacts between children with special educational needs and their peers (Whitaker, 1994; Walsh *et al.*, 1996).

'S' is also involved in a link scheme in which all members of his class are integrated into their local mainstream school and taught alongside their mainstream peers for one half-day per week. Such programmes have been developed in the UK over many years, and of the 898 special schools which took part in a research survey reported in 1994, 83 per cent were involved in collaborative arrangements with ordinary schools (Fletcher-Campbell, 1994). These schemes vary from 'one-way visits', 'reciprocal' and 'regular but infrequent' to 'weekly' and 'daily'. The most successful (Lewis, 1995; Shelvin, 1992; Shelvin and Walsh, 1994) encouraged shared activity based on common interests. Pupils from the different schools are paired if they share a common enthusiasm for a subject or an activity, and as part of the planned integration programme are allowed either formally or informally to develop their interests collaboratively (Tilstone, 1996). Sebba's (1997) research with Sachdev shows that settings in which social interaction is actively encouraged by adults are also likely to be highly beneficial in developing social inclusion. She found that it was the examples set of the appropriate way to behave (by staff showing that they equally valued all children in the class) and the use of structured group work which were of most benefit. Sebba, however, is sceptical about link schemes in general leading to full inclusive practices. She maintains that

> the proportion of pupils from each special school participating in links was quite small and their involvement tended to include social activities, music, physical education and school trips rather than participation in the full curriculum.
>
> (p.31)

However, the benefits of developing positive relationships and of changing attitudes through link schemes cannot be denied.

CONCLUSION

As the literature from a range of countries shows, inclusion is a highly complex phenomenon (Hegarty, 1993; Clark *et al.*, 1995). Ainscow *et al.*

(1994) and Ainscow (1995) are amongst the researchers in the UK who have considered integration through school improvement. They believe that the ability to improve schools (which includes providing an appropriate education for all children, including those with special educational needs) hinges on the six basic conditions of:

- effective leadership;
- the involvement of school staff, students and the community in the development of policies and the making of decisions;
- a commitment to collaborative planning;
- effective co-ordination strategies;
- attention to the potential benefits of enquiry and reflection;
- a policy for staff development.

(p. 66)

They argue that such conditions increase collegiality, opportunities for professional learning and increased responsibility for the education of all children. Such conditions, however, must be worked on alongside changes to the curriculum in order that the diversity of all children can be recognised and celebrated. Other chapters in this book explore this perspective in detail.

There is, however, another fundamental condition, which is particularly relevant for children with severe learning difficulties, but is often overlooked in the academic literature. Structured attitude change is of crucial importance to the acceptance of children like 'J' and 'S'. If they had been born thirty years ago, not only would they have been considered 'ineducable', but it is likely that they would be living in long-stay hospitals segregated from the wider community. This historical legacy has left its mark, for, although around three-quarters of the population have never met a person with severe learning difficulties, the popular images of *mental* handicap (so easily confused with 'mental illness') are 'locked doors', 'doctors', 'psychiatrists' and 'violent behaviour'. Unfortunately, attitudes not only depend on contacts in the present, but are also determined by the feelings, reactions and beliefs of the past and, unless they are challenged, are likely to be handed down from one generation to another.

Although neither 'J' nor 'S' is experiencing inclusion in the true sense of the word, their carefully planned and structured activities are helping to break down fear and prejudice. Information and research evidence is available on policies of inclusion, but there tends to be an assumption that society is *ready and waiting* to receive all those with special educational needs. It is not, and it can hardly be blamed for being reticent. As McConkey (1996) emphasises, widely distributed information about the rights and needs of people with disabilities is unlikely to affect the attitudes and behaviour of members of the public, particularly when they have never had contact with children with severe learning difficulties. In the case of 'J' and 'S', the special school staff did recognise that the first step in facilitating true inclusion was the changing of attitudes through positive experiences and the creative use of functional and social integration. Their ideological commitment to inclusive education has encouraged them to explore what is practical within a time frame and to build upon and extend current practice. In Sebba's (1997) terms they have considered the evidence of 'what works' in both intended and unintended outcomes. Criticisms can be levelled that the intended outcomes are based on the assumptions surrounding integration rather than full inclusion. It is our view that it is important to celebrate and learn from the positive steps being made in both special and mainstream settings.

REFERENCES

Ainscow, M. (1995) 'Special needs through school improvement; school improvement through special needs', in C. Clark, A. Dyson and A. Millward (eds) *Towards Inclusive Schools?*, London: David Fulton.

Ainscow, M., Hopkins, D., Southworth, G. and West, M. (1994) *Creating the Conditions for School Improvement*, London: David Fulton.

Barton, L. (ed.) (1988) *The Politics of Special Educational Needs*, London: Falmer Press.

Beasley, F. and Upton, G. (1989) 'Effectiveness of locational integration for children with moderate learning difficulties', in N. Jones (ed.) *Special Educational Needs Review (Vol. 2)*, Lewes: Falmer Press.

Centre for Studies on Inclusive Education (CSIE) (1997a) *Inclusive Education: a Framework for Change*, Bristol: CSIE.

Centre for Studies on Inclusive Education (CSIE) (1997b) *A Trend Towards Inclusion (Statistics on special school placements and pupils with statements in ordinary schools in England. 1992–1996)*, Bristol: CSIE.

Clark, C., Dyson, A. and Millward, A. (eds) (1995) *Towards Inclusive Schools?*, London: David Fulton.

Department for Education and Employment (1997) *Excellence for All Children: Meeting Special Educational Needs*, London: The Stationery Office.

Department of Education and Science (1978) *Special Educational Needs: Report of the Committee of Inquiry into the Education of Handicapped Children and Young People* (The Warnock Report), London: HMSO.

Dessent, T. (1987) *Making the Ordinary School Special*, London: Falmer Press.

Farrell, P. (1996) 'Discussion: integration – where do we go from here?', in J. Coupe O'Kane and J. Goldbart (eds) *Whose Choice? Contentious Issues for Those Working with People with Learning Difficulties*, London: David Fulton.

Fletcher-Campbell, F. (1994) 'Special links? Partners in provision? Collaboration between ordinary and special schools', *British Journal of Special Education* 21(3): 118–20.

Hegarty, S. (1993) 'Reviewing the literature on integration', *European Journal of Special Needs Education* 6(2): 87–99.

Holm, P., Holst, J. and Perlt, B. (1994) 'Co-write your own life: quality of life as discussed in the Danish contex', in D. Goode (ed.) *Quality of Life for Persons with Disabilities: International Perspectives and Issues*, Cambridge, MA: Brookline Books.

Hornby, G., Atkinson, M. and Howard, J. (1997) 'Integration of children with special needs into mainstream schools – inclusion or delusion?', in G. Hornby, M. Atkinson and J. Howard (eds) *Controversial Issues in Special Education*, London: David Fulton.

Inclusion International (1996) *Inclusion: News from Inclusion International*, Brussels: Inclusion International.

Lewis, A. (1995) *Children's Understanding of Disability*, London: Routledge.

Lindsay, G. (1989) 'Evaluating Integration', *Educational Psychology in Practice* 5(1): 134–43.

Lindsay, G. (1997) 'Are we ready for inclusion?', in G. Lindsay and D. Thompson (eds) *Values into Practice in Special Education*, London: David Fulton.

McConkey, R. (1996) 'Seen through a glass darkly: modifying public attitudes', in P. Mittler and V. Sinason (eds) *Changing Policy and Practice for People with Learning Disabilities*, London: Cassell.

Norwich, B. (1990) *Reappraising Special Needs Education*, London: Cassell.

O'Connell, R. (1994) 'Providing integration works, how effective is the integration of students with PMLDs into the mainstream of an SLD school in increasing their opportunities for social interaction?', in J. Ware (ed.) *Educating Children with Profound and Multiple Learning Difficulties*, London: David Fulton.

O'Hanlon, C. (1997) Personal communication.

Reiser, R. (1994) 'An opportunity not to be missed: 1994 inclusive school policies', *New Learning Together Magazine* No.1: 8–13.

Sebba, J., with Sachdev, D. (1997) *What Works in Inclusive Education?*, Ilford, Essex: Barnardos.

Shelvin, M. (1992) 'Fast friends: shared classroom activities for students with and without learning disabilities', *Frontline Magazine* Summer: 10–11.

Shelvin, M. and Walsh, P. N. (1994) *On Equal Terms*, Dublin: St Michael's House Research.

Swain, J., Finkelstein, V., French, S. and Oliver, M. (1993) *Disabling Barriers – Enabling Environments*, London: Sage.

Tilstone, C. (1991) *Teaching Pupils with Severe Learning Difficulties: Practical Approaches*, London: David Fulton.

Tilstone, C. (1996) 'Changing public attitudes', in B. Carpenter, R. Ashdown and K. Bovair (eds) *Enabling Access: Effective Teaching and Learning for Pupils with Learning Difficulties*, London: David Fulton.

Tilstone, C. and Barry, C. (1998) 'Advocacy and empowerment: what does it mean for pupils with pmld?', in P. Lacey and C. Ouvry (eds) *Interdisciplinary Work with People with Profound and Multiple Learning Disabilities: a Collaborative Approach to Meeting Complex Needs*, London: David Fulton.

Tomlinson, S. (1982) *A Sociology of Special Education*, London: Routledge & Kegan Paul.

Walsh, P. N., Shelvin, M., O'Moore, M., de Lacey, E. and Stritch, D. (1996) 'In-service training for teachers involved in link schemes: a consultative process', *British Journal of Special Education* 23(2): 75–9.

Whitaker, P. (1994) 'Mainstream students talk about integration', *British Journal of Special Education* 21(1): 13–16.

Chapter 12

A wider role for special schools?

Alan Wiltshire

In this chapter Alan Wiltshire considers ways forward for special schools in promoting inclusion which builds on existing practices.

It has been acknowledged that an increasing proportion of pupils with learning difficulties are being educated in mainstream schools and the Green Paper (DfEE, 1997) makes it clear that the government intends a further increase, although there is no immediate prospect of the closure of all special schools. Nevertheless, special schools will need to change their roles, and special and mainstream schools will need to work more closely together and to support each other. These changes will lead to the establishment of special schools as an integral part of an increasingly inclusive system.

THE SPECIAL SCHOOL: THE ARGUMENTS FOR AND AGAINST

There are considerable variations throughout the UK in special school provision: some local education authorities (LEAs) have continued to cater for discrete groups of children with special educational needs; others have created generic special schools in order to cater for a wide range of needs. The policy in others has been to reduce the number of special schools, in some cases as a means of cutting costs (Chapman, 1994), or to close them altogether as in Newham (Jordan and Goodey, 1996).

If the aims of education are the same for all children, as emphasised in the Warnock Report (DES, 1978), what characterises special schools and why are they necessary for some pupils? Special schools have:

- smaller numbers of pupils;
- higher staff/pupil ratios;

- possibly greater access to a whole range of experts – specially trained and qualified teachers and therapists, including speech and language therapists, physiotherapists and occupational therapists;
- specially adapted environments and specialised equipment and resources.

Historically children and people with severe learning difficulties (SLD) have been segregated and marginalised (Pritchard, 1963; Preen, 1976; Cole, 1989; Tilstone, 1991a), and consequently special schools are now seen as separate or different owing to the context in which they have developed.

The extreme polarisation of views on inclusion and segregation can inhibit developments in the education of all children. A realistic way forward will take into account both points of view. Although the principle of inclusion, based on human rights, is appealing and appropriate, it is essential to proceed with caution as it is impractical to assume that all children can be catered for in mainstream classes in the immediate future, particularly those pupils with multisensory impairments (deaf–blind), autism, profound and multiple learning difficulties or severe emotional and behavioural disorders. For example, Tilstone (1996: 273) suggests that special schools are not redundant and that:

> In a society committed to 'education for all', there will always be a small proportion of children who will need the protection of a sheltered environment, but that many children are at present excluded from mainstream due to fear and prejudice.

Farrell (1997) supports the view that some pupils with SLD and profound and multiple learning difficulties (PMLD) will continue to need some kind of segregated provision and, in 1996, pointed out that the United Nations Rights of the Child (Article 23) states that: 'Children should be helped to become as independent as possible, and to be able to take a full and active part in everyday life'. The paper does not state, however, that children need to be prepared for independence in ordinary schools. Farrell, in considering the Statement, recognises the positive ethos of many special schools where children enjoy rich and stimulating experiences and are provided with a range of opportunities. This opinion needs to be treated with caution as its critics (e.g. Tyne, 1993; Hall, 1996) have suggested that it can lead to low expectations and a patronising approach.

Farrell (1996) summarises some of the arguments put forward in support of segregated special schools and suggests that:

- it is unrealistic to expect some children with special needs to learn from the same curriculum as other children;

- the degree of individual planning to meet some special needs is only possible in special schools;
- as teachers choose to teach children with severe learning difficulties, their motivation is usually high;
- parent support is more forthcoming in segregated settings [a simplistic assumption which many teachers will wish to challenge];
- pupils will have classmates of a similar age and ability;
- vulnerable children are safer in segregated special schools;
- segregated provision is the most cost effective.

The arguments against special schools are also persuasive and have been influenced by medical, social and professional interests (Hall, 1996; Tomlinson, 1982).

As children with SLD were outside the education system before 1971 and were the responsibility of the health authorities, the medical model promoted segregation. Hall (1996) and Wood and Shears (1986) are amongst those who argue that the consequent focus was on disability and what was wrong with the child. It can also be seen as leading to the creation of the large institutions which it has been argued still influence thinking and practice in special education today (Hall, 1996).

Tomlinson (1982) suggests that special education is a form of social control, and, by admitting those pupils who pose a challenge to the smooth operation of the mainstream, special schools operate as 'safety valves'. Consequently, they can be perceived as having a lower status and reduced expectations for their children. It is also believed that special schools provide poor role models and, by their very existence, encourage negative labelling and social isolation. Cole (1989), however, although accepting parts of the argument, suggests that some of the evidence is selective and overlooks the influences of more humanitarian approaches. Nevertheless, it is widely agreed that the less able and the more vulnerable are still not valued in the same way as other children (Dyson, 1997; Lindsay and Thompson, 1997).

It has been argued that the professionals involved in special education have created a separate discipline, and that professionalisation has filled the lives of children and families, a point further developed by Skrtic (1991) and Hall (1996). People with learning difficulties have themselves become increasingly critical of the ways in which professionals, including their teachers, underestimate their abilities (Barton, 1989; Tilstone, 1991b).

The question arises, therefore: can the existing special schools aid inclusion? Ainscow (1997), Ainscow et al. (1994) and Sebba with Sachdev (1997) argue that transplanting special education thinking and practice into mainstream may lead to difficulties and the promotion of further segregation. They assert that the way to inclusion is through the school improvement movement, a view also supported by Zigmond and Baker (1997) and Rouse and Florian (1996). Ainscow (1993, p. 15) suggests that the key areas for school improvement are:

- teacher learning;
- leadership;
- student involvement;
- vision;
- celebrating success.

Rayner (1994, p. 170), on the other hand, identified an alternative way forward:

> The special school, and the support service, should aim to create a new interest in partnerships between schools, which may provide support for SEN in a far more successful way than was previously realised. Ideally this relationship is not one based on conflict and competition, but on mutual benefit, which involves a business-like organisation of provision, serving a clearly defined educational community.

Interestingly these arguments echo the Warnock Report (DES, 1978), which stated that special schools need to take on new roles and that firm links need to be established between special and ordinary schools. By the early 1990s many special schools had established links with neighbourhood schools (see Chapter 11 by Christina Tilstone). Nevertheless, some authors suggest that there needs to be even more collaboration between special and ordinary schools (Fish, 1985; Tilstone, 1996; Bovair 1989; 1993) in order that staff can give each other support and assistance. The Green Paper (DfEE, 1997) also stresses the importance of close partnerships. At present these might include:

- classes or small groups of children visiting other schools (special or mainstream) for shared learning activities, such as music, PE and drama;
- children on shared placements between mainstream and special schools;
- special school staffs offering advice and support for children with special needs in mainstream schools;
- pupils using other schools' specialist facilities and resources;
- joint curriculum development projects, covering a wide continuum of learning needs and styles;
- joint professional development or in-service training activities;
- access to extra-curricular activities;
- shared projects or events, such as 'French days' or 'weeks', art weeks, music festivals.

Partnerships, however, need to go beyond 'activity-based' events towards more coherent programmes. Many special schools have provided 'outreach' services to mainstream schools (Day, 1989), offering advice and support on teaching strategies, planning and resources. Outreach, however, may seem to imply one-way traffic as it takes expertise and resources from the special school into the mainstream. Bovair's (1993, p. 117) ideas of 'affiliation' take the notion of outreach a step further, involving the:

> encouragement of a greater collaboration between ordinary schools and special schools. This relationship, it was hoped, would lead to a gradual assimilation of the special school into the ordinary setting. It would be a natural growth process, led by the practitioners involved, with the children as the leading force. Using joint resources and settings it was hoped that a natural integration process would take place.

Unfortunately the culture of competition in education in recent years has not been conducive to 'partnership and collaboration'. League tables, grant-maintained status and the implications and pressures of Ofsted inspections have tended to make schools autonomous and separate and isolated.

The increasing focus on 'clustering' or collaboration between groups of schools, nationally and internationally, may be seen as a significant move toward more inclusive schools (Meijer and Stevens, 1997). Clusters are defined by Lunt *et al.* (1994, p. 17) as:

> A grouping of schools with a relatively stable and long-term commitment to share some resources and decision-making about an area of school activity. The arrangements are likely to involve a degree of formality such as regular meetings to plan and monitor this activity and some loss of autonomy through the need for negotiated decision-making.

The research undertaken by Lunt *et al.* (1994) shows how, through collaboration, resources can be enhanced to meet pupils' needs. The work is based on the recommendations in the Fish Committee Report (ILEA, 1985) which suggest establishing clusters with the following functions:

- sharing responsibilities for special needs which arise in the clusters, and developing means of identifying and meeting them;
- providing a continuity of concern over children's education from under fives through to secondary education;
- assisting local decision-making about the forms of provision to meet SEN which are most appropriate for a group of schools;
- providing a focus of service delivery so that members of all services advising and supporting schools and associated tertiary provision, including health and social services, can deploy staff to work with a

small group of schools. Schools in their turn would be enabled to
work with a known group of supporting professionals.

(ILEA, 1985, quoted in Lunt *et al.*, 1994, pp. 6–7)

These functions match well with Bovair's (1993) concept of assimilation and
the idea of working together in seamless systems.

Another aspect of the development of the special school is as a 'Resource
Centre' or 'Centre of Excellence' highlighted in the Warnock Report (DES,
1978). It was suggested that within each local authority area special schools
should act as resource centres, or centres of specialist expertise to undertake
research into special education. It also stated that some special schools
should be designated 'specialist centres', for rare or complex disabilities, and
developed and run by groups of LEAs.

Hegarty (1994, p. 25) supports the notion of the special school as a
multipurpose institution that would, for example:

- be a source of information on all matters relating to special educational needs;
- conduct assessment, particularly in difficult cases;
- provide advice, consultancy and support;
- engage in curriculum and materials development;
- evaluate software, equipment and other materials;
- conduct research and run experimental projects;
- contribute to professional development, whether through in-service
  training courses, attachments, workshops or joint working;
- be a resource for parents;
- provide counselling and careers advice for older students.

He advocates the creation of a new kind of institution which:

takes us well beyond the familiar notion of a school, be it special or
otherwise. It entails elements of numerous existing agencies such as
teachers' centres, and advisory services, a library and information
service, a pilot project, a resource centre, a training institution and a
careers service. Such an institution would have an indirect responsibility
for a wide range of matters relating to special educational provision in
its own community.

Such ideas on centres of excellence may appear to imply that the staff of the
centre have all the expertise. The notion of true partnership, however, with
schools working together, sharing their experiences, learning from each
other, and analysing events, is not developed. Perhaps a more radical
proposal as part of a vision for the future in the current economic climate is
the setting up of a learning centre, which would take on many of the

features described: research, professional development, resourcing (e.g. library), facilities for parents and families and multi-agency support. In North America, for example in Calgary, Canada, the Learning Centre, which is located next to a special school, is a base for research, training and a wide range of professionals working throughout the system with pupils with learning difficulties. The professionals are also involved in a range of settings across the city (Samuels and Brown, 1989).

The Green Paper (DfEE, 1997) recognises the importance of increased opportunities for staff development and in-service training. The Warnock Committee had previously singled out teacher education as an area of expansion and improvement (together with its proposals on integration), but unfortunately the closure of specialist initial training courses for teachers of children with SLD and the fact that the Committee's anticipated post-experience courses did not materialise meant that specialist opportunities were severely limited. By 1986 the situation had become serious as the recruitment of teachers to full-time professional courses for teachers of children with special educational needs had declined by two-thirds (Miller and Garner, 1996). Hinchcliffe (1997) reported that although in 1988 there were twenty-six institutions offering training in the teaching of children with SLD, in 1996, there were only seven (Tilstone, 1998). Consequently there is now a widespread shortage of qualified teachers of children with SLD and it is therefore necessary to use the skills of the qualified in order to provide, at the very least, some basic training. Bovair (1989; 1993) acknowledges that special schools could play a significant role in providing both in-service and initial teacher education of this type. It is also crucial that opportunities for professional development are also available for learning support assistants (LSAs).

Special schools may, in the future, extend their role of providing professional development opportunities in 'partnership'. There is a danger, however, that the skills and approaches may be designed specifically for a segregated setting and consequently may inhibit moves towards more inclusive school systems.

MEETING THE CHALLENGE: THE JOINT RESPONSE OF TWO SCHOOLS

It seems clear that there will be a need for special schools in the foreseeable future, although if they have proved effective the number of pupils will be certain to drop. And, even if it is unlikely that they will be closed *en masse*, radical changes to their working practices, to their presentation and to their marketing strategies will be essential if they are to play an increasingly important role within the wider community.

Two neighbouring special schools in Kent have recently formed a partnership. The following statement taken from the Vision and Development Document articulates a commitment to:

Quality and improvement: where improvement in, and the enhancement of, the quality of education for each child is at the centre of every development undertaken, with the aim of improving the quality of teaching and learning for all children, not just those in the two special schools, but throughout their catchment areas.

The head teachers believe that this commitment leads to the development of a more inclusive educational experience for all children with special educational needs:

Inclusion: where the organisation of the education system needs to recognise the diversity of the learning needs of all pupils. We believe that special schools need to play a part in the preparation of pupils for education in an ordinary class in their neighbourhood school. This particular partnership entails work with other schools and agencies to develop skills, attitudes, cultures, strengths and structures to ensure inclusion.

It has been agreed that the most effective way of achieving these aims is through partnership and co-operation, where:

- professional partnership extends beyond the two special schools and involves other schools and agencies,

- partnership through co-operation will recognise and celebrate diversity by planning educational provision (using Individual Education Plans) that defines pupils in terms of their curricular needs and strengths in the most inclusive settings possible,

- the centre of this collaboration is a reworking of both special schools' roles and a sharing of their respective expertise,

- where partnership and integration between schools provides opportunities for collaboration between staff and meaningful interactions between pupils.

An agreed concept of community, for learning, development and support, is established on a number of different levels:

- community of children, in which a broad and balanced education is delivered and enhanced for a wide community of need, taking advantage of the greater expertise and flexibility offered on a campus, including children from both schools as well as those who may visit for some specialist input (i.e. the concept of 'in-reach');
- a community of professionals, by which a broad and balanced education is delivered and enhanced by the staff from the schools, as well as professionals from different agencies (Education, Health and Social Services), offering enhanced opportunities for partnership;
- a community resource, through which facilities, resources and expertise are made available to parents, families, people from the neighbourhood and other carers.

Features of the new role

The special school will continue to develop its 'core business' for specific groups of pupils who need time within a specialist provision. In 'partnership' with other schools, special schools will be involved in mutually supportive roles including the provision of:

- advice and support on policy, organisation and practices;
- advice and consultancy aimed to support either individuals or small groups of pupils;
- expertise, specialist facilities and resources;
- professional development opportunities for the whole range of school staff;
- high-quality shared learning experiences for pupils, including those on a joint placement between special and mainstream schools;
- joint curriculum developments, involving staff partnerships and covering a wide continuum of need and ability;
- mutual developments of and the of use of schemes of work or areas of the curriculum for individuals or groups of pupils;
- formal and regular opportunities for two-way exchanges of staff between schools (e.g. secondments and job swapping);
- opportunities for pupils from mainstream schools to benefit from the resources, expertise and facilities of the special school.

The staff of the special school will want to learn from, and work much more closely with, mainstream colleagues.

Making the vision a reality

The importance of professional development

It has already been pointed out that special schools need to play a significant role in teacher education and that programmes and opportunities will need to be devised for the whole range of staff in order to provide training for untrained and unqualified LSAs in all settings. Bovair (1989) and Ainscow (1997) express disappointment that so many untrained assistants have worked with vulnerable children with complex learning difficulties and it has been claimed that in many mainstream settings their (the assistants') presence is indicative of integration. It is welcome, therefore, that the Green Paper has recognised the importance of training (DfEE, 1997).

In order to provide further training for the wide range of professionals working with pupils with learning difficulties, a multidisciplinary element is essential: training in working together and sharing expertise in all contexts (see Chapter 15 by Penny Lacey). Walker and Apter (1997) describe the setting up of an 'Early Childhood Inclusion Network', which focused on a training initiative involving special educators and child care providers. The work of the group, including the production of a supporting manual, provides useful indicators and innovative ways of sharing and developing perspectives, knowledge, expertise and strategies. Smith and Hilton (1997) present some important pointers to what is needed in terms of professional development. They suggest that training must involve all members of the education community, including professional support staff, secretarial staff, bus drivers, students and parents, and should cover a knowledge of disabilities, the encouragement of appropriate attitudes, legal and ethical issues, collaboration and methods of friendship development.

In addition, teachers and administrators will need to acquire knowledge of, and skills in, assessment, advanced collaboration, effective practices for direct instruction and service delivery, and the evaluation of educational outcomes. The appropriate opportunities have to be planned and depend upon a partnership with other schools and agencies, LEAs, institutes of higher education, voluntary agencies and other interest groups.

Ainscow (1995) calls for a radical rethinking of teacher education, incorporating his view that school improvement initiatives are the only way forward in attempting to establish inclusive practices. He also maintains (1997, p. 6) that, in teacher education:

Emphasis will be placed on the importance of collaboration between pupils, teachers and parents as a means of developing schools for all . . . such initiatives build on evidence that schools which are effective in responding to diversity do so through an intensification of teamwork, including co-operative planning and, where possible, partnership teaching in the classroom.

CONCLUSION

Throughout this chapter it has been argued that although special schools should be undergoing rapid changes, they are unlikely to disappear completely in the immediate future as they will continue to be needed for certain groups of pupils for whom full-time placement in mainstream schools is not appropriate at present. Their role will, however, change and they will be required to work in 'partnership' with a range of schools and other agencies in order to promote inclusion. One of their major functions should be to provide an element of professional development within a framework which at present has not been defined. It will need government backing and funds if inclusive education is to be realised. Thomas (1997, p. 176) provides an imaginative and practical response to present problems and suggests a pattern for teacher education to encourage inclusion based on five main elements:

- specific short courses on needs associated with particular disabling conditions – so-called 'low-incidence' SEN;
- training for all Learning Support Assistants;
- an expansion in continuing professional development (including distance and open learning) for those coordinating SEN provision in schools;
- professional masters degrees and doctorate of education programmes dedicated to inclusive education;
- specific provision for SEN in initial teacher education.

This is but one example of a kind of future role for special schools that will render them part of a seamless, inclusive education system.

ACKNOWLEDGEMENTS

The author is grateful to Brian Shelley for permission to reproduce the unpublished Vision and Development Document, prepared by Brian Shelley and Alan Wiltshire.

REFERENCES

Ainscow, M. (1993) *Towards Effective Schools for All*, Stafford: NASEN.

Ainscow, M. (1995) 'Special needs through school improvement; school improvement through special needs', in C. Clark, A. Dyson and A. Millward (eds) *Towards Inclusive Schools?* London: David Fulton.

Ainscow, M. (1997) 'Towards inclusive schooling', *British Journal of Special Education* 24(1): 3–6.

Ainscow, M., Hopkins, D., Southworth, G. and West, M. (1994) *Creating the Conditions for School Improvement*, London: David Fulton.

Barton, L. (ed.) (1989) *Disability and Dependency*, London: Falmer Press.

Beveridge, S. (1993) *Special Education Needs in Schools*, London: Routledge.

Bovair, K. (1989) 'The special school: a part of, not apart from the education system', in D. Baker and K. Bovair (eds) *Making the Special School Ordinary?* (Volume 1: Models for the Developing Special School), Lewes: Falmer Press.

Bovair, K. (1993) 'A role for the special school', in J. Visser and G. Upton (eds) *Special Education in Britain after Warnock*, London: David Fulton.

Cole, T. (1989) *Apart or A Part? Integration and the Growth of British Special Education*, Milton Keynes: Open University Press.

Chapman, N. (1994) 'Caught in the crossfire: the future of special schools', *British Journal of Special Education* 21(2): 60–3.

Day, A. (1989) 'Reaching out: the background to outreach', in D. Baker and K. Bovair (eds) *Making the Special School Ordinary?* (Volume 1: Models for the Developing Special School), Lewes: Falmer Press.

DES (1978) *Special Educational Needs: Report of the Committee of Inquiry into the Education of Handicapped Children and Young People* (The Warnock Report), London: HMSO.

DfEE (1997) *Excellence for All Children: Meeting Special Educational Needs* (The Green Paper), London: The Stationery Office.

Dyson, A. (1997) 'Social and educational disadvantage: reconnecting special needs education', *British Journal of Special Education* 24(4): 152–7.

Farrell, P. (1996) 'Integration: where do we go from here?', in J. Coupe O'Kane and J. Goldbart (eds) *Whose Choice?*, London: David Fulton.

Farrell, P. (1997) 'The integration of children with severe learning difficulties: a review of recent literature', *Journal of Applied Research in Intellectual Disabilities* 10(1).

Fish, J. (1985) *The Way Ahead*, Milton Keynes: Open University Press.

Hall, J. (1996) 'Integration, inclusion: what does it all mean?', in J. Coupe O'Kane and J. Goldbart (eds) *Whose Choice?*, London: David Fulton.

Hegarty, S. (1994) *Response in Planning and Diversity: Special Schools and Their Alternatives*, Stafford: NASEN.

Hinchcliffe, V. (1997) 'A Bermuda Triangle for training: the case for severe learning difficulties', in J. D. Davis and P. Garner (eds) *At the Crossroads: Special Educational Needs and Teacher Education*, London: David Fulton.

Inner London Education Authority (1985) *Educational Opportunities for All* (The Fish Report), London: ILEA.

Jordan, L. and Goodey, C. (1996) *Human Rights and School Change – the Newham Story*, London: CSIE.

Lindsay, G. and Thompson, D. (1997) *Values into Practice in Special Education*, London: David Fulton.

Lunt, I., Evans., J., Norwich, B. and Wedell, K. (1994) *Working Together: Inter-School Collaboration for Special Needs*, London: David Fulton.

Meijer, C. J. and Stevens, L. M. (1997) 'Restructuring special education provision', in S. J. Pijl, C. J. W. Meijer and S. Hegarty (eds) *Inclusive Education: a Global Agenda*, London: Routledge.

Miller, O. and Garner, M. (1996) 'Professional development to meet special educational needs', *British Journal of Special Education* 23(2): 70–4.

Preen, B. (1976) *Schooling for the Mentally Retarded*, Brisbane: University of Queensland Press.

Pritchard, D. (1963) *Education and the Handicapped: 1760–1960*, London: Routledge & Kegan Paul.

Rayner, S. (1994) 'Restructuring reform: choice and change in special education', *British Journal of Special Education* 21(4): 169–73.

Rouse, M. and Florian, L. (1996) 'Becoming effective and inclusive: cross-cultural perspectives', in L. Florian and M. Rouse (eds) *School Reform and Special Educational Needs*, Cambridge: University of Cambridge Institute of Education.

Samuels, M. and Brown, R. (eds) (1989) *Research and Practice in Learning Difficulties: a Demonstration Model*, Toronto: Lugus Productions.

Sebba, J., with Sachdev, D. (1997) *What Works in Inclusive Education?*, Ilford: Barnardos.

Skrtic, T. (1991) *Behind Special Education: a Critical Analysis of Professional Culture and School Organisation*, Denver, CO: Love Publishing.

Smith, J. and Hilton, J. (1997) 'The preparation and training of the educational community for the inclusion of students with developmental disabilities: the MRDD position', *Education and Training in Mental Retardation and Developmental Disabilities* 32(1): 3–10.

Thomas, G. (1997) 'A blueprint for the future: special educational needs and teacher education in the 21st century', in J. D. Davis and P. Garner (eds) *At the Crossroads: Special Educational Needs and Teacher Education*, London: David Fulton.

Tilstone, C. (1991a) 'Historical review', in C. Tilstone (ed.) *Teaching Pupils with Severe Learning Difficulties*, London: David Fulton.

Tilstone, C. (1991b) 'Pupils' views', in C. Tilstone (ed.) *Teaching Pupils with Severe Learning Difficulties*, London: David Fulton.

Tilstone, C. (1996) 'Changing public attitudes', in B. Carpenter, R. Ashdown and K. Bovair (eds) *Enabling Access: Effective Teaching and Learning for Pupils with Learning Difficulties*, London: David Fulton.

Tilstone, C. (1998) 'The education of children with severe learning difficulties: responding to challenge and change in curriculum teaching and learning and teacher development', PhD thesis, University of Birmingham.

Tomlinson, S. (1982) *A Sociology of Special Education*, London: Routledge & Kegan Paul.

Tyne, A. (1993) 'The great integration debate: part 3', *Mental Handicap* 21(4): 150–2.

Walker, P. and Apter, D. (1997) 'One community's efforts to promote child care inclusion', *TASH Newsletter* 23(4): 14–16.

Wood, S. and Shears, B. (1986) *Teaching Children with Severe Learning Difficulties: a Radical Re-appraisal*, London: Croom Helm.

Zigmond, N. and Baker, J. (1997) 'Inclusion of pupils with learning disabilities in general education settings', in S. J. Pijl, C. J. W. Meijer and S. Hegarty (eds) *Inclusive Education: a Global Agenda*, London: Routledge.

Chapter 13

Inclusion in national standards

Allan Day

Ensuring school effectiveness is an important consideration when tackling issues which could obstruct inclusion. Allan Day examines how special schools can evaluate their own practice in ways that are more closely aligned to mainstream schools.

There are increasing pressures from all sectors of education to include special schools within a community of shared educational concepts and accepted good practice, particularly in the areas of school effectiveness and school improvement in line with major national initiatives. In the 1997 White Paper *Excellence in Schools* (DfEE, 1997a), for example, it is stated that: 'A strategy to improve provision and standards for children with SEN must therefore be an integral part of other national policies for improving standards' (p.33, para 44). This emphasis is indicative of one element in a long-term process initiated by the special schools themselves to develop statutory inclusive practices.

In recent years, attempts have been made to develop closer links between special and mainstream schools via pupil, staff and curricular activities; outreach schemes; and school development groups or clusters (Jowett *et al.*, 1988; Day, 1989) (see Chapter 6 by Jim Wolger and Chapter 12 by Alan Wiltshire). Such organisational links have brought professionals and pupils together in ways which break down barriers and encourage shared values and practices. More recently, government policy has sought to accelerate the inclusion of special schools in clusters with mainstream schools as part of a national drive towards inclusion (DfEE, 1997b).

The National Curriculum itself (DfEE, 1995) has, without doubt, pulled special schools forcefully into the mainstream of curriculum thinking. It has led to a plethora of curriculum development work initiated largely by special education specialists who have sought to redefine their own practices within the National Curriculum framework (Fagg *et al.*, 1990; Tilstone, 1991; Carpenter *et al.*, 1996) (see Chapter 3 by Richard Rose), or who have attempted to devise new conceptual models to allow therapeutic needs and broader personal and social objectives to be considered together with the National Curriculum (Sebba *et al.*, 1995; Rose *et al.*, 1996).

Administratively and managerially, Local Management of Special Schools (LMSS) has brought special school financial and development planning into line with mainstream processes (Touche Ross, 1990; DES, 1991). LMSS is, in fact, an excellent example of the inclusion of special schools in mainstream processes, with access being allowed by modifications to formulae and procedures. In this case, funding is mainly place led, rather than pupil led, and based on type of need, rather than on age weighting. A further confirmation of the extent to which special schools are now being considered within mainstream frames of reference is their inclusion in the national school inspection process under Ofsted, and the application of inspection criteria which are almost identical to those applied to mainstream schools (Ofsted, 1995). This *Guidance on the Inspection of Special Schools* includes clear messages about inclusion within a mainstream values framework, and consequently special schools are attempting to establish practices which will allow them not only to survive inspections based on a mainstream model, but also to use inspections as part of a school improvement process (Sebba *et al.*, 1997).

All these developments have challenged special schools to identify a need to move away from a model of separate values and ethos, towards one which is more closely aligned to mainstream schools and the school evaluation systems accompanying them. It is important to locate special schools themselves more clearly within a mainstream evaluation frame of reference, which focuses on school effectiveness.

School effectiveness is, by definition, a measure of the effect which schools have on their pupils; as opposed to the contextual factors which pupils bring to the school, such as family and environmental background, prior achievement, gender and disability. It involves a consideration of educational outcomes and some means of assessing and evaluating them within two main frames of reference.

The first is the school's own statement of its aims and objectives, which involves a person-centred definition of effectiveness, such as the one given by Georgopoulos and Tannenbaum (1957):

> the extent to which any organisation as a social system, given certain resources and means, fulfils its objectives without incapacitating its means and resources and without placing undue strain upon its members.

> (p.535)

Even when stated in a person-centred way, this concept of effectiveness is inseparable from a formulation of objectives and a means of evaluating outcomes. LEA special schools are required under Section 370 of the Education Act 1996 (DfEE, 1996) to make a statement of their curricular aims, having consulted their LEA policy. This requirement, however, does not extend beyond the curriculum and does not specify objectives which can be evaluated. One obvious way to guarantee effectiveness is for the school to formulate clear aims and objectives, an approach considered in more detail later in this chapter.

The second frame of reference for evaluating school effectiveness is a school's comparative performance. Originally, this orientation developed from American studies such as that of Coleman *et al.* (1966) which suggested that a child's home background influenced educational outcomes far more than the school. Researchers such as Edmonds (1979) attempted to identify factors which enabled some schools to be more effective than others in securing higher attainments for the urban poor. The overriding concern with social disadvantage in the 1960s and 1970s is in stark contrast to the dominant, market-forces orientation of the 1980s and 1990s. Now, a major motive for publicly identifying effective schools, in the UK at least, is to inform powerful parent-choosers in a survival-of-the-fittest schools market regime.

Somewhere between the two lies the possibility of using effectiveness findings to inform the improvement of all schools, and the two major studies of UK secondary schools (Rutter *et al.*, 1979) and junior schools (Mortimore *et al.*, 1988) generated considerable data. Further research has led to an improving knowledge base and conceptual framework, which ought to benefit all school management, including that of special schools. The factors identified by Mortimore *et al.* (1988) were:

- purposeful leadership of the staff by the head teacher;
- involvement of the deputy head in policy matters;
- involvement of the teachers in planning;
- consistency among teachers;
- structured sessions and structured work;
- intellectually challenging teaching with high expectations;
- work-centred environment;
- limited focus within sessions;
- maximum communication between teachers and students;
- record keeping;
- parental involvement and partnership;
- a positive climate and reinforcement.

The narrower issue of teacher (as opposed to school) effectiveness in a survey of thirty-one special schools in twenty-three LEAs by HMI in 1995 led to a series of conferences on 'Effective Teaching Observed in Special Schools'. Although this work was not published, its findings in relation to the 103 best lessons observed pointed to eleven key areas of teacher expertise which were considered to be linked to effectiveness across all age and ability groups:

- subject knowledge and expertise;
- skills in managing the disability;
- skills in lesson planning and preparation;
- the effective organisation of teaching;
- skills in using questions to promote language;
- skills in giving feedback and praise to pupils;
- skills in enabling pupils to make choices and work independently;
- realistically high expectations of pupils;
- the skilled assessment of pupils' achievements;
- the ability to co-ordinate the contribution of other adults;
- the ability to set the right climate for learning.

These areas of expertise can be seen as closely related to areas identified in the general teacher effectiveness literature. They also relate to the 'competencies' identified for SEN contexts by the Special Educational Needs Training Consortium which was funded by the Department for Education and Employment in 1995 to consider how training for teachers of pupils with special educational needs could be improved (SENTC, 1996).

ESTABLISHING FRAMES OF REFERENCE FOR SPECIAL SCHOOL EVALUATION

Special schools therefore need to work within two main frames of reference in order to define and improve their effectiveness. Firstly, their own key aims and objectives need to be effective. Secondly, they must define their practice and outcomes in relation to those agreed by the wider educational community as indicative of effective schools. In the case of special schools, there is a great deal of development work yet to be done on agreed educational outcomes and the methodology of evaluation, but it is possible to use a framework which will allow maximum involvement in effectiveness development, and will incorporate new data and methodologies as they become available.

Internal reference: analysing performance in relation to educational objectives

A way forward is for the special school to attempt to define its:

1   overall mission/reason for being;
2   culture and core values;

3   key aims and objectives;
4   criteria and indicators;
5   quality assurance procedures.

It is important that the staff and governors of special schools, in partnership, are closely involved in the development of these specifications. Items 1 and 2 should be defined in conjunction with the LEA (or parent organisation for non-LEA schools). Statements of mission and core values are important, but will vary from school to school. A school which provides outreach support, for instance, will need to incorporate 'outreach' as part of its core function and purpose; similarly, one which offers twenty-four-hour care will develop a statement essentially different from that of a day school.

If these definitions are arrived at collaboratively with governors and the LEA, the school will have an initial value frame of reference which will both aid development planning and inform external inspection. This is an important point, which raises questions about the current Ofsted special school inspection framework, for which inspectors have their own rigorous inspection criteria. Nevertheless, the overall emphasis may vary. A clear statement by the school, in conjunction with its LEA, can be a positive influence on an inspection team.

Aims and objectives should also be stated in a way which incorporates agreed effectiveness criteria and allows for the evaluation of outcomes. Specification of an objectives model begs the question of how objectives should be stated in order to be useful, and what criteria are required for the evaluation of outcomes. Dror (1973) provides a technical framework for the evaluation of outcomes in any enterprise in terms of primary and secondary criteria and associated standards. Primary criteria are a direct measure of the objectives set (e.g. examination results); secondary criteria are used when a direct measure of outcomes is not possible, owing to their complexity or intangibility (e.g. school ethos). Secondary criteria are thought to be positively correlated with, and more measurable than, the net output; for example, the proportion of staff with advanced qualifications might be thought to correlate with the quality of teaching. Secondary criteria are therefore indicators of success or effectiveness, rather than direct measures. In the context of school planning, bearing in mind the inevitability of external inspection, it could make sense for a school to use the Ofsted inspection framework as a basis for its aims and objectives. Consider the 'Aspects of the School' (Ofsted, 1995, p.4):

4.   **Educational standards achieved by pupils at the school**
4.1. Attainment and progress
4.2. Attitudes, behaviour and personal development
4.3. Attendance

5.   Quality of education provided
5.1. Teaching
5.2. The curriculum and assessment
5.3. Pupils' spiritual, moral, social and cultural development
5.4. Support, guidance and pupils' welfare

6.   The management and efficiency of the school
6.1. Leadership and management
6.2. Staffing, accommodation and learning resources
6.3. The efficiency of the school

If 'Curriculum areas and subjects' (Ofsted, p.4) are added, the four main headings could be converted into key aims; the subdivisions converted into key objectives; and the inspection criteria modified and embedded in the school's own self-evaluation processes. An example of one special school's three-stage process is:

Stage I

Identify a small number of key aims related to the main functions of the school as an organisation:

Key aim 1: Teaching and learning

To provide all pupils with the highest-quality teaching, classroom support, care and therapy to meet their special educational needs and to ensure high standards of achievement and quality of learning.

Key aim 2: Environment

To ensure a safe, healthy and supportive environment in which learning can take place.

Key aim 3: Management and administration

To establish efficient, effective management, and administrative and financial systems as a basis for strategic planning and the day-to-day running of the school.

Stage 2

Expand each aim to specify key objectives whose outcomes can be evaluated.

Key aim 1: Teaching and learning

To provide all pupils with the highest-quality teaching, classroom support, care and therapy to meet their special educational needs and to ensure high standards of achievement and quality of learning.

Key objectives:

1.1 To develop and sustain a highly motivated, well-trained teaching and support staff, working within clear staffing structures, job descriptions, a supportive professional development framework and an equal opportunities ethos.
1.2 To promote high-quality effective teaching.
1.3 To provide a curriculum which incorporates National Curriculum elements as appropriate, but which is modified to meet the special needs of individual children with a wide range of learning diffi-culties and which gives due emphasis to personal and social development.
1.4 To sustain high levels of pupil attainment, progress and behaviour across all age groups and types of special need.
1.5 To maintain all necessary links with health and social services and other support services to ensure that effective multidisciplinary planning and action takes place.
1.6 To establish open and co-operative relations with parents, both as customers receiving services and as partners in the education process.
1.7 To foster appropriate links with the local and the wider commu-nity.

Key aim 2: Environment

To ensure a safe, healthy and supportive environment in which learning can take place.

Key objectives:

2.1 To devise, implement and monitor clear health and safety policies and procedures.
2.2 To ensure proper site management.
2.3 To ensure the competent supervision of children within the terms of a clear, written policy framework.
2.4 To implement a care and control policy which promotes the well-being of all pupils.

Key aim 3: Management and administration

To establish efficient, effective management, administrative and financial systems as a basis for strategic planning and the day-to-day running of the school.

Key objectives:

3.1 To establish and maintain the necessary governors' finance, and personnel and policy systems to ensure effective and cost-effective administration under LMSS.
3.2 To establish and maintain an effective school development planning cycle in collaboration with the head and staff.
3.3 To establish and maintain an active partnership between governors, head and the management team.
3.4 To ensure that the head and the governors are supported by high-quality administrative and clerical staff.
3.5 To establish, wherever possible, procedures for monitoring and improving standards and quality within all organisational areas of the school (Quality Assurance Systems).

Stage 3

Add criteria and standards where possible, and identify monitoring and evaluation mechanisms. (A selection from key objective 1.1 is given below as an example.)

Key objective	Effectiveness focus	Criteria and standards	Monitoring and evaluation
1.1 Teaching and support	Staffing structure and salaries	Staffing structure and line management reflect current school size and department structure	Head and SMT review annually and report to governors' committee
		All roles and responsibilities are made explicit and are reviewed annually in consultation with staff	
		All staff have up-to-date job descriptions which are reviewed annually	Head undertakes annual check. Files open to all staff
		Governors undertake an annual salaries review	Pay or Finance Personnel Committee reports to the full governing body in the summer or autumn term
		Governors have in place a performance review for heads and deputies	
	Teamwork	Teams are well defined, effectively led and achieve results	Annual team review by head of department
		Teaching and non-teaching staff understand and are committed to their respective roles and support each other	
		Teamwork is regularly addressed as a development focus and improvements pursued	HoDs follow up annual team review with a meeting with the head

Professional development	The governors and head work towards establishing a teaching staff who all have advanced SEN qualifications. This policy is pursued in the appointment of new staff, and financially supported where possible	
(a) Training and qualifications (b) INSET (c) Appraisal (d) Equal opportunities	All classroom support staff have appropriate qualifications or are being supported by the school to gain qualifications as a part of a systematic professional development process	Head reports annually to Governors' Finance and Personnel Committee
	The INSET budget is effectively managed and linked to school development priorities	INSET co-ordinator presents an annual evaluation report to SMT each February
	All teachers take part in an ongoing appraisal cycle and set targets to improve performance	Annual evaluation by head monitored by the Chair of Governors
	An equal opportunities policy is in place and is systematically monitored	Named governor undertakes Annual Review and reports to full governing body

It is important to note that this model entails objectives, not targets; that the criteria and standards are written as reasonable expectations, not as attempts to improve on existing performance; and that the monitoring and evaluation procedures are meant to be built in and ongoing. The main point of this approach is to provide a framework for sustainable, cyclical action within a school. Within this framework, it is possible to select some objectives and to set specific targets for them, a natural part of school development planning. This is not to be confused with the setting of annual academic performance targets based on national standards, as advocated by SCAA (School Curriculum Assessment Authority) (1997a), discussed later in this chapter.

Within the key objectives model, there is also scope for attempting a more rigorous analysis of aspects of pupil performance, provided that detailed assessments can be scored in some way. In common with mainstream schools, special schools will be critically interested in pupil attainment and progress, and will increasingly seek to establish assessment systems which allow inclusion in mainstream evaluation processes.

When evaluating special school pupils' attainment and progress, we need to be clear about our intentions. The first level of focus in assessment is on the individual pupil and our primary purpose may be to establish what we should teach the pupil next (i.e. formative assessment), a common vehicle for which is a range of curriculum-based performance items in graded, small steps. A second purpose may be to chart and to report on a child's progress, which will entail occasional summative assessment and the measurement of change.

Our second level of focus, while still for internal reference, is systems review and improvement, and will involve the analysis of aggregated performance data, by gender, year groups, classes, departments, or other subgroups considered relevant. Raw National Curriculum attainment levels will be relevant and useful for some higher-performing special school pupils, although it may be difficult to provide enough discriminatory (and therefore useful) information for most of the pupils, who are likely to be working within a small number of levels over an extended period.

The two main reference frames for school effectiveness indicate that the implementation of an aims and objectives model can ensure the evaluation of special school effectiveness in relation to a school's own objectives, and that these objectives can incorporate widely accepted effectiveness indicators within a rigorous framework. Furthermore, provided that the progress made by pupils with special educational needs can be scaled, similar data analysis to that used in mainstream schools can be applied to special schools, thereby allowing inclusion in mainstream developments.

EXTERNAL REFERENCE: ANALYSING SCHOOL PERFORMANCE IN RELATION TO THE PERFORMANCE OF OTHER SCHOOLS

Inclusion in mainstream effectiveness frameworks also requires the examination of interschool comparisons of pupil attainment and progress. In doing so, however, two features of mainstream effectiveness thinking may create dilemmas for special schools. The first is a pervasive emphasis on outcomes of pupil learning in terms of norm-referenced attainments and model behaviours (both called 'standards'), which, if measured against mainstream norms or expectations (in the absence of like-for-like comparisons), will automatically define special schools and their pupils as failing. The second feature of mainstream effectiveness thinking is the implication that numerically measurable results can be subject to statistical analysis, which, in mainstream and special schools alike, will tend to restrict the analysis of effectiveness to a narrow range of performance outcomes, at the expense of qualitative evaluation.

Currently, the dominant mainstream analytical tool which special schools can use is 'value-added' analysis, involving comparisons of the progress of one sample of pupils over a given period with the average progress of a larger sample of pupils (SCAA, 1997b, p.3). The Value Added National Project (Final Report) and the ongoing national framework are concerned with value-added indicators relating to externally measured attainments (SCAA, 1997c, p.13). Current mainstream value-added developments will begin with Baseline Assessments (SCAA, 1997d; 1997e), which are based on the Desirable Outcomes for Children's Learning identified in relation to the six areas of learning for under 5s (SCAA, 1996a). The link with the National Curriculum is as follows:

Six areas of learning for under 5s	National Curriculum progression
Language and literacy	English
Mathematics	Mathematics
Personal and social development	English, PE, maths, science, RE
Knowledge and understanding of the world	Geography, history, science, design and information technology
Physical development	PE
Creative development	Art and music

Schools and LEAs will chart pupils' progress through a range of performance measures from Reception to Year 11 (including various standardised tests, the end of Key Stage National Curriculum assessments and GCSE results). An individual school's 'effectiveness' (within the range of attainments selected) can then be calculated in relation to other schools in its LEA, national averages, or any other relevant part of the whole sample.

Mainstream value added is itself fraught with theoretical problems, particularly in relation to its fairness. Not surprisingly, the theoretical problems are compounded for special schools (Saunders, 1997) and comparison with progress made by pupils in mainstream education will be, by definition, counter-productive. On the other hand, comparison with other pupils with special educational needs will require at least the following:

- a valid and agreed set of baseline assessment measures of outcome measures;
- a database established over a period of several years using large numbers of pupils with SEN, with enough detail to discriminate outcomes differentially for pupils with a range of disabilities and backgrounds;
- large and stable enough cohorts within a given school to establish statistical significance.

There are challenges associated with each of these requirements:

- any group of special schools working together (e.g. regionally) will have to agree to use the same baseline assessment scheme;
- for pupils with learning difficulties, it will be necessary either to extend the Baseline Assessment scales and continue to use the six Areas of Learning format over several years, or to devise new scales for older pupils using a different, more relevant format. In either case, it will be necessary to break outcomes down into smaller steps than National Curriculum levels, and to reach agreement on outcomes;
- a viable SEN database must be established over several years by a large enough group of schools using agreed baselines and outcome data;
- populations and cohorts within special schools are anomalous, and pupils will enter special schools at different ages. There may well be a systematic shift in the type of need catered for within a special school over time (whether by design or 'drift'), and, if the trend is towards more complex needs, the measured effectiveness of the school may (erroneously) appear to be deteriorating. As cohorts in special schools are small, SCAA's own research conclusions were that:

Value added measures fluctuate from year to year, particularly those for small groups of pupils. Consideration of present research, and of findings from other researchers led to a rough rule of thumb: a group should contain at least thirty pupils before the data could be regarded as sufficiently reliable. It also led to a view that looking at value added measures over a three year period would be more reliable than looking at one year at a time.

(SCAA, 1997b, p.9)

On the grounds of small cohorts alone, almost all special schools would be disqualified if the data was used to compare schools' performances in accountability terms.

Taken together, these considerations suggest that true value-added comparisons for special schools may not be feasible. However, if the purpose of the exercise is primarily a matter of school self-improvement, rather than school comparison, then there may still be a justification for investment in quasi-value-added analysis. It may entail clusters of special schools working together to share data and methodologies, thereby increasing the size of the database and improving mutual awareness of effectiveness issues.

BENCHMARKING AND TARGET SETTING

Whether information on school performance is truly value added, there is a strong impetus from central government for schools to 'raise standards' by comparing their pupil performance with that of similar schools via bench-marking, and linking targets for improvement to national targets. Underlying the notions of target setting is a transformation from norms to expectations, which allows policy-makers to insist that 80 per cent of pupils will be expected to achieve the standards set for their age (DfEE, 1997b, p.19, para 21). Whatever the results of imposing such systems on schools as a national policy, it is clear that they idealised expectations and mainstream norms, which are of little use, as they stand, to special schools. Nevertheless, in the interests of inclusive practice, it would be beneficial if a model could be devised to identify a continuum of target-setting practice which would work across both mainstream and special schools. If this is to be of relevance to special schools, and to pupils with special educational needs in ordinary schools, the first requirement would be for target setting which was not restricted to a narrow band of pupil attainments. This could be achieved by recognising the three dimensions of target setting, as follows:

Dimension	Type of outcome relevant to target setting
1 Attainment	Measurable performance outcomes in agreed curriculum areas
2 Behaviour	A) Outcomes which are considered to be indicators of organisational effectiveness B) Outcomes which describe social skills and attitudes relevant to children's needs
3 Experience	Outcomes which describe experiences which can be considered to be providing entitlement or access

Setting targets for improvement in relation to measurable attainment will be more problematic, the more severe the learning difficulty, and the more fundamental the in-child processing impairments. Therefore entitlement or access targets of an experiential, rather than attainment, type will be more appropriate, the closer the pupils are to the severe end of the learning diffi-culties continuum. Provided that the dimensions have a continuum of outcomes, ranging from normative expectations (for the most able pupils) to personal and pupil-centred outcomes (for those with more severe learning difficulties), and provided that more weight can be given to experiential rather than attainment outcomes for the pupils with severe learning difficul-ties, a workable model can be constructed. The following table shows how the emphases might vary over the full SEN range.

		Attainment	Behaviour	Experience
Mild to moderate learning difficulties	*Normative expectations*	***	**	*
Moderate to severe learning difficulties	*Mixed*	**	**	**
Severe to profound learning difficulties	*Personal and child-centred outcomes*	*	**	***

Applying this schema to real school situations would allow a variation in target setting by the selection of outcomes relevant to pupils' needs and abilities. For example:

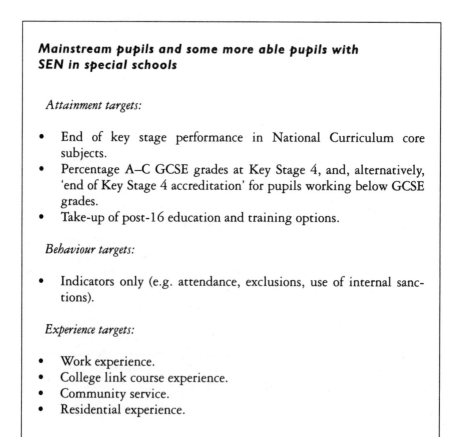

Mainstream pupils and some more able pupils with SEN in special schools

Attainment targets:

- End of key stage performance in National Curriculum core subjects.
- Percentage A–C GCSE grades at Key Stage 4, and, alternatively, 'end of Key Stage 4 accreditation' for pupils working below GCSE grades.
- Take-up of post-16 education and training options.

Behaviour targets:

- Indicators only (e.g. attendance, exclusions, use of internal sanctions).

Experience targets:

- Work experience.
- College link course experience.
- Community service.
- Residential experience.

Special school pupils with moderate to severe learning difficulties

Attainment targets:

- End of Key Stage performance in National Curriculum core subjects: 'small steps', rather than full levels (see below).
- End of Key Stage 4 accreditation below GCSE level in a range of subject areas (see SCAA, 1996b).
- Take-up of post-16 education and training options.

Behaviour targets:

- Attendance, exclusions, use of internal sanctions.
- Social skills targets relevant to key stages and range of learning difficulties.

Experience targets:

- Work experience (where relevant).
- College link course experience.
- Residential experience, links with mainstream schools, community involvement.

Special school pupils with severe to profound and multiple learning difficulties

Attainment targets:

- End of key stage performance in National Curriculum core subjects: small steps only.

Behaviour targets:

- Life and social skills targets relevant to key stages and range of learning difficulties.

Experience targets:

• Experiences defined as entitlements appropriate to each key stage and pupil developmental level.

All of the above are only possible if National Curriculum core subject attainment levels can be broken down into a nationally agreed 'small steps' framework. Behaviour and experience targets could be the subject of nationally co-ordinated development work, but could also be developed by groups of schools within a benchmarking cluster.

Given the variability of the special school pupil factors discussed above in relation to value added, there would be doubts about the validity of expressing targets in terms of year-on-year improvements or raising the average levels achieved by all pupils each year. It would be reasonable, however, to set targets in a given year for the proportion of pupils attaining certain levels of performance and for a range of 'entitlement experiences'. Benchmarking (SCAA, 1997f) across special schools will have to be a tentative matching process, but need not be a major issue if the resulting comparisons are used to create special school clusters for in-house school improvement. Crude benchmarking of special schools to create special school league tables or as a basis for inspection judgements would be unsound.

The above model for special school target setting would enable them to be included within the same school improvement processes as mainstream schools, but with modifications to the content in order to make the process viable and meaningful.

CONCLUSION

This chapter began with an assertion that special schools can and should be involved in a rigorous evaluation of effectiveness, linked as far as possible to mainstream frameworks, and an attempt has been made to explore how this might be undertaken to allow the maximum inclusion in evaluative processes. The first requirement is an objectives framework which will allow evaluation of outcomes in terms of the special school's own perceived tasks. The framework can then be developed with reference to a broader-based school evaluation and inspection framework, and can therefore be based on criteria considered to be valid within the wider educational community. There is also the possibility of developing special school information networks and databases which will allow a quasi-value-added analysis of a partial range of their work, for the purpose of school evaluation, planning and improvement. This development work should be seen as a matter of extended research. The unusual features of special school pupils' characteristics and educational objectives will preclude a true value-added analysis and target setting based on mainstream schools' national pupil performance expectations. Nevertheless, the extension of outcome measures along continua to include pupils of all abilities is a theoretical and practical possibility, and could lead to more relevant evaluation and target setting for pupils with learning difficulties in both special and mainstream schools.

The latter is perhaps the crucial point. In our efforts to achieve inclusive practice, it is important to be clear that inclusion is not simply the assimilation of an out-group into an in-group's frame of reference. An in-depth exploration of issues which apply to pupils with special educational needs ought to feed back into mainstream thinking, and genuine inclusive practice should involve an expansion of the whole frame of reference and a new synthesis in order to challenge mainstream as much as special schools.

REFERENCES

Carpenter, B., Bovair, K. and Ashdown, R. (eds) (1996) *Enabling Access: Effective Teaching and Learning for Pupils with Learning Difficulties*, London: David Fulton.

Coleman, J. S., Campbell, E., Hobson, C., McPartland, J., Mood, A., Weinfeld, F. and York, R. (1966) *Equality of Educational Opportunity*, Washington, DC: National Center for Educational Statistics.

Day, A. J. (1989) 'Reaching out: the background to outreach', in D. Baker and K. Bovair (eds) *Making the Special Schools Ordinary?*, Lewes: Falmer Press.

Department for Education and Employment (1995) *The National Curriculum*, London: HMSO.

Department for Education and Employment (1996) *The Education Act, 1996*, London: HMSO.

Department for Education and Employment (1997a) *Excellence in Schools*, London: The Stationery Office.

Department for Education and Employment (1997b) *Excellence for All Children: Meeting Special Educational Needs,* London: The Stationery Office.

Department of Education and Science (1991) *Local Management of Schools: Further Guidance*, Circular 7/91, London: DES.

Dror, Y. (1973) *Public Policy making Re-examined*, Bedford: Leonard Hill Books.

Edmonds, R. (1979) 'Effective schools for the urban poor', *Educational Leadership* 44(8): 13–19.

Fagg, S., Aherne, P., Skelton, S. and Thornber, A. (1990) *Entitlement for All in Practice: a Broad, Balanced and Relevant Curriculum for Children and Young People with Severe and Complex Learning Difficulties in the 1990s*, London: David Fulton.

Georgopoulos, B. S. and Tannenbaum, A. S. (1957) 'A study of organisational effectiveness', *American Sociological Review* 22(5): 534–40.

Jowett, S., Hegarty, S. and Moses, D. (1988) *Joining Forces: a Study of Links between Special and Ordinary Schools,* Windsor: NFER-Nelson.

Mortimore, P., Sammons, P., Stoll, L., Lewis, D. and Ecob, R. (1988) *School Matters: the Junior Years*, Wells: Open Books.

Ofsted (1995) *Guidance on the Inspection of Special Schools*, London: HMSO.

Rose, R., Fergusson, A., Coles, C., Byers, R. and Banes, D. (eds) (1996) *Implementing the Whole Curriculum for Pupils With Learning Difficulties*, Revised edition, London: David Fulton.

Rutter, M., Maughan, B., Mortimore, P. and Ouston, J. (1979) *Fifteen Thousand Hours*, London: Open Books.

Saunders, L. (1997) *How Relevant is 'Value-Added' to Schools in the SEN Sector?* (Topic, Issue 17, Spring 1997) Slough: NFER.

School Curriculum and Assessment Authority (1996a) *Desirable Outcomes for Children's Learning*, Hayes: SCAA Publications.

School Curriculum and Assessment Authority (1996b) *Assessment, Recording and Accreditation of Achievement for Pupils with Learning Difficulties*, Hayes: SCAA Publications.

School Curriculum and Assessment Authority (1997a) *Target Setting and Benchmarking in Schools* (Consultation Paper), Hayes: SCAA Publications.

School Curriculum and Assessment Authority (1997b) *Value Added Indicators for Schools* (Consultative Paper: Secondary), Hayes: SCAA Publications.

School Curriculum and Assessment Authority (1997c) *The Value Added National Project: Final Report*, Hayes: SCAA Publications.

School Curriculum and Assessment Authority (1997d) *The National Framework for Baseline Assessment*, Hayes: SCAA Publications.

School Curriculum and Assessment Authority (1997e) *Baseline Assessment Scales*, Hayes: SCAA Publications.

School Curriculum and Assessment Authority (1997f) *Target Setting and Benchmarking in Schools* (Consultation Paper), Hayes: SCAA Publications.

Sebba, J., Byers, R. and Rose, R. (1995) *Redefining the Whole Curriculum for Pupils with Learning Difficulties* (Revised edition), London: David Fulton.

Sebba, J., Clarke, J. and Emery, B. (1997) *Enhancing Special School Improvement Through Inspection in Special Schools* (Ofsted Publication), London: HMSO.

Special Educational Needs Training Consortium (1996) *Professional Development to Meet Special Educational Needs*, Stafford: SENTC.

Tilstone, C. (ed.) (1991) *Teaching Pupils with Severe Learning Difficulties: Practical Approaches*, London: David Fulton.

Touche Ross (1990) *Extending Local Management to Special Schools*, London: HMSO.

Chapter 14

Routes to inclusion

Jonathan Steele

Promoting inclusion within the community whilst retaining the specialist input afforded by special schools or units is part of the challenge special schools are facing as they become community special schools. In this chapter, Jonathan Steele explores the potential of community, business, professional and school links as routes to inclusion. He discusses examples of links, their potential outcomes and the process involved promoting inclusive practice. Particular consideration is given to the factors that can influence the successful establishment of links.

The inclusion of pupils with learning difficulties within their communities depends on many complex factors, with educational placement being only one of these. Concepts of integration and segregation are not poles on a linear continuum, but even if they were, the concept of true inclusion would not appear anywhere on such a line. The factors which influence inclusion alter with time as changes and developments are made in different aspects of community provision. Such changes can be effected by simple movement or appointment of key personnel. Attitudes have a major effect on expectations and the way people with special needs are treated (Johnson and Johnson, 1986). The range of attitudes to, and expectations of pupils with, severe learning difficulties (SLD) will be clear to those involved in the field; variations can be observed within and between schools and communities as well as at different points in time. This chapter considers ways of promoting more inclusive practice through the exploitation of links between special schools and a range of mainstream or community environments.

Links with mainstream schools have been long accepted as vital aspects of good special school practice and provide one way of promoting inclusion within the community. Around a decade ago, Jowett *et al.* (1988) reported that 80 per cent of heads of schools for pupils with SLD were developing such links. The importance of these links has continued to be recognised,

Fletcher-Cambell (1994) noting that they have been maintained despite the competing pressures of issues such as National Curriculum, local management and the likelihood that SLD schools are taking pupils with greater or more complex learning difficulties. Descriptions of link schemes between special and mainstream schools are frequent in the literature (e.g. Beveridge, 1996; Turner, 1996; Information Exchange, 1995; Steele and Mitchell, 1992; Ware et al., 1992). However, links may be forged between bodies other than schools or colleges. For many pupils, it is the links with broader community facilities or businesses that are important. In addition, links established at a professional level have been found to be useful by many establishments.

EXAMPLES OF COMMUNITY LINKS

The diversity of links with community facilities creates numerous opportunities to promote inclusive practice. Special schools have developed a tradition of links with their local community. For example, with local athletics clubs or sports facilities, organisations that work with young people such as youth clubs, Scouts or Guides, and local church organisations. These community links are two way. Often special schools have resources that may be useful to the wider community and can be shared on a formal or informal basis.

For example, one special school had the possibility of releasing a room for one session each week and, realising the pressure that the local child development centre was under in providing day placements for under 5s, suggested that an additional session could be run at the school. This not only provided access to specialist equipment and resources otherwise unavailable to the children at the child development centre but helped break down misconceptions about the school within the local community. Other special schools have established integrated nursery provision, bringing children with and without learning difficulties and their parents together against the background of a specialist establishment with its range of resources and expertise.

Community links may be supported by school staff as part of a curricular provision, by social services or youth services staff outside schools, or other voluntary agencies. However such support is given the success of such schemes may depend on effective communication between the supporting agency, home and school. The importance of staff meeting together to discuss such links and visiting school or home to get to know the pupils is therefore paramount.

EXAMPLES OF BUSINESS LINKS

Opportunities for linking with businesses, both through Education Business Partnerships (EBPs) and individual local contacts, have improved over recent years. Many examples of good practice exist in a wide range of schools, encouraged by the EBP 'Aim High' Awards (TES, 1997). The Secretary of State for Education has identified three types of activity in this area: student mentoring, work experience and study support (Blunkett, 1997). The careers services have an important role in facilitating such experiences and several case studies have been noted (DfEE, 1997). Business links can also help in the areas of improving staff management skills and assisting in general school development. Some practical examples of how business links have helped special schools take a more active role in the wider community are given below.

Work experience

Businesses have been involved in providing work experience for pupils with SLD for some considerable time. Schools have developed work experience programmes with the assistance of a number of agencies including local Training and Enterprise Councils, EBPs, TVEI clusters, social services (e.g. post-school resource centres) and individual contacts. Safety of pupils is always a concern with any work experience for mainstream or special schools; senior staff should be able to ensure this by following their LEA guidance and gaining the appropriate insurance.

Placements that demand different levels of independence, skills and support can be organised to meet the needs of individual pupils. Schools may operate supported employment placements close to, or even within, the school (see Chapter 17 by Jan Tyne). Placements at local supermarkets, garden centres, libraries, local radio stations, animal sanctuaries, to name but a few possibilities, have all been arranged. The encouragement of positive community attitudes, and the opportunity for many pupils with SLD to provide a positive input to businesses, is a particularly important outcome. Some pupils may even go on to longer-term work placements or employment in the community.

It is also possible for special schools to provide work experience placements for mainstream pupils. This can be an important part of ensuring that positive attitudes are engendered and that participants do not develop a patronising or elitist approach to those with learning difficulties.

Study support

It is possible for businesses and other outside agencies to support pupils with their curriculum. Financial support in providing equipment has traditionally been one way of doing this, although it can lack the personal contact over a period of time that is important if pupils are to become known and understood within the community.

Several well-known businesses do provide educational resources and input for pupils in mainstream and special schools. However, this may not provide local contact. It is local contact that is important to the process of inclusion, as pupils need to become known and respected within their own communities. Some special schools in Lancashire are developing Joint Accreditation at 16–19 with local firms. In this situation, local firms are contacted and key senior personnel are persuaded to become co-signatories on certificates of achievement for particular curriculum areas. Appropriate links are made between businesses and curriculum areas (e.g. banks and budgeting work, bookshops and literacy work, etc.). Visits to school are arranged to discuss the degree of involvement (e.g. regularity of visits, work to be seen, etc.) and introduce the pupils. Pupils may also visit the businesses involved and may undertake some type of work experience there.

This particular system of linking with business has the advantage of providing information about the pupils' abilities to the local community. Whilst this example's accreditation scheme is not nationally recognised, it can be argued that local recognition is more important. Many nationally recognised schemes may not be well known to local employers; however, the local schemes are recognised and understood by a range of employers, by virtue of their involvement in the scheme.

The TES (1997) reported another example of study support where a local company supported a horticulture project through sponsorship and by providing a retail outlet for plants produced within the company's park grounds. The company also provided work for adults with special needs within the park grounds, probably as a result of increased awareness of special needs through the school/business links.

Student mentoring

Golden and Sims (1997) recently reviewed industrial mentoring schemes in schools. These schemes are supported by EBPs, Training and Enterprise Councils or Compact schemes typically to address the needs of pupils who underachieve. Of the studies reviewed 12 per cent involved pupils with special educational needs. The potential relevance and benefits of these schemes are clearly spelled out in the following objectives:

- enhancing students' personal development (e.g. awareness of world of work, self-confidence through someone taking an interest in them, etc.);
- supporting and improving students' school achievement (e.g. attendance, punctuality, application to study, relevance of study to future, etc.);

- providing benefits to mentors and their company (learning about young people, the education system, gaining recruits, etc.).

Like other links, mentoring is a two-way process that may not only inform and encourage pupils through the individual interest that is taken by the mentor, but may also encourage businesses to consider utilising the skills of some of the pupils with learning difficulties in work placements. Golden and Sims report a number of features common to successful schemes that may be summarised as follows:

- objectives are clearly identified and defined;
- clear criteria are set for the selection of students;
- clear terms of reference and roles are set for all those involved;
- mentors are recruited from a range of companies;
- mentors are offered training and support and do have sufficient time to undertake mentoring;
- the experiences of other schools involved in mentoring are taken into consideration;
- there is a clear monitoring, evaluation and review process;
- support is provided to the school, particularly with recruiting mentors, identifying achievable objectives.

In one special school involved in Joint Accreditation with local companies an informal type of student mentoring is developing, with individual accreditors taking a particular interest in the work of one or a number of students and discussing it with them. It is not difficult to see how such arrangements or other less formal links with businesses could be developed into more structured mentoring schemes, following the above guidelines and given the appropriate support.

Improving management skills/school development

Links between school staff and business staff have been usefully deployed as an aid to management development. Teacher placements within industry are well known and supported by some LEAs. Further links with industry may be developed through schemes such as Investors in People, which aims to improve the effectiveness of an establishment through ensuring there is a commitment to staff training and development. This scheme, often supported by Training and Enterprise Councils, may have area networks where a range of schools and businesses can discuss issues of development; sharing strategies and approaches.

EXAMPLES OF PROFESSIONAL LINKS

The expertise of staff within special schools has been mentioned as a valuable resource and should be utilised to develop links with the wider community.

Special school teachers can, and do, provide input on national teacher training courses. The input of experienced specialist teachers on national courses is important, but equally important is establishing the special school as a centre of expertise in its local environment. Good practice may consist of staff with a range of different roles and responsibilities sharing their expertise through local college, university or education authority courses. Hence not only teachers, but special support assistants and other staff may be involved in providing input to courses for the training of professionals.

Many special schools also enhance links with their local community professional training centres by providing placements for students during their course. Apart from trainee teachers, special schools provide placements for students studying to become special support assistants, nursing staff, therapists, paediatricians, etc. One enlightened paediatric consultant insists that junior doctors spend some time in the local school for children with SLD and with parents of the pupils.

EXAMPLES OF LINK SCHEMES WITH MAINSTREAM SCHOOLS

Links aimed at primarily developing positive attitudes

Initiated by a mainstream comprehensive school in the mid 1980s, this type of scheme involved running a short course about SLD based on guidance provided by McConkey and McCormack (1983). The emphasis was on exploring and challenging attitudes using questionnaires, discussion, role play and video. This was followed by shared activities with the local special school. Questionnaires before and after the course revealed:

- A clearer concept of the meaning of severe learning difficulties.
- A more positive and accepting attitude towards social contact with people who had SLD.

This scheme was noteworthy in its effect on changing negative attitudes towards disability through the presentation of clear information and sharing mutually challenging social activities. The success of this scheme was reflected in the fact that shared activities continued at lunch-times and an integrated camping weekend followed shortly after the course. Interest by mainstream staff also led to the development of shared curricular activities (Steele, 1985).

Links involving curriculum

One school where this type of scheme was particularly well developed assigned teachers with a specific responsibility for integration to negotiate placements and to support small groups of pupils. Pupils with SLD joined their mainstream peers for a wide range of activities including PE, music, English, art, cookery, science, outdoor pursuits and basic construction (bricklaying, plumbing, painting and carpentry), as well as the evening and residential extra-curricular activities of mainstream schools. The special school's residential facility was used on a number of occasions for integrated activity weekends, particularly involving younger pupils.

The 'integration teachers' also ran courses for college and mainstream staff and students to promote positive attitudes to those with learning difficulties, as well as negotiating the timetabling of integration across the school in a way that did not result in major curriculum imbalance for individual pupils. Of course, in the past it has not been uncommon for teachers in SLD schools to support the majority of integrated placements, sometimes on a one-to-one basis. Now, however, this is unlikely to be seen as an effective way of deploying staff. Special support assistants are now far more likely to be deployed as support staff, with appropriate training and monitoring from senior teaching staff who negotiate the initial placement and may undertake a range of additional tasks related to the promotion of positive attitudes. There are a number of positive outcomes to developing this role for special support assistants. Apart from being able to introduce greater numbers of pupils to integrated placements, more staff can be involved in integration and observation of a wider range of educational practices. This generated ideas for discussion and professional development.

The advantage of the above link schemes is that they can be developed in a collaborative way involving parents and professionals, ensuring that the activities to be undertaken are selected in a way to facilitate positive outcomes and yet still be challenging. A less focused approach to developing links runs the risk of inappropriate matches of pupils to activities resulting in possible breakdown of the scheme with, at best, no development in positive attitudes to people with SLD.

The need for refinement of link schemes in the light of the National Curriculum and Local Management of Special Schools has not prevented schools continuing links over a wide range of curriculum areas throughout the age range (Fletcher-Cambell, 1994). However, greater clarity about the outcomes for individuals may be required. The type of activity chosen is then more likely to depend on the individual needs of each pupil, as identified through the usual range of multiprofessional discussions that should include the pupil and their parents wherever possible.

OUTCOMES OF LINK SCHEMES

The outcomes of link schemes can be grouped into three main areas.

Curriculum

Curriculum opportunities may be extended through sharing resources. A greater range of subject specialist personnel and physical resources may be available in the mainstream school. The special school can contribute by sharing expertise in the field of learning difficulties, possibly suggesting specialist approaches and teaching methods where appropriate. The value of involvement in a mainstream curriculum is not accepted by all. Some (i.e. Jenkinson, 1993) have concluded that it is not possible for pupils with SLD to follow meaningfully a differentiated mainstream curriculum. However, this was not the experience of the schemes described above. Improvements in gross motor skills were seen in pupils attending mainstream PE, developments in language and ability to work within groups were reported for pupils attending mainstream science lessons, as well as the more usually expected developments in socialisation, play and independence skills (Steele and Mitchell, 1992). However, Ware et al. (1992) note that such professional impressions do not always stand up to closer scrutiny, particularly in the area of language development. They observe that there seems to be no advantage, in terms of amount of interaction, for pupils with SLD who are involved in integrated sessions. Ware et al. also note that there seems to be a higher level of response to pupils' language in a segregated setting, which may motivate language use. However, they conclude that the crucial factors seem to be the type and structuring of activities, rather than the presence or absence of mainstream pupils.

For inclusive education to be meaningful, pupils with SLD in mainstream schools should be closely monitored to ensure that they are benefiting and that information on their progress is communicated clearly so that it can inform future planning. This has time and training implications for staff involved in integration support.

Social learning

The possibility of widening opportunities for social learning through contact with mainstream pupils is another significant benefit of a range of link schemes. Mainstream pupils, who represent 'competent peers' can form powerful role models (Beveridge, 1996). Hence pupils from a special school are provided with practical experience of learning a range of social skills that have been taught, assessed and recorded in a more formal and precise way within the special school.

Positive community attitudes

Contact between pupils with SLD and the wider community is clearly vital if the positive attitudes necessary to allow participation in society are to be engendered. This is discussed by McConkey and McCormack (1983). More recently, Helmstetter *et al.* (1994) reported a range of positive attitudes towards pupils with moderate or severe learning difficulties following integration experiences. There seems little reason to believe that acquisition of such positive attitudes should be limited to students; staff and others involved with links may also be affected.

The reader should not be lulled into the comfortable belief that the development of more positive attitudes is an inevitable outcome of the passage of time. A few examples from history may help us remember that positive and negative attitudes have co-existed over time (Stratford and Steele, 1985; Stratford 1989; Steele, 1990).

It is a salutary lesson to consider the prevailing attitudes towards learning difficulties of the ancient Olmec culture, living around the Gulf coast of Mexico between 1500 BC and 300 AD. There is evidence (Milton and Gonzalo, 1974) to show that their carved quartz figures, with many features of people with Down's syndrome, represented individuals who were considered to be god–human hybrids. Whilst this report may seem strange in our modern context, it cannot be considered as an example of negative attitudes towards learning difficulties from the distant past. More recently, the unusually low prevalence of Down's syndrome reported in 1930s' Germany (Doxiades and Portius, 1938) did not reflect some breakthrough in prevention, but the abhorrent way in which the Nazi regime of the time treated such individuals. A better appreciation of the range of attitudes that have been held through history may guard against complacency and should encourage us to continue efforts to maximise the inclusion of people with learning difficulties within our current society.

WORKING TOWARDS INCLUSION

Inclusion as a process

Various schemes at different stages of development have been cited in this chapter. Positive attitudes to integration are noted to be central to successful schemes, yet professionals involved will come across a wide range of attitudes, some clearly less positive than others. The discrepancy between the attitudes and values of experienced professionals committed to inclusion and those of others can be difficult to deal with and may sometimes be discouraging. Therefore it is important to remember that inclusion is a process that occurs over time. The process is characterised by four stages: anxiety, 'charity', acceptance and, finally, true inclusion. Each stage is briefly discussed below.

Anxiety stage

Some anxiety is experienced by most people when a novel or unusual situation arises, the intensity of this anxiety no doubt being proportional to the individual's perception of threat. Inclusion of pupils with learning difficulties may be a novel experience for mainstream staff or pupils. Fears can be allayed to some extent by clear joint planning, effective communication between mainstream and special schools or establishments and particularly by providing evidence of successful projects elsewhere. Where appropriate, pupils can be introduced to the concept of learning difficulties as in the link schemes described earlier. However, whilst specific anxieties must obviously be addressed, it is highly unlikely that anxiety can be completely removed.

Charity stage

At this stage the attitude to pupils with learning disabilities is positive, but can be somewhat oversympathetic. This can lead to a devaluation of the skills and abilities of people with learning difficulties. At this stage interventions tend to centre around providing help, often physical help, to pupils. Behaviour that is usually unacceptable may be excused or ignored by those who are overly sympathetic. However, this stage can represent part of the process towards true inclusion and, provided it is worked through, should not be seen in a negative light. Skilled support is vital to promote progress at this stage as is exemplified by the following situation:

In one mainstream school a weekly unsupported integration scheme was in existence. For the local newspaper, the teacher wrote proudly about 'John' (a 10 year old with SLD) and 'Jane', a mainstream child:

> Suddenly there is a dash for the door, rules forgotten for the moment in Jane's eagerness to greet John. What happens next is so moving, especially to those who have never witnessed this before. Jane assists him with his coat; he responds with an affectionate hug!

Leading him to the table she opens up his lunchbox and pours out his drink, fussing over him like a mother hen! John waits, however, and Jane has gained a special friendship which, hopefully, she will always treasure.

'John' was, in fact, well able to remove his own coat, pour his own drink and open his own lunchbox. Lack of skilled and diplomatic support here prevented the mainstream school from moving to the realisation that 'John' needed to practise these skills for himself. He also was working on learning appropriate greetings. Naturally enough, he was quite happy for someone else to do the work for him!

Acceptance stage

This stage is characterised by a reduction in the amount of attention focused on the pupils with learning difficulties. Care must be taken at this stage to ensure that this reduction in attention is not misinterpreted as a backward step in the move to inclusion. Closer observation will not reveal an increase in negative interactions, as might be expected if the situation was moving towards a breakdown. The pupils with learning difficulties are simply being accepted as part of the group. They will be welcomed when they arrive, but the 'fussing' referred to above will not occur; the novelty of their attendance at the mainstream class has worn off. Expectations from mainstream pupils and staff will gradually become more appropriate as they get to know the individuals concerned. The pupils with learning difficulties will be included in some of the wider activities of the school, although invitations to these activities may be offered through the support staff rather than to the pupil him- or herself.

True inclusion stage

Pupils from the special school will be liked or disliked for their personality rather than their intellectual ability. Whilst pupils with learning difficulties will have developed positive relationships with a number of mainstream peers by this time, it must be remembered that it is not normal for everyone to get on perfectly in school. Hence pupils with learning difficulties will be included in games and social interactions by their friends, who will expect them to act in an appropriate way yet sensitively take account of their difficulties in understanding. Conversely, they will be excluded by those who get on with them less well. Appropriate amounts of responsibility will be given by mainstream peers and staff, and pupils with learning difficulties will be expected to take part in the extra-curricular activities of the school. As Smith and Hilton (1997) note, true inclusion welcomes pupils with special needs into all aspects of the school: the curriculum, the environment, and social life.

FACTORS AFFECTING INTEGRATION LINKS

Having discussed examples of links, their potential outcomes and the process involved in the move towards inclusion, it is useful to consider six factors that can also influence the successful establishment of links. All six factors apply to links between special and mainstream schools, but several of them also apply to business, community and professional links.

Early integration

Many authors (e.g. Steele and Mitchell, 1992; Farrell, 1997) have noted improved chances of successful inclusion where children join their mainstream peers at as young an age as possible. This may be due to younger mainstream pupils having fewer preconceptions of people with learning difficulties than older pupils.

Correct age group

Ideally, pupils should join their correct chronological age group; certainly they should not be more than a year behind. Whilst working outside these age recommendations may seem acceptable during the early years, it can lead to inappropriate social skills and behaviours. Clearly, as the pupil gets older, inappropriate behaviour presents an increasingly obvious problem and can severely disadvantage a teenager with learning difficulties in a range of social settings.

Ability

More able pupils with learning difficulties who do not present challenging behaviours are reported to have better chances of successful integration (e.g. Farrell, 1997). Personal experience has shown practitioners to take this viewpoint for granted, with attitudes towards pupils with more profound learning difficulties or emotional problems being less positive (Moberg, 1997).

Limited numbers

Numbers of special school pupils joining a class should be limited to two or three; this appears to decrease the likelihood of these pupils forming an isolated group within the class. In their American study, Ellis *et al.* (1996) found that social interactions between mainstream pupils and those with moderate or severe learning difficulties in PE classes were much improved when smaller numbers of pupils with learning difficulties were involved. When larger numbers (a class of ten) attended, they tended to retain their group identity and engaged in far less social interactions.

Shared participation

The activities that are chosen should allow some degree of shared participation and promote ability rather than disability. The importance of shared activities, particularly working towards shared goals, was identified in early work on integration (e.g. Rynders 1980). McConkey and McCormack (1983) also make many practical suggestions about shared activities that are still relevant to those developing integrated activities today.

Skilled support

Personal experience has shown that there are rare individuals who are naturally able to work successfully alongside mainstream teachers, adapting teaching to pupils' needs using appropriate methods as well as balancing their structured intervention with facilitating broader integration within the class group. However, training and professional supervision are increasingly important both for professionals whose skills do not yet match those above and as encouragement to the more skilled supporter. Pupils must be provided with skilled support, so that interactions can be promoted and facilitated throughout the range of activities. For example, support staff should not sit next to the pupils with learning difficulties all the time. This approach has been shown to be a barrier to interactions (Lincoln *et al.*, 1992) and certainly seems more likely to emphasise disability than ability. Skilled support requires much more. Farrell (1997) provides a detailed discussion of this topic.

The notion that systematic and structured teaching methods are important factors in successful integration is not without its critics. Ainscow (1997) questions the appropriateness of simply transferring special school teaching methods, particularly the emphasis on individual planning, to the mainstream setting. He is apprehensive that such an approach may distract from the need to emphasise concern for, and engagement with, the whole class. However, as is noted above, the skilled supporter must be sensitive to these issues and will facilitate the conditions that allow pupils to interact and make a positive contribution to the tasks set.

Of course, the need for skilled support will be well known to those promoting inclusive practices. Examples of this are not difficult to find. In one situation a mainstream teacher had asked a pupil with SLD to attend without support. Some time later, a video was made that included this unsupported situation. It was interesting to note that interactions between the pupil with learning difficulties and mainstream peers in the unsupported situation were less frequent or lengthy than in supported situations, indicating that skilled support may be important in facilitating interactions and could serve as a model for initial interactions and appropriate behaviour expectations.

CONCLUSION

At this point the reader may be wondering: 'Is this author for or against placing pupils within special schools?' I am neither for nor against such placements *per se*. I stand for providing the very best learning environment and developing pupils' ability to lead as happy and independent a life as possible. Of course, the vast range of pupils with learning difficulties should be educated in their local mainstream schools. Furthermore, help and support should be provided to ensure this is a beneficial and positive experience. However, there will be a number of pupils whose needs realistically cannot be met in this way at a particular place or time. Such pupils often may have more severe or profound learning difficulties or more extreme behavioural difficulties, and will benefit from some separate specialist input. What is vital is that where special schools do exist they should not be isolated from their local community. Some of the links outlined in this chapter should be achievable by the vast majority of such schools. A special school placement can and should represent a positive option for a specialist facility which, in specific individual circumstances, is best able to provide the pupil with improved prospects for educational development and consequent true inclusion. It must be acknowledged that the educational placement of pupils with special needs is not a simple matter and the answers will vary depending on people, places and time.

REFERENCES

Ainscow, M. (1997) 'Towards inclusive schooling', *British Journal of Special Education* 24(1): 3–6.

Beveridge, S. (1996) 'Experiences of an integration link scheme: the perspectives of pupils with severe learning difficulties and their mainstream peers', *British Journal of Learning Disabilities* 24(1): 9–19.

Blunkett, D. (1997) 'We need business to help us raise standards', *Times Educational Supplement* 13 June: 3.

DfEE (1997) 'Better Choices', *Careers Education and Guidance for Young People with Learning Difficulties and/or Disabilities*, London: DfEE.

Doxiades, L. and Portius, W. (1938) 'Zur Ätiologie des Mongolismus unter beson-
    derer Berücksichtigung der Sippenbefunde', *Zeitschrift für Konstruktiv Lehre* 21:
    384–446.
Ellis, D. N., Wright, T. and Cronis, T. G. (1996) 'A description of the instructional
    and social interactions of students with mental retardation in regular physical
    education settings', *Education and Training in Mental Retardation & Developmental
    Disabilities* 31(3): 235–42.
Farrell, P. (1997) 'The integration of children with severe learning difficulties; a
    review of recent literature', *Journal of Applied Research in Intellectual Disabilities*
    10(1): 1–14.
Fletcher-Cambell, F. (1994) *Still Joining Forces?*, Slough: NFER.
Golden, S. and Sims, D. (1997) *Review of Industrial Mentoring in Schools*, Slough:
    NFER.
Helmstetter, E., Peck, C. A. and Giangreco, M. F. (1994) 'Outcomes of interactions
    with peers with moderate or severe disabilities: a state-wide survey of high school
    students', *Journal of the Association for Persons with Severe Handicaps* 19(4): 263–76.
Information Exchange (1995) 'Two way communication', *Information Exchange* 4:
    16–17.
Jenkinson, J. C. (1993) 'Integration of students with severe and multiple learning
    difficulties', *European Journal of Special Needs Education* 8(3): 320–35.
Johnson, D. W. and Johnson, R. T. (1986) 'Classroom learning structure and atti-
    tudes toward handicapped students in mainstream settings: a theoretical model
    and research', in R. L. Jones (ed.) *Attitudes and Attitude Change in Special Educa-
    tion: Theory and Practice*, Reston, VA: The Council for Exceptional Children.
Jowett, S., Hegarty, S. and Moses, D. (1988) *Joining Forces: a Study of Links Between
    Ordinary and Special Schools*, Windsor: NFER-Nelson.
Lincoln, J., Batty, J., Townsend, R. and Collins, M. (1992) 'Working for the greater
    inclusion of children with severe learning difficulties in mainstream secondary
    schools', *Educational and Child Psychology* 9(1): 145–51.
McConkey, R. and McCormack, B. (1983) *Breaking Barriers. Educating People about
    Disability*, London: Souvenir Press.
Milton, G. and Gonzalo, R. (1974) 'Jaguar cult – Down's syndrome – Were-jaguar',
    Expedition 16(4): 33–7.
Moberg, S. (1997) 'Inclusive services as perceived by prospective special education
    teachers in Estonia, Finland and the United States', *International Journal of Reha-
    bilitation Research* 21(1): 29–40.
Rynders, J. (1980) 'Producing positive interactions among Down's syndrome and
    non-handicapped teenagers through co-operative goal structuring', *Journal of
    Mental Deficiency Research* 85: 268–74.
Smith, J. D. and Hilton, A. (1997) 'The preparation and training of the educational
    community for the inclusion of students with developmental disabilities', *Educa-
    tion and Training in Mental Retardation & Developmental Disabilities* 32(1): 3–10.
Steele, J. (1985) 'Report of an integration exercise at William Rhodes School',
    Unpublished professional report.
Steele, J. (1990) 'Investigation into the prevalence of Down's syndrome', PhD
    thesis, University of Nottingham.
Steele, J. and Mitchell, D. (1992) 'Special links with mainstream', *Special Children*
    55: 14–16.

Stratford, B. (1989) *Down's Syndrome. Past, Present and Future*, London: Penguin Books.

Stratford, B. and Steele, J. (1985) 'Incidence and prevalence of Down's syndrome – a discussion and report', *Journal of Mental Deficiency Research* 29: 95–107.

TES (1997) 'Business links', *Times Educational Supplement* 13 June.

Turner, A. (1996) 'Cromwell and two trees: an integration project involving secondary aged students with severe learning difficulties and mainstream peers', *SLD Experience* 14: 11.

Ware, J., Sharman, M., O'Connor, S. and Anderson, M. (1992) 'Interactions between pupils with severe learning difficulties and their mainstream peers', *British Journal of Special Education* 19(4): 153–8.

Chapter 15

Multidisciplinary teamwork

Penny Lacey

Through an in-depth case study of one special school Penny Lacey looks at aspects of collaborative work and suggests strategies to promote inclusive practice.

Many people are involved, and have parts to play, in the care and education of children with learning difficulties: teachers, support assistants, special educational needs co-ordinators, therapists, learning and psychological services staff, members of the medical profession and parents. Attempts to integrate their work may lead to problems unless staff in schools and centres (and families) are actively encouraged to work together in multidisciplinary teams and to share their knowledge and expertise (Davie, 1993). The relevant literature indicates that there are no easy solutions to the problems of integrating skills and that strategies must be devised to support and motivate individuals responsible for managing and providing services (Orelove and Sobsey, 1996; Gregory, 1989; Lacey and Lomas, 1993).

Pupils with learning difficulties are educated in a variety of different settings and the extent to which they are included in mainstream education will vary according to the needs of individual pupils and the amount of support they receive from both internal and external services. It could be argued that, owing to the larger numbers of pupils in any segregated setting, services will operate more effectively and efficiently than in an inclusive provision but there is no evidence to suggest that this is so. Collaborative multidisciplinary teamwork is difficult to achieve whatever the setting (Davie, 1993; Orelove and Sobsey, 1996).

As part of a research study, staff in both mainstream and special schools were asked about their teamwork difficulties. They identified a lack of time, staff shortages, large caseloads and an inflexible curriculum as major problems, to which, after further probing, they added that difficulties can arise over incompatible service priorities, disagreements over resources, an inaccurate definition of roles, and poor communications (Lacey, 1997).

The central part of this chapter is a study of multidisciplinary teamwork in a special school where many of the team members are in daily contact with each other. The study not only illuminates procedures in that school, but also helps to inform practice in other settings. The implications for inclusive practice will be explored at the end of each section.

THE STUDY

An ethnographic study was carried out over four years, mainly in one special school for children with multiple disabilities, but supported with evidence from six other sites. The school explored in this chapter was given the pseudonym Pear Tree School. There are approximately 100 children on roll, all of whom have physical disabilities, and most have a range of learning difficulties. The staff include teachers, assistants and therapists.

Data for the study was collected through participant and non-participant observations and unstructured interviews, some of which focused on specific aspects of multidisciplinary teamwork. Transitions into and out of school and the implications of the Code of Practice were considered in detail, and participants were encouraged to set their own agendas and to talk about their perceptions. Interviews were transcribed and a field diary, designed to record perceptions of the problems and possibilities faced by teachers and therapists working together on a daily basis, was used for observations. The data was analysed using qualitative techniques, ranging from simple categorisation to metaphorical analysis and diagrammatic relationships (Miles and Huberman, 1994; Hammersley and Atkinson, 1995; Dey, 1993).

MULTIDISCIPLINARY TEAMWORK AT PEAR TREE SCHOOL

The fourteen teachers, seventeen classroom assistants, seven therapists and two therapy assistants at Pear Tree School work together in a variety of ways. Close relationships between education and health staff, leading to the sharing of knowledge and expertise, are a distinctive feature of the nursery stage, during which the children's abilities and disabilities are assessed and individual programmes jointly devised. Several examples are given below.

Example 1

Sarah was being assessed for access to the computer through a switching system. The occupational therapist and speech and language therapist worked together after consulting the class teacher about a suitable computer program for assessment purposes. The two therapists worked for over an hour trying a variety of positions and switches before they arrived at one that was possible for Sarah. They met both the physiotherapist and the class teacher after the session to share their findings.

Although there is joint work at all stages of the children's schooling, there is generally more collaboration at Pear Tree School in the early years than in the secondary department. There is a conscious reduction in therapy in the upper school, mainly because the positioning and physical management which have been established can be continued with only minor adjustments. This is a situation which will change in the future as children with degenerative and other multiple disabilities move up the school.

Although collaboration, manifested in shared and joint work, has been suggested as a desirable way in which teachers and therapists can work together, it is by no means the only way.

Example 2

In the senior department, Paul, who has Duchenne muscular dystrophy, needs to be placed in a standing frame for part of every day. After training classroom staff to place Paul in his frame, the physiotherapist is only responsible for occasional monitoring. Paul goes to the physiotherapy department for his daily exercises, where, privately, he works to maintain his mobility.

Example 3

When pupils leave Pear Tree School, the County Disability Officer becomes involved in their transition to adult life. Before this she does not meet the pupils and has no input into their care or education, although she is available for consultation and liaison, primarily to give the school details of the services and facilities available to leavers.

Relationships between multidisciplinary team members can be daily, weekly or only occasionally, as in the case of the Disability Officer. However, at the point of contact, it is important for them to share their skills and knowledge. When the Disability Officer is working with individual pupils and their families, she is sharing her expertise and making joint decisions with other members of the team. When she has completed this work, she moves on.

Several other services are likely to be called upon from time to time to contribute to the work of the team, for example medical staff, therapists, educationalists, psychologists, social workers and technicians. Some may work directly with individual children; others in an advisory capacity. It is, however, important that, at the point of contact, a collaborative mode of working is employed, as individuals working in isolation can easily undermine the process.

COLLABORATION AT PEAR TREE SCHOOL

The following list focuses on the positive aspects of the collaborative work at Pear Tree, which may imply that the school is a shining example of excellent practice, a claim that none of the staff would wish to make. Later in the chapter some of the problems that they had to face have been addressed.

The blurring of roles: Although teachers and therapists may have distinct roles, some can be shared. For example, although an occupational therapist is a specialist in dressing and undressing, anyone who works with children in school or at home is aware of their levels of achievement and can help them to practise these particular skills as part of their day-to-day activities.

The joint planning of objectives: At annual multidisciplinary teamwork meetings, teachers and therapists jointly decide on objectives for each child. However, it is also possible for amendments to be made informally and more frequently.

Concentrated input in the early years: The close collaboration between therapists and teachers, established at the nursery stage, continues throughout the infant stage, but begins to change as programmes are developed and routines, for positioning and the use of equipment, are established. Therapists then take on a monitoring role, although if a child undergoes an operation, intensive therapy may be needed.

Staff observing each other at work: As therapists work mainly in classrooms, they are able not only to pass on their skills to other staff, but also to develop additional skills.

Joint training: In addition to the opportunities for within-classroom training, there are also timetabled sessions for therapists and teachers to train each other or to be trained together.

Intensive work with one child: If necessary, several members of a team can collaborate on solving the problems of individual children, for example in devising an augmentative communication system.

Close physical locality: At Pear Tree School, the therapists are all based at the school even if they have an additional community caseload. Thus it is relatively easy for teachers and therapists to communicate with each other, and meetings can be quickly arranged.

Most of the work is undertaken in the classroom: Although traditionally therapists withdraw children and work with them in isolation, at Pear Tree School (particularly in the primary department) most of the work is undertaken in the classroom, as education and therapy are regarded as interdependent.

Joint interviews of new families: When children are about to be admitted to the school, parents attend a joint meeting with teachers and therapists in order to reduce unnecessary repetition of information.

The management's active support of teamwork: The head teacher supports teachers and therapists as they work together. For example, he arranges cover for meetings.

Senior staff responsible for the co-ordination of multidisciplinary teamwork: One of the senior posts contains specific reference to:

- the encouragement of multidisciplinary involvement
- liaison with schools and external agencies.

Thus one senior member of staff is responsible for the systems and processes designed to encourage teachers and therapists to work together.

The commitment of the co-ordinator and of the majority of other staff: The majority of staff at the school, teachers, therapists and assistants, are committed to the policy of collaborative work as a means of meeting the needs of the children.

A *willingness to share:* There is very little evidence of professional boundary guarding. Individuals are willing to share their expertise with colleagues wherever possible.

Implications for inclusive practice

All the above thirteen points have relevance for promoting inclusive practice. The integration of education and care, and the sharing of information and skills, are vital ingredients in collaboration wherever it is practised. It is particularly important to facilitate these approaches in the early years of schooling, when needs are being recognised and programmes devised. Management systems which support collaboration, such as annual multidisciplinary team meetings, and a senior member of staff with responsibility for multidisciplinary teamwork, are essential in inclusive schools. They contribute considerably to raising the profile of both the needs of pupils with learning difficulties and the significance of a collaborative approach.

CHALLENGES TO COLLABORATION AT PEAR TREE SCHOOL

Although there is the potential for collaborative teamwork at any school, there are difficulties and compromises need to be reached. Examples from Pear Tree are given below.

Management systems

There are fundamental differences between the management systems of education, health and social services which, at school level, can result in communication problems. At Pear Tree School two management systems run side by side, one for teachers and support staff and another for therapists and therapy assistants. The head teacher is responsible for all that goes on in the school, including the therapy, although this is not total responsibility as he has no direct lines of management with the therapists. All communication with them is dependent upon goodwill. Therapists operate completely independently from the school management system, although there are very strong links to ensure that, for example, therapy is timetabled in sympathy with individual children's curricula. The head teacher is not consulted at service level concerning the number of therapists, nor the actual people involved. Difficulties may arise in multidisciplinary teams not only as a result of different management systems but also owing to differences in thinking and practice. Teachers are expected to remain in the classroom (engaged exclusively with pupils) whereas therapists use an appointments system which gives them flexibility and enables them to move from class to class. These differences in practice can result in misunderstandings if therapists interrupt lessons and there is a lack of time to exchange information.

A multiplicity of teams

Another difficulty at Pear Tree School is caused by the large number of different teams to which all staff are expected to contribute. This is a particular problem for the therapists and can be illustrated by the difficulties experienced by a physiotherapist who is a superintendent within her Trust and a member of at least five different teams. She also has an advisory role within the school and the wider community. This situation leads inevitably to conflicts of loyalty within the various teams and difficulties in the equitable apportioning of time.

Time

Everyone interviewed, as part of the research, stressed the challenge of managing time within multidisciplinary teams. An analysis of informants' responses revealed a strong metaphorical language, relating time to games of power, to gambling or to the criminal world. For example, the speech and language therapist talked of 'this magic day' when the nursery teacher was given time to talk to her. She went on to say that the teacher then 'lost it' (meaning the time to talk). It was as if time had taken on a life of itself, leaving people powerless in the hands of chance.

The feeling of unacceptable time pressures is particularly intense at present. There have been many recent changes in special education as well as in therapy. For example, therapy caseloads have increased dramatically, forcing therapists to devise new ways of working which leave little time for working with individual children. Working practices have also been affected by the development of a consultancy model, in which therapists work with staff rather than with individual children. Although this model can be said to have been developed as an expedient in times of declining resources, there is actually much to recommend it, as it contributes to effective collaborative teamwork.

Example 4

The speech and language therapist at Pear Tree School spent a considerable amount of time working alongside classroom staff, exchanging skills and developing understanding. Together they wrote integrated programmes in order that, in her absence, the classroom staff could carry out some of the required speech and language therapy.

In addition to her work at Pear Tree School, the speech and language therapist has a managerial role across the Trust. During one term, her management duties prevented her from spending much time at the school and, as a consequence, she adopted a monitoring role and classroom staff continued the jointly written programmes.

It is easy for staff to resent the loss of a speech and language therapist, but in this case, previous training and shared work enabled them to continue the therapy in her absence.

Collaborative teams

Generally, the move from individual and unconnected care and education towards collaborative teamwork has involved considerable changes in ways of working. Collaborative teams are built on flatter structures than traditional hierarchical management systems. At their most effective, all members of the team feel that they have equal voices, although their roles are likely to be different (Drucker, 1974).

Katzenbach and Smith (1993) suggest that *real* teams can be identified by the ability of their members to take risks, to use conflict positively, to trust each other and to work interdependently, using mutual accountability to evaluate their practice. Everyone has a role and is, in fact, a co-manager because there is little distinction between workers and managers. This has implications for the way in which such teams are run, and most importantly, how they are led. Leadership in collaborative teams is not hierarchical and does not rely upon dominance but involves the provision of direction and co-ordination of the work. Good team leaders enthuse about their work, lead by example, trust members, feel personally responsible for resources, are active in setting a direction and accept the risks of leadership (Adair, 1983; 1984; 1986). Adair is clear about the importance of a good leader to an effective team:

Teamwork is no accident, it is the by-product of good leadership.

(p.125)

Leaderless teams

Despite the overall leadership of the school through the head teacher, class-room multidisciplinary teams at Pear Tree School do not have formal leaders. Some teams have enabled leaders to develop but these are unofficial and largely untutored. If Adair is right concerning the fundamental impor-tance of good leaders to effective teams, then leaderless multidisciplinary teams in special education are always likely to run into difficulties. There is no tradition of appointing leaders and all members are expected to work through goodwill and a commitment to collaboration. Many such teams do function well, but it is naïve to expect this to happen with neither a leader nor training.

Whilst seeking evidence of leadership at Pear Tree School, the effective-ness of the nursery class teacher was monitored. She was also a member of the senior management team with responsibility for multidisciplinary team-work. Although she had seniority within the school, she was not officially appointed as a leader of the nursery multidisciplinary team, which consisted of a teacher, a nursery nurse, an intervenor (for one child who is deaf–blind), a physiotherapist, an occupational therapist, a speech and language therapist and a speech and language therapy assistant.

Example 5

Pam describes her management style as 'up-front' by which she means that she discusses her ideas, and those of others, in a direct manner. Team members move in and out of the class freely and opinions are expressed openly. Communication is informal as team members work alongside each other. Pam believes that 'teamwork is a philosophy' and demonstrates this in the way in which she works jointly with colleagues. She trusts members to work inde-pendently and encourages them to lead when their specialisms are needed.

Although Pam is undertaking many of the duties of team leadership identified by the literature, a more formal recognition of the role would enable her to extend her responsibilities to include the initiation of teamwork training, the setting of performance targets and the devising of an evaluation system.

Implications for promoting inclusive practice

All the challenges faced by those at Pear Tree School can be mirrored in mainstream schools. Differences in management systems, cultures and working practices can present almost insurmountable barriers to effective collaboration. Vocabulary can be particularly divisive, and incomprehensible jargon has the potential to ruin promising relationships.

The combination of team members working in many other teams and the pressures of time is universal across segregated and inclusive schools. Such problems can lead to particular difficulties in large secondary schools where pupils meet many different teachers and visiting professionals with heavy caseloads in other schools. Poor understanding of the meaning of teamwork and the lack of formal team leaders can also be found in mainstream schools, but both need to be addressed if collaboration is to flourish.

STRATEGIES FOR ENCOURAGING EFFECTIVE COLLABORATIVE TEAMWORK

This chapter will be concluded with suggestions on ways of supporting the multidisciplinary teamwork found in special schools, based on some of the successes and challenges evident at Pear Tree School. The suggestions will also be related to the situations likely to be found in mainstream schools.

Senior management teams

From the case study, it can be inferred that giving responsibility for multi-disciplinary teamwork to a senior member of staff is important, as it then becomes part of his or her responsibility to create and maintain the systems which encourage effective teamwork. He or she can be responsible for liaison with services, for organising meetings, for negotiating non-contact time, and for ensuring that multidisciplinary teamwork is monitored and evaluated.

Senior management team support can also be seen as essential to the success of multidisciplinary teamwork and, as collaboration requires a change in working practices, it is very difficult to achieve without assistance from decision makers. Individuals can and do work together with little management support, but with clear, well-thought-out systems and personal encouragement, a whole school approach can be accomplished.

If the presence of two management systems in one school is to be effective, it may be helpful to include a therapist (in a rotating post, involving all therapists) on the senior management team (SMT). Such an appointment would encourage fuller communication between health and education at school level.

Creating collaborative teams

To collaborate, it appears to be essential for team members to share aims, information, knowledge and skills, and to support and trust each other in their work as they may need to work jointly on specific aspects of meeting pupil needs. Team structures should ensure not only that every member's contribution is valued, but that each can take on several roles within the team. For example, in a partnership between a class teacher and a support assistant in an inclusive classroom, the assistant may need to work not only with pupils with learning difficulties, but also with the most able pupils, in order that the teacher can concentrate on the less able.

Time flexibility

If collaborative teams are to carry out their work and share information, it appears that time will need to be viewed more flexibly. Teachers who have no non-contact time cannot easily meet multidisciplinary team members who are only available in class time and both need to reallocate their time. For example, if team members are able to visit a classroom for several days at a time, instead of once a week for twenty minutes, they will have the opportunities to assess children's needs, to share information with classroom staff, to write joint programmes and to share some of their expertise. Cover will need to be provided for meetings during lessons and it may be necessary to continue after school hours, requiring compromises and a reallocation of time.

'Clustering time' could also be effective for working with support teachers in inclusive schools as they could then target specific classes for extended periods. The ensuing work can then be monitored until the next allocation of support teacher time.

Appointing and training leaders

It is clear from the research that effective teams need leaders, and therefore that it would be helpful for multidisciplinary teams to appoint or elect their own (possibly rotating) leaders. There is a valid argument for appointing class teachers or pastoral tutors as leaders as they are in daily contact with pupils, but they will require some training.

Investment

Working collaboratively cannot be achieved instantly. It requires investment of time and resources for pay-off in the future. Team members require time to understand each other's roles and skills and to learn how to work together. Teams of people who know each other well, trust each other and share what they can do are seen to be successful (Katzenbach and Smith, 1993) and this closeness cannot be achieved without working, meeting and talking together.

CONCLUSION

The ethnographic study used to underpin this chapter has provided examples of good practice in collaborative teamwork as well as the foundations to discuss possible improvements. Although an in-depth study of only one school should be treated with caution, the suggestions for ways in which organisations view their teamwork practices may be of value in other circumstances.

From the research, it would appear that there are two prerequisites when forming and running a collaborative, multidisciplinary team:

- collaborative teams need time to talk;
- a collaborative team requires investment.

It was found that almost all staff in the schools studied were committed to teamwork as a way of meeting the needs of the children in their care, but that they lacked a supportive management system. They were frustrated by inflexible time management, a lack of training, leaderless teams and a general misunderstanding of teamwork. Although the central case study concentrates on a segregated special school, it has afforded the opportunity to consider the practice of multidisciplinary teamwork, wherever that might take place. There is fear that moving towards inclusive schooling for all pupils will adversely affect the good relationships built up between teachers and therapists in special schools. However, although the best special schools have developed excellent collaborative partnerships, there are many which do not work effectively, as they tend to be overwhelmed by the challenges facing them. It is also important to recognise that the best practices can be transferred to mainstream schools. In doing so, however, previous customs will have to change and time and resources will need to be invested.

REFERENCES

Adair, J. (1983) *Effective Leadership*, London: Pan Books.

Adair, J. (1984) *The Skills of Leadership,* Aldershot: Gower Press.

Adair, J. (1986) *Effective Teambuilding*, London: Pan Books.

Davie, R. (1993) 'Implementing Warnock's multi-professional approach', in J. Visser and G. Upton (eds) *Special Education in Britain after Warnock*, London: David Fulton.

Dey, I. (1993) *Qualitative Data Analysis*, London: Routledge.

Drucker, P. (1974) *Management: Tasks, Responsibilities, Practices*, Oxford: Butterworth–Heinemann.

Gregory, E. (1989) 'Issues in multi-professional co-operation', in R. Evans (ed.) *Special Educational Needs: Policy and Practice*, Oxford: Blackwell/ NARE.

Hammersley, M. and Atkinson, P. (1995) *Ethnography: Principles and Practice*, 2nd edition, London: Tavistock.

Katzenbach, J. and Smith, D. (1993) *The Wisdom of Teams*, New York: Harper Business.

Lacey, P (1997) 'Multidisciplinary teamwork in special education: practice and training', PhD thesis, University of Birmingham.

Lacey, P. and Lomas, J. (1993) *Support Services and the Curriculum: a Practical Guide to Collaboration*, London: David Fulton.

Miles, M. and Huberman, M. (1994) *Qualitative Data Analysis*, London: Sage.

Orelove, F. and Sobsey, D. (1996) *Educating Children with Multiple Disabilities: a Transdisciplinary Approach*, 3rd edition, Baltimore, MD: Paul Brookes.

Part IV

Towards a more inclusive way of life

Planned transition from education to employment for young people with severe learning difficulties

Caroline Broomhead

In this chapter Caroline Broomhead describes a three-year project which looked at the means by which students with severe learning difficulties could be prepared for post-school inclusion in the workplace.

> How sad to hear a young man of 19, in answer to the question 'Where would you like to work?', say: 'My dad's going to look after me.'

For some time it has been apparent that vocational opportunities for young people with severe learning difficulties are extremely limited. There is a need to actively extend the range of opportunities provided to pupils and to prepare young people with learning difficulties for the choices and challenges that could be available to them at 19 years of age. Until such time as major changes in post-school provision are made, the move towards a more inclusive society will remain little more than a future aspiration.

Recent years have seen a major shift in attitudes, perceptions and expectations. The 1970s saw the start of a focus on the rights of people with learning difficulties to engage in productive work (UN, 1971). At the same time integration into mainstream education was seen by Warnock (DES, 1978) as a natural extension of the comprehensive ideal of equality of opportunity for all pupils, with a new focus upon learning together. Being categorised out of 'normal' education often results in those who receive 'special' education being destined for a 'special' career and lifestyle in terms of their employability and self-sufficiency. They are consequently denied occupational success and social mobility (Tomlinson, 1982).

As Whelan and Speake (1981) stated, 'a job is not everything in life, but in our society it is an important part of being human'. It is regarded as part of human nature to work. People with severe learning difficulties have traditionally been regarded as dependent members of a society in which employment is seen as the main source of income, status and social relations, and an integral part of our lives. It influences the range of experiences we have, even the range and nature of our friendships and other relationships. Employment provides a structural framework to our lives and helps us to value our leisure time, to measure ourselves against others, and to learn accepted behaviours in the workplace. It is a myth to suggest that people with severe learning difficulties want a life of leisure; evidence shows that many people who are currently occupied in adult training centres want jobs (Kings Fund, 1984).

Preparation for employment starts in childhood when occupational roles are acted out and when families discuss 'what do you want to be when you grow up?' The expectation within western society is that a person will work. An individual's expectations of him- or herself are developed in the context of family and society expectations. The family role in developing self-image, in relation to employment or 'economic dependence', is crucial. By depriving people of the right to employment, we are depriving them of much more.

Traditionally, post-school opportunities for people with severe learning difficulties were limited, with attendance at an Adult Training Centre (ATC) providing a typical placement, though in extreme instances there was little option other than to stay at home. Young adults with learning difficulties were mostly excluded from the labour market as it was felt that employers demanded a workforce which could function independently with minimal support and guidance (Kings Fund, 1984). Research by Todd et al. (1991) into the destinations of 118 people with severe disabilities who were aged between 16 and 24 found that there was a high incidence of vocational inactivity for this group. The majority transferred from school into segregated day centres, and only a few entered the employment market, although this remained an ambition for many and they expressed dissatisfaction with the very limited options available. However, Corrie (1985) had earlier warned that the declining job market could lead to a belief that disabled young people should not expect to obtain employment and should seek a life outside economic activity.

A variety of local and national schemes were set up during the 1980s with an aim of promoting supported and integrated employment. Unemployment amongst people with severe learning difficulties was 95 per cent, compared with an overall national rate of 13.4 per cent (Kings Fund, 1985). Research conducted at this time concluded that people with severe learning difficulties valued their jobs and wanted to work. Furthermore, it was demonstrated that this group can successfully enter open employment and become reliable and efficient employees (Kroese et al., 1990), particularly when they receive appropriate support (Griffiths, 1994). The Kings Fund Centre (1985) was impressed by the ability of people with severe learning difficulties to remain cheerful and positive despite all the disadvantages and the difficulties which they had been forced to overcome.

The 1980s may be seen as a decade of innovation for disabled people. The Department of Employment (1990) referred to 'major progress' having been made in helping disabled people to find employment and training alongside non-disabled people. The accuracy of such a statement is open to challenge. A person's employability has been the subject of national research involving the Further Education Unit (FEU), and others (Griffiths, 1988). The 'Employability Package' which was developed at this time identified those qualities seen as desirable in potential employees, such as reliability, conscientiousness and punctuality. Barriers to employment were also identified, such as prejudice, or a lack of an adequate understanding of what work is about. Support from the family and commitment to the concept of work was recognised as a major factor in the success or failure of a young person at work. The UK went into the 1990s with the knowledge that people with severe learning difficulties can, and want to, contribute to the economy through meaningful employment. Despite this, unemployment is currently two and a half times greater for people with disabilities than it is for those without (Tomlinson Committee, 1996). Inclusion clearly remains a distant target.

All the moves towards integrated employment which were seen as a success of the 1980s and 1990s must be seen in the light of the national policy of providing care and support to help people achieve independence and to live in their local community. It is recognised that supporting people in employment must also have a full regard for the role which they are able to play within the local community. Younger people with learning difficulties need help in establishing relationships, securing employment and achieving an active role in society alongside their peers (Lavendar, 1988). Schools clearly have a major role to play in preparing their pupils for such post-school expectations. Peckham, in Whelan and Speake (1981), recommended that schools should take a more active role in preparing young people for employment. He identified job sampling, job search skills, and interview skills as activities in which schools should engage their pupils.

Traditionally the function of special schools has been seen by many as one of preparing young people for life in an ATC, and this inevitably limited teacher expectations with regards to the employability of their pupils (Kings Fund, 1984). Schools are seen as providing the starting point for transition to adult life, which is made up of a number of small stages over a period of time. It is a mistake to view such transition as being manageable through one single event (Griffiths, 1994). The school curriculum must recognise the need to begin preparation for post-school life at an early stage. There has been justifiable criticism of the special school curriculum by Tomlinson (1982) and others. Not least amongst the perceived shortcomings are the assumptions which seem to be built into curriculum design that students with moderate learning difficulties should be prepared for employment, whilst those with severe learning difficulties receive training in social skills.

Corbett and Barton (1992) posed the question of who decides what is 'appropriate' social behaviour. They were critical of the fact that the personal lives and feelings of people with learning difficulties were open to public scrutiny in a way which would not be tolerated when addressing the needs of people without learning difficulties. The introduction of the National Curriculum (DES, 1988) enshrined in law the entitlement of pupils with learning difficulties to a curriculum and its associated assessment which is broadly in line with that provided to their able peers. It was further accepted that this was to be seen within the context of a wider curriculum which would address individual needs. For students aged 16 to 19 years, there is a recognised need for a focus on preparation for adult life.

With a renewed focus upon curriculum priorities, practitioners became involved in the national debate about developing a vocational purpose in the 14 to 19 curriculum for all students. It was suggested that such a curriculum could enable students to develop generic skills such as team working, communication and the appreciation of technology (NCC, 1993). Griffiths (1988) recommended that, as professionals, we need to challenge reduced expectations of the contribution disabled people make to our community. It was suggested that a change in expectations can bring about new ideas and opportunities. The view was held that the school curriculum should, through planned interaction with non-disabled peers, both prepare young people for work and enable them to develop the skills to live independently in the local community (Griffiths, 1994). Of course it is not only the special schools that have segregated young people with severe learning difficulties from their non-disabled peers as well as from the 'ordinary' curriculum. Colleges of further education have perpetuated that exclusion. There was criticism of the cost, content and ultimate goals of 'special' college courses with no clear progression routes planned. The money could be better used to finance individuals with disabilities doing what they would rather do – supporting them in paid jobs, in real leisure activities, and in real training for an ordinary life, and all in appropriate settings (Brandon, 1991).

A number of colleges did address the issue of including vocational preparation in their courses for students with severe learning difficulties. In Tyneside, a three-year course was offered which aimed to develop personal competence. From there students joined an 'Education to Work' programme which further developed their vocational skills and arranged placements in work settings (FEU, 1988). An integral aspect of the transition curriculum must be to support young people by enabling them to sample a range of vocational areas before committing themselves to real employment (Griffiths, 1994). It was clearly recommended (Griffiths, 1988) that 'school and post-school educational experience must be based on the assumption that employment is the aim for all young people', a view supported by the Tomlinson Committee (1996).

The Further and Higher Education Act of 1992 was regarded as a 'landmark' in the development of education policy for people with learning difficulties. It placed them fully within the scope of further education in the way that the 1981 and 1988 Education Acts did for school age pupils. It emphasises the need for planned transition from school to adult status. Young adults with severe learning difficulties could have difficulty achieving this if they do not have access to an appropriate range of enabling learning experiences (Griffiths, 1994). As the Tomlinson Report (1996, p. 7) states:

> students with learning difficulties should be helped towards adult status. This requires the achievement of autonomy and a positive self image realistically grounded in the capacity to live as independently as possible and to contribute both to the economy and the community.

Employers' understanding of the learning difficulties label is not always accurate and often communicates negative images. Terms such as 'mental handicap' which persist in use not only are derogatory, but present to potential employers a negative stereotyped image. Several concepts can be seen to underlie employers' perceptions of their employees. People with severe disabilities are expected to perform better than their non-disabled counterparts in job satisfaction, genuineness, grafting and loyalty, but less well on productive capacity, supervision and risk, and learning capacity (Harrison, 1990). Employers strongly endorse the use and value of work experience.

The role of parents during transition and thereafter is crucial. Transition is a difficult time for young people with disabilities, but is equally difficult for their families. They can experience anxiety, isolation, and lack of control of the situation. Professionals, such as teachers, social workers and careers officers, are aware of the need to involve families in joint planning and decision making long before the school leaving date and on from there through the transition into adulthood. Parental expectations of the vocational potential of their children do not always agree with the professional expectations that most persons who have severe learning difficulties can move into open employment. Research from the USA (Hill *et al.*, 1987) concluded that parental expectations regarding employment will only be raised when they can see examples of consistently successful placements.

PLANNING A WAY FORWARD

The author was involved in a three-year action research project to develop a curriculum for 16 to 19 year old students with severe learning difficulties which aimed to prepare them for successful, supported transition to employment at 19. It also included the creation of a wider range of post-19 options than had hitherto been available. A group of seven students were involved in the project, which was based at a further education unit for thirty 16 to 19 year old students with severe learning difficulties, on the site of an all-age special school.

In 1989 an audit of the needs of the students in the unit and of the curriculum which was being offered at this time was conducted. This resulted in the design of an 'Entitlement Curriculum' which sought to ensure that students had appropriate experiences to prepare them for their individual transition to adulthood. The curriculum framework incorporated communication and numeracy skills, home/independence skills, personal/social/health education, vocational skills, technology, environmental and scientific awareness, creative development, and physical and leisure skills. The underlying principle which still pervades this unit is that students learn by being actively involved in 'real' experiences. They learn to shop and cook by doing all the shopping for the unit each week, and making meals for all students and staff each day. They learn about money by using it in real-life situations. They learn to adopt appropriate behaviour for a range of situations by being exposed to a wide variety of experiences, such as getting the bus to the market to buy vegetables. They regularly plan and prepare buffets for visitors to the unit, thereby developing the confidence required for a range of social situations. Students take part in residential holidays including visits abroad to destinations such as Germany and the South of France. These trips make use of a variety of accommodation which include hotels and youth hostels. Basic skills such as communication are developed in context, for example by writing letters to friends at a link school in Germany, or using the word processor to make newspapers and booklets, or telephoning the optician to make an appointment for an eye test.

It was decided to place a greater emphasis on the vocational aspects of the curriculum. In order to pursue this aim a project involving the unit, a local mainstream school, and a local further education college was established. This collaborative approach was seen as a means of providing increased opportunities for access to mainstream provision for students who had spent most of their educational lives in segregated provision. The course was extended to include a wider range of contacts with industry and employers generally, to broaden the concept of work to include paid and unpaid work, and to develop further the work preparation aspects of the programme, including supported work experience. The intention was that students would learn about the world of work by actively interacting with it. It was a primary goal of the course to prepare students for entry to employment, should they choose this option at 19.

Students took part in a range of planned experiences with the aim of investigating the world of work in, for example, manufacturing, retailing, packaging, advertising, consumer protection legislation, transportation, and local services. Students were involved in planning and participation in visits, designing and completing questionnaires and surveys, and taking part in role play situations followed by further development of the skills learned by putting them to use in real-life contexts. The investigation and observation of the world of work was followed by a focus, through discussions and videos, on the concept of work in relation to the students themselves and an exploration of their strengths, interests and aspirations. Students participated in a mini enterprise project for a full week to enable them to be assessed on work-related skills. They received a financial reward for their work. Work shadowing was introduced at the end of the first year of the course as a means of enabling the students to 'sample' a range of work situations of interest to them as individuals. These experiences were carefully planned in terms of level of challenge and associated risk taking, to ensure students had a successful experience. Collaborative working with people outside of education was a key feature of this course. Careers officers, Compact staff, specialist employment services, employers and voluntary agencies all had important roles to play throughout the planning, delivery, assessment and evaluation of the course. This way of working gave students a wide range of opportunities to become involved in and with the wider community, and to make use of its resources. It also enabled students to become aware of the support services which would be available to them in adult life.

Core skills were developed as an integral part of the course. These included communication, numeracy, information technology, and social skills. Where students experienced speech and language difficulties, they were taught to use alternative forms of communication such as symbols. Intensive unit-based teaching sessions focusing on appearance and personal presentation skills through the use of role play, video and pictorial catalogues were also organised. The significance to these students of pictorial and photographic means of recording experience and achievement became apparent during the course. Students were involved in agreeing and recording their personal targets, assessing and recording their progress, and contributing to their Annual Review Reports and Records of Achievement. Pupil self-assessment enabled them to gain a greater understanding of their own needs and the actions which they would be required to take in order to address these. (See Chapter 7 by Richard Rose.) During their final year in the unit students were involved in a range of experiences which enabled them to focus on their individual aspirations in relation to transition from the unit at 19, with particular reference to their employment potential. They made visits to places which they were interested in moving to when leaving the unit, such as youth training centres and colleges.

During the previous two years at the unit, students from this group had been given opportunities to join mainstream classes at a local comprehensive school, with support from unit staff. The aim had been to develop social and communication skills as well as transferable skills such as problem solving, memory improvement, recording of data, and handling of equipment. In the final year at the unit, the students were given the opportunity to join mainstream courses at the local college, and in this venture they were supported by unit staff. The emphasis during these sessions was on the development of practical vocationally focused skills, specifically related to the interests of the individuals concerned. Where appropriate, students were assessed against NVQ criteria along with mainstream peers. These carefully planned and supported mainstream experiences each had a significant effect on the development of the student's ability to cope in a range of contexts and learning situations. Parallel to this, back at the unit, the students focused on the development of job search skills, in conjunction with the careers officer and speech therapist. These skills included the development of interview techniques, identification of and search for job vacancies, completion of application forms, answering the telephone, learning to give personal details in response to oral questions, developing awareness of the importance of time, recognition of the range of jobs available and their associated working conditions and qualities needed by employees. Video was used as a means of recording and analysing the interviews, which took place in the unit and at the employer's premises. Students had by this stage become familiar with the purpose and content of their profile folders and readily used them in these mock interviews.

Further work-shadowing experiences took place (one day's duration), again in open employment situations. Work experience placements of two weeks' duration were organised and associated preliminary visits, and independent travel programmes, were completed. Factors taken into account when planning placements included previous experience on work-shadowing placements, any specific occupational skills the student had been developing at college, the advice of the specialist employment service officer in relation to the local labour market situation, the interests of the students, and the availability of sympathetic employers. The study found that there is a great deal of goodwill amongst employers in relation to helping young people to realise their interests and potential in the work situation, provided the aims and roles are clearly understood by all those involved.

In addition to the vocational emphasis given to the course, the students' other curriculum experiences were planned to give them opportunities to make decisions and face challenges in daily life in community settings. Planned and regular use of community facilities developed appropriate personal and social skills, as well as core skills. The personal, social, health and sex education programme helped students to become emotionally mature and aware of the physical changes they were experiencing during their adolescence. A carefully structured independent mobility programme not only enabled young people to travel between destinations, but greatly increased their need to make their own decisions, to be self-reliant, to be aware of their surroundings and of time, to relate to other people in an appropriate way, and to develop personal organisation skills – all felt to be important requirements for successful employment (Griffiths, 1988). The provision of access to mainstream accreditation opportunities was also a key policy decision. Students were awarded a City and Guilds Certificate of Pre-Vocational Education (CPVE) on completion of their course. In 1992 the CPVE was replaced by the Diploma of Vocational Education at foundation level. This then became the main form of accreditation until 1997 when a decision was taken to replace it with RSA National Skills Profile plus vocational modules. One of the main aims of the RSA course is to 'assist in the development of personal and practical work skills which can be used to facilitate social and vocational effectiveness'. GCSE Art and Design, and the Institute of Environmental Health Basic Food Hygiene Certificate, were also used in accrediting these aspects of the curriculum. All students in this group received the Record of Achievement on leaving the unit. Students were able to gain units towards NVQ, but none was able to reach a full level 1 qualification, owing to the levels of skill required to reach competency at the most basic employment level. Regular meetings were held between the unit staff and the specialist employment service staff concerning the curriculum being offered and its appropriateness for those students aiming for open employment.

The study highlighted the issue of whether the school's role is one of innovator or responder. Whose job is it to create a wider range of opportunities? If the students were prepared for a move into adulthood in employment, then it was essential to ensure that the appropriate opportunities were available to them on reaching the age of 19. As there was no established procedure or structure to facilitate this, it had to be developed. The school took on the role of bringing together the various agencies which were in a position to provide those opportunities, and providing a forum for detailed discussion and planning. The range of transition routes was extended to include: further education college, youth training, supported employment, residential college, and the SEC. All those involved were aware of the potential difficulties families could face regarding entitlement to benefits if the students went into youth training or employment. These were discussed with families and DSS benefits officers.

Throughout the three-year project there was ongoing contact with parents concerning the range of planned activities in which students were involved. Additional meetings were held with careers officers, college staff, specialist employment service staff, and unit staff to explain to students and their parents the various options open to them on leaving the unit. There was considerable interest by parents in the supported employment option, with a link to a lifelong specialist employment service. Parents were also interested in finding out what their sons or daughters would be doing if they chose the college option. Without exception, parents had concerns about the long-term prospects for their sons and daughters and welcomed reassurances from the careers officer that there would be a point of contact for the future. Parents' views and expectations were a significant influence on the transition choices made by young people at 19. Informal conversations with students and their families over the three years showed that throughout life these youngsters may have been grouped with other disabled people to take part in appropriate leisure activities aimed specifically at a clientele with special needs. Of course these experiences would not have been the same for each individual, but nevertheless the unit staff inherited a dependency culture which had in some instances been sustained for sixteen years in each family. It is understandable that the parents of many young people with special needs have created a protective environment in which their son or daughter has been sheltered from the rigours of the real world. Where parents had wanted their sons or daughters to have as normal a life as possible, this was reflected in the extent to which they were themselves encouraged to be involved in the decisions made about all aspects of their everyday lives. The study showed that parents have a crucial role to play in preparing and supporting these young people during transition. Indeed, earlier research (Kings Fund, 1985) showed that the level of support needed to ensure success in employment was not related to the degree of special educational need, but was more influenced by the support given by the family.

At the end of the project, one student accepted supported employment, four went to the local college of further education for two years full-time study, and two students went to an out-of-district residential college. The professional opinion of the head of unit was that five of the seven students who left the unit would have been capable of going straight into supported youth training, leading to supported open employment. The full-time two-year course at the local college was offered for the first time in the year these students were leaving and this had a significant impact on their choice of first destination, preferring to participate in a further two years of full-time education prior to entering the world of work. The specialist employment service guaranteed these students that their services would be available to them when they left college at the age of 21.

For the students who took up the college option, the transition was not as smooth as it should have been, given the level of liaison which took place between the unit, students, parents and college staff. The issue of transport for non-independent travellers caused considerable worry (a factor reflected in the work of the Tomlinson Committee, 1996). None of the students were travelling to and from college independently despite doing so on a daily basis whilst at the unit. This was essentially a parental decision. Despite some of the students having had experiences of the mainstream college courses on a supported infill basis whilst at the unit, none of them attended any mainstream classes as part of their full-time programmes. Given the level of pre-vocational preparation which the students experienced at the unit, logical progression towards employment would require a substantial emphasis in the college programme on vocationally focused training and work placements. There was concern in 1992 that the students may not have had the opportunities to continue with this vocational focus whilst at college. The current options at the local college for students leaving the unit include a vocational opportunities course funded by the Further Education Funding Council which incorporates up to four days per week planned, and if appropriate supported, work placements. This programme takes account of the previous experiences of the students during their three-year vocational education course at the unit.

Teacher expectations played a significant part in the success of this project. There was an acceptance that the curriculum would be similar in purpose and nature to that for most 16 to 19 year olds, but that the students with learning difficulties would require high levels of support and differentiation to ensure access. There was an absence on the part of teachers of any preconceived ideas about future destinations. Earlier work by Griffiths (1988) and Beresford *et al.* (1982) confirmed the need for professionals to challenge low expectations.

Since 1993 the unit curriculum has been updated and has continued to focus on independence and vocational preparation. However, there is a recognition now that further educational provision at the local college is a natural extension of this vocationally orientated curriculum, and is to be encouraged as part of a planned transition to employment in adult life. The study showed that for such a transition from education to employment to be successful, there are certain fundamental principles which must be incorporated into the philosophy, policy making, planning, delivery and evaluation of an appropriate curriculum for students who experience severe learning difficulties. These are a commitment to:

- inclusion;
- independence;
- progression;
- curriculum relevance;
- interactive/experiential learning strategies;
- integral development and application of core skills in context;
- community-based learning of a normalising nature wherever possible involving collaborative working between education and other agencies;
- appropriate support provision;
- high expectations of students in relation to employment in adulthood;
- meaningful student involvement in setting targets, assessing personal progress, recording achievement, and decision making;
- access to a valued national system of qualifications and accreditation.

These principles have implications for schools, families, employers, professionals in education, social services, and health, as well as to the individual. The importance of rooting the curriculum in the realities of the outside world cannot be overemphasised. The 'employability curriculum' must, through an appropriate range of experiences, empower the students, give them the skills to make choices and decisions, enable them to develop social skills appropriate to non-segregated adult settings, provide the basic vocational and technical skills needed to enter the labour market, and it should encourage appropriate risk taking.

The principle of inclusion must be viewed in curriculum planning terms, in its widest sense. Access to mainstream education and training, and to all aspects of life within the community, to a range of employers, to leisure facilities, to community services, and to consumer services must become the norm rather than something provided by a benevolent society. As the Tomlinson Report (1996) states: 'The aim of all provision must be inclusion in our communities'. The development of independence must be carefully planned across all learning experiences. This must be achieved in relation to the aims, range, type, depth, context of learning experiences, levels of challenge, and the levels of personal autonomy in decision making espoused by the systems in which we work. It will be dependent upon the level and type of support provided, and the focus of this support, to ensure progression from general transferable to vocational-specific skill development.

Access to nationally recognised vocational qualifications and accreditation through structured progression routes from pre-foundation to advanced level is essential. It is hoped that the proposed 'Entry Level' in key skills and other qualifications will be accessible to students with the whole range of learning difficulties. For too long, these pupils and students have been 'working towards', but never reaching, the minimum level of competence required to attain the first rung of the qualifications ladder. The RSA National Skills Profile is intended as a route into mainstream qualifications for those experiencing barriers to learning. The proposed 'Skills for Adult Life' award is also a possible step in the right direction. An inclusive education system must incorporate an inclusive system of assessment, qualifications and accreditation. Interactive and experiential learning strategies must be incorporated into the transition curriculum. Whenever possible, interaction should take place in community-based settings which enable young people to have experiences of a 'normalising' nature. Of particular significance is the opportunity to model and develop appropriate social skills in context. It is only in a real-life context that a person can 'experience' the expectations others have in relation to behaviour, and can 'test out' the boundaries of acceptability. However, without support at an appropriate level, this can be a disastrous experience for a young person.

The issue of support is important for the young person during education, training and employment. Support must be planned and budgeted for according to individual need and based on the intention that the young person should be moving towards greater levels of independence. A careful distinction must be made between the individual support a young person needs in particular situations, such as on independent travel programmes, and support required to access a mainstream course, such as differentiated curriculum materials or means of demonstrating competence and achievement. Support for the mainstream lecturer or employer may be as important as support for the young person. Careful analysis of support needs should identify the professional expertise required in each situation and provide indicators with regards to its most effective deployment. It has been suggested that if this support could be provided at the end of high-quality pre-vocational education and training, and at the outset of employment following the principles described earlier, 'young people with disabilities would have the best possible chance of gaining and sustaining employment' (Griffiths, 1988). Unless this support is provided much of the investment made in the individual by the family, school and college may be wasted or put at risk (Tomlinson Committee, 1996).

Following changes in legislation during 1992 some colleges expanded to take in students with more severe difficulties. The majority of students saw college as part of their progression towards work. The challenge to colleges, employers and politicians is to develop not only access to college but also real access to work (Harrison, 1996). It is clear that students with severe learning difficulties can benefit significantly from a planned vocational education programme from 16 to 21 involving school and college, incorporating the principles discussed in this chapter, with the ultimate goal of supported employment leading to open employment. Supported work experience and school–college links could be integral aspects of such a programme. The Tomlinson Committee (1996) recognised the difficulties caused by the FEFC funding criteria and emphasised the importance of link courses continuing. They are 'crucial in helping many students to feel at ease and to be successful in their transition to further education'.

In the wider community context, employers need to be aware of the strengths and abilities of people with severe learning difficulties. They can only develop this awareness through active engagement with young people who fall into this category. Employers' experiences need to be positive. They need support in addressing the requirements of employees with special needs and this can be provided through agencies such as specialist employment services, school staff, or careers officers. Schemes such as the Sheltered Placement Scheme can help through offsetting the worry of undertaking what may be perceived as a new and high-risk venture.

We continue to be faced with uncertainty. As a system of common funding for all 16 to 19 year olds is put into place there continues to be a range of anxieties with regard to the ways in which procedures may be adapted to meet the needs of all school leavers (Melville, 1997). There are many views about ways in which inclusive learning can be realised. The Tomlinson Committee (1996) had visions of a system that is inclusive and which will require 'many mansions', referring to a combination of integrated and discrete forms of provision within an inclusive philosophy, a view supported by Weddell (1995). The three-year study described in this chapter demonstrates how this can be achieved in practice, and can make a real contribution to the greater inclusion of young people with learning difficulties into society. The important principle to keep in mind is that we must create a climate within which inclusive practice can be developed across all phases of education, training and employment (Ainscow, 1997).

REFERENCES

Ainscow, M. (1997) 'Towards inclusive schooling', *British Journal of Special Education* 24(1): 3–6.

Beresford, P., Booth, T., Croft, S. and Tuckwell, P. (1982) 'An ESN (s) school and the labour market', in T. Booth and J. Statham (eds) *The Nature of Special Education*, London: Croom Helm.

Brandon, D. (1991) 'Colleges favourites to win the new Nobel prizes', *Community Living* January: 8.

Corbett, J. and Barton, L. (1992) *Students with Special Needs in Transition to Adulthood: a Struggle for Choice*, London: Routledge.

Corrie, M. (1985) *After Special School*, Scottish Council for Research in Education, Working Paper 3.

Department of Education and Science (1978) *Special Educational Needs. The Warnock Report*, London: HMSO.

Department of Education and Science (1988) *Education Reform Act*, London: HMSO.

Department for Employment (1990) *Employment and Training for People with Disabilities*, London: HMSO.

Further Education Unit (FEU) (1988) *New Directions – a Curriculum Framework for Students with Severe Learning Difficulties*, London: NFER.

Griffiths, M. (1988) *Enabled to Work*, London: FEU.

Griffiths, M. (1994) *Transition to Adulthood – the Role of Education for Young People with Severe Learning Difficulties*, London: David Fulton.

Harrison, B. (1990) 'Employers' attitudes to the employment of people with mental handicaps; an empirical study', *Mental Handicap Research* 3(2): 196–213.

Harrison, J. (1996) 'Accessing further education: views and experiences of F.E. students with learning difficulties and/or disabilities', *British Journal of Special Education* 23(4): 187–96.

Hill, J., Seyfarth, J., Banks, D., Wehman, P. and Orelove, F. (1987) 'Parents' attitudes about working conditions of their adult mentally retarded sons and daughters', *Exceptional Children* 54(1): 9–23.

Kings Fund Centre (1984) *An Ordinary Working Life*, London: Kings Fund.

Kings Fund Centre (1985) *The Employment of People with Mental Handicap*, London: Kings Fund.

Kroese, B. S., Lowe, S., Irchens, A., Sidway, N. and Cragg, R. (1990) 'Employment opportunities for people with mental handicaps', *Mental Handicap* 18: 143–5.

Lavendar, P. (1988) *Care and Education in the Community*, London: FEU.

Melville, D. (1997) 'Small sixth forms under threat', *Times Educational Supplement* October 17.

National Curriculum Council (NCC) (1993) *A Curriculum Perspective. 14–19 Education in Schools and Colleges*, York: NCC/FEU.

Todd, S., Evans, G. and Beyer, S. (1991) 'Into adulthood: the vocational situation of young people with severe learning difficulties', *British Journal of Mental Subnormality* XXXVII: Part 1, 5–15.

Tomlinson Committee (1996) *Inclusive Learning: Report of the Learning Difficulties and/or Disabilities Committee*, London: FEFC.

Tomlinson, S. (1982) *A Sociology of Special Education*, London: Routledge & Kegan Paul.

UN (1971) *United Nations Declaration on Human Rights of Mentally Retarded Persons*, New York: United Nations.

Weddell, K. (1995) 'Making inclusive education ordinary', *British Journal of Special Education* 22(3): 100–4.

Whelan, E. and Speake, B. (1981) *Getting to Work*, London: Souvenir Press.

Chapter 17

Growing up – moving on

Jan Tyne

If inclusion is about the opportunities for disabled people to participate fully in all the educational, employment, consumer, recreational, community and domestic activities that typify everyday society, then inclusive education should be seen as the beginning to a good start in life. In this chapter, Jan Tyne focuses on the importance of friendship and support systems when the school years are over and pupils enter into adulthood. Several case examples are drawn upon to illustrate just how difficult and how promising life can be for young people with severe learning difficulties and their families.

Joyce

Seven of us have gathered for Joyce's annual 'life care' meeting. We have been invited by Joyce and the staff of the hostel where she lives to review what she has been doing at the day centre. The meeting is rather like an end of term review. The managers of the centre, the hostel, and key worker have prepared written reports. I am Joyce's friend and Citizen Advocate. Another friend, Joan (recruited through the hostel befriender scheme) is also present. We have been asked for comments on our friendship with Joyce.

We are sitting together in the common room of the hostel. It is a pleasant enough room: pictures on the walls, bright and clean paintwork, a few assorted ornaments on the dresser, dining table and chairs, three sofas. Fifteen young people can use this room to relax and have a chat, yet it is all very tidy. I cannot help but notice the lack of personal clutter: there are no magazines, no piles of CDs, videos, tapes, discarded clothes, none of the things that say who lives here.

Joyce is congratulated on her progress, she can wash her hair with the minimum of help, make a sandwich, a cup of tea, tidy her room. She still needs help to have a bath, to do her washing, to make more complicated meals and to go into town. She is popular, friendly and chatty, but people are complaining she is too nosey when the family and friends of other residents visit the hostel. Sometimes there are arguments, she is not very friendly with a couple of the other residents. But staff do say they like 'teaching' her, and that she is good fun and enjoys a laugh. All of this is fine they say but they must remember to check the tasks she does to see if they have been finished. At the end of the meeting Joyce is asked directly what plans she has for her future. She replies without hesitation: 'A home of my own. I want to work in a Cafe.' Joyce is 27.

Like many others with learning disabilities, Joyce relies on an organised human services for the important things in her life. Such things include whether she can have a job, meet and make friends, and where she lives regardless of whether it is with people she wants to be with or who want to be with her. Joyce's request for a home of her own, and a job, away from the day centre, which is less than 100 yards (90 metres) from the residential hostel, is talked through diligently. It is quite obvious that the service on which she depends will not be able to help her to achieve her dream for a very long while, if ever. The usual concerns about lack of resources, people, money, time, and risks, are all mentioned, then finally: 'if you want to work in a cafe you must understand how to handle money, let's make that our next goal. We will put that down on this form.'

Events have brought me back into Joyce's life again after a break of eight years, since both she and I left the special school she attended. I first taught her fifteen years ago. Together over the years we cooked, caught buses to town, went shopping, polished, hoovered, dusted, washed and dried up the dishes. We enjoyed swimming, horse riding, and walks in the country. I have helped her to write her name, to recognise money. We have been on outings and on holiday together, and we thought long and hard about how to behave appropriately in company, and much more. Everything that we did was carefully planned as part of a typical life-skills curriculum. As I sat listening to the reports and the discussion about setting and agreeing new goals I realised they were exactly the same as those we chose we all those years ago.

What is the difference in Joyce's life now? All that work that we did at school together – was it wasted? Has she really forgotten how to do those things? If the same things are being written into her life-care plan that I wrote as aims and objectives in my lesson plans then surely something has gone wrong somewhere. Perhaps they didn't know about those things we did together. Have they ever had her school records? Shouldn't we be looking for another way of doing things?

SUPPORT FOR ADULT LIFE

Throughout life and in different ways, people need varying degrees of help and assistance from others in order to safeguard the independence and autonomy that comes with being an adult. Yet support is seen by some as being incompatible with adult status and inconsistent with autonomy. Having full responsibility for oneself, managing one's own affairs, making decisions and being accountable for the consequences of one's actions are commonly accepted markers of adult status. For young people who are severely disabled these markers of adulthood can be difficult and sometimes impossible to achieve because the required level of support often signals a degree of dependency and disability that suggests the person with severe learning difficulties can never be truly independent or self-sufficient. In other words, the severity of the disability renders adult status impossible and the individual becomes frozen in childhood, always dependent on parental or some other form of care (Wertheimer, 1981).

Over the past twenty-five years there has been a growing agreement that there are other perspectives on caring and on what constitutes support for people with learning disabilities. Towell (1997: 91) summarises this clearly:

> there is increasing agreement that people with disabilities should be offered the support and opportunities necessary to:
>
> * grow up in a family;
> * learn with other children;
> * experience good health;
> * live in ordinary flats, houses, in the neighbourhood;
> * access continuing education;
> * have a real job and pay;
> * enjoy life with friends;
> * choose for oneself;
> * and be accepted as a citizen.
>
> In short to live an 'ordinary life' (p. 91).

The phrase 'an ordinary life' has become shorthand symbolising the philosophy which should guide the provision of services for people with disabilities. Unfortunately, longstanding beliefs about the limitations of people with severe disabilities make it a difficult philosophy to put into practice. The professionals who work alongside Joyce and others like her are not uncaring people, but all too often their work is based on preconceived assumptions about what is possible and desirable. Thus we hear comments such as:

> Sophie has the developmental age of a two year old, she could never get a job, or own her own house.

Or:

> They are better and happier being with people like themselves. It is more cost effective to offer a similar services to groups.

Organisations often find it hard to think about one person at a time even though the legal framework to do it is in place. The Statutory Education Reviews at 14+ provide an opportunity to collect and review all available information from the relevant services needed to shape post-school provision. However, it is unlikely that the representatives of all relevant adult service agencies such as Supported Employment Agencies, or Housing Associations, or local FE colleges will participate in the review unless the meeting's Convenor makes a special effort to involve them. As a result, many teenagers with severe learning disabilities miss out on vital planning time.

Anyone who spends time talking to people who have a learning disability soon realises how far they can feel excluded from the many everyday experiences and opportunities that we all take for granted and expect. They feel they have been denied opportunities in education, in getting a job, in housing arrangements, leisure and travel pursuits, as well as opportunities to make friends and relationships – all the things which for the majority of us ensure we can have the kind of life style that we choose. It is a simple wish to want to be treated like everyone else and to hope that people will treat you as they would like to be treated themselves. There are examples both here and abroad where the joint efforts of families, well-designed support services, and a willingness of communities to welcome and include, show that substantial improvements in the quality of life can be achieved given the chance.

Clare

Clare lives in a small staffed house, near her family, with two other young people with severe learning disabilities, all in their late teens to early twenties. The house is owned and managed by an agency situated in a suburb of a big town. Until last year, Clare went to school with the other two residents. They have all been in the same class group doing the same things together since they were six. They know each other very well but they don't really like each other much!

Although Clare does not speak or communicate in a conventional way those who know her well understand what she likes and dislikes. Each day, staff take Clare out to go swimming, to aromatherapy, to have a drink, meet up with friends in town and to visit others. Some of her assistants are her friends and have introduced her to their friends. Clare's Mum and Dad want her to move out of the staffed house and are exploring ways that will help her to buy her own house but continue with the assistance which enables her to enjoy day to day life. Her parents feel she should not have to live with people she doesn't like, living where she does for no other reason than the professionals thought all the young residents had the same level of need.

Clare's parents insisted that they help to write the Care Plan with Clare's social worker that resulted from the Community Care Assessment. It was not easy for them, but there is opportunity now embodied in the Community Care Act, that Social Services work in partnership with families, so that they can stay involved in the care of their disabled family member and not be made to feel deskilled and uninvolved as used to be the case.

Anna and Wendy

Until five years ago, Anna lived in a group home where she was deeply unhappy. Over her lifetime she has been sent away from family many times: to residential homes, to a psychiatric hospital, to group homes, each new placement bleaker than the last. When

asked at a review meeting what she wanted Anna replied unequivo-
cally that she wanted her own home, a key to her door. She was very
clear. Fortunately, staff at the local Council Housing Department
recognised the security that home ownership could offer Anna.

Anna has lived in her own home for four years now. She buys
part of the value of her house through a mortgage using the
DIYSO scheme (Do It Yourself Ownership scheme) operated and
facilitated by her local Borough Council, in partnership with a
local Housing Association. She uses some of her Disability Living
Allowance to do this. It is Anna's name on the mortgage agreement. She lives with her friends Wendy and Zoe who are her
tenants. Brenda and other assistants come in each day to help
Anna with her daytime activities.

Individualised supported living arrangements have been pioneered in the
USA for more than twenty years. 'Options in Community Living' in
Madison, Wisconsin, was one of the first. 'Options' enables people with
severe learning difficulties to live with and alongside non-disabled tenants
in ordinary housing. The contracts between each tenant, support tenants,
and the organisation are drawn up to suit each individual. The experience of
many tenants has been documented by O'Brien and Lyle O'Brien (1992).
Similar schemes operate in many parts of the UK (Kinsella, 1993).

However, as these schemes have become established, it is becoming
increasingly obvious that many people are still very lonely and isolated.
They are not as included as much into their local communities as the phrase
'living in the community' conjures up in our minds. Concern is growing
that the friendships most people take for granted are missing from the lives
of people with severe disabilities.

GROWING UP AND MAKING FRIENDS

Anna has Wendy and Zoe and all of their friends as well as the friends she
brings into their lives. Clare has her family nearby and sees them regularly.
She also has the same regular assistants that take her out, not just on 'official' trips, but to the pub in the evenings with their friends. She's part of
their gang. But Joyce is a lonely person despite living in a large hostel with
twenty-four other residents. The difference between Anna and Clare and
Joyce is that Joyce has no friends who are there *just for her*. Reflecting on the
importance and value of friendship, Strully and Strully (1993) write:

It is friendship that will ultimately mean life or death for our daughter. It is her one and only hope for a desirable future and protection from victimization.

(p.214)

Shawntell Strully

Shawntell is a young woman with very limited verbal communication, and with both physical and visual impairments. Her friends read her responses to their shared activities as a mark of friendship. They take meals together, stay over at each other's homes, holiday together, drive around, and generally hang about together. They speak of sharing confidences together identifying Shawntell's preferences and interests as being distinct from their own. They identify themselves to others as friends.

Shawntell's developing friendships would have been impossible if she had been segregated from mainstream schooling. To be able to enjoy common interests, mutuality and respect with individuals with severe learning difficulties for some people is almost unthinkable, and schools do not pay high regard to encouraging this as part of the regular curriculum. Yet friendships are at the heart of what we all need. The skills we learn as a child about how to make friends, we take with us into adult life.

It is our friendships that enable us to be active and productive community members. Friendships help ensure that being part of a community rather than just being in the community is a reality for everyone.

(Strully and Strully, 1989, p.68)

When people live in congregate care settings it is difficult for their individualism to be noticed. Sensitive assistants realise that the rich support and improved quality of life that comes from joining clubs and associations will only happen if someone facilitates it. A good community builder or facilitator can change someone's life dramatically. It does not matter whether this facilitator is a personal assistant, friend or relative. What is important is that there is somebody there working to make it happen.

Pam and Betty

Pam works as a community support worker. She is attached to a small group home where four ladies live. The women have spent most of their lives in a long stay institution and are now in their late sixties to early seventies. When they took up residence at the local authority group home, none of them had family or friends outside the home. Pam noticed that the local Community Centre hosts a knitting circle for the over sixties club. Aware that Betty could knit, Pam introduced her to the other ladies. Within a few months Betty became a fully fledged member of the knitting circle and other members collect Betty from her home every week to go to the club. Pam does not need to go anymore, she just calls by from time to time. Often Betty is invited to another lady's house for tea. She also goes to the local church with friends in the circle and stays for coffee afterwards. She is now on one of the committees at the church.

As a result of Pam's initiative, Betty found new friends for herself, and they are visiting her and the other ladies in her home. It was all made possible by Pam understanding and getting to know the particular skills that Betty had and giving her the chance to use them.

Diane and Toby

Diane is getting to know Toby. He is 20, and left his last Special School two years ago. The Special Schools he attended, were more than ten miles away. Toby now goes to a Further Education College each day during term time, 25 miles from where he lives. The college nearest to his home did not offer the kind of course he wanted to do. In the town where he lives with his parents, he knows nobody of his own age and is reliant on his parents for going places and doing things. Diane has found Toby likes birdwatching, going for long walks, helping his father with practical jobs, and swimming. Diane introduced Toby to the local Duke of Edinburgh Award Group, and the Conservation Volunteers. Now he goes with a member of the D of E to do local conservation work. Without Diane's help Toby would not have met these other young people.

Encouraging people who are disconnected from their community to become friends and actively included back into local community associations requires time, patience, and above all someone recognising the need, and being willing to help out.

CIRCLES OF FRIENDS – CIRCLES OF SUPPORT

Most of us have *circles of friends* made up of people we rely on for many reasons: advice, friendship, companionship, assistance. They constantly form and reform as people move away and our paths cross with others throughout our lives.

> Circles both expand and contract at different stages of our lives, they are both a continuing process and outcome of the lives we lead, the jobs we hold, the connections we make. Different circles have different compositions – some are mainly family members, others are bound by friendship. We take our friendships for granted, and don't spend long hours listing who are in our circle. It is only in times of distress and tension that we consciously think who is part of our circle. It is at these times that we need to know who will stand up and be counted with us.
>
> (O'Brien, 1992, p.50)

Sometimes a more structured and formal approach is necessary. *Circles of Support* involves a range of people. It begins when these people come together with the specific intent of assisting somebody who is at the centre wanting help in some way (Mount, 1988). Circle members meet frequently to try to figure out how best to solve problems that are being faced or troubling the person. Facilitators have a role helping a person to organise a circle, guiding everyone in realising what the person's dream is and making personal commitments to assist the realisation of that dream.

> Circles of Support offer people structure for discovering and working together with someone who would otherwise be unable to realise their dreams; circle members remember the human interdependence that forms the foundation of civilised life.
>
> (O'Brien, 1992, p.55)

As a circle works it shrinks and grows. People come and go as their influence changes. However, many members stay in contact as 'concerned friends'. They become part of a 'circle of friends'.

GROWING UP: GETTING A JOB, SUPPORTED EMPLOYMENT

If we assume that people will never work they will not be given the chance to work. The thought that people with severe learning difficulties can work and keep a paid job is often greeted with scepticism. Yet having a job gives people high status and regard in our society. People with severe learning disabilities want to enjoy the benefits as much as anyone else. However, the perpetuation of low expectations create barriers to progress in employment for people with severe learning difficulties.

As discussed by Caroline Broomhead in Chapter 16, supported employment schemes have been developed specifically to assist adults with severe learning difficulties into employment. The key concepts on which supported employment is based are:

- employment gives workers self-esteem;
- employment contributes to productivity and happiness;
- employers generally feel that people with disabilities are good employees;
- workers with disabilities may be more reliable than many workers without disabilities;
- supported employment is a way to help people with more severe disabilities get and maintain a job;
- productive work helps people achieve independence;
- employment promotes empowerment and choice;
- anyone who wants to work should be given the chance to try.

Supported employment schemes based on these ideas have been in operation in the UK for at least ten years. They originated in the USA based on the pioneering work of Marc Gold and Mike Callahan (Callahan, 1990). There are now many stories of people with jobs who are enjoying the improvement to their lives, not just in material terms but in terms of their status, self-esteem, contribution and inclusion into the communities in which they live.

In the UK there are about a hundred Employment Agencies. Specialist staff often known as job coaches are trained to assist people with learning disabilities to find and keep work. Jobs are found and terms negotiated in the same way as for any employee in a company. Pay is decided at the usual competitive rates. The success of supported employment depends on a close understanding between the agency staff, the person seeking work and the employer. Where agency staff have been able to become closely involved during the 'transition years' before students leave school, there has been marked success in getting the students into work as opposed to placement at the local day centre. Evaluation studies show how life changes for the better for people who have been helped to find jobs (Lister, 1992; Wertheimer,

1992; 1993). The National Association for Supported Employment (AfSE), together with support from the Employers Forum on Disability, can assist and give information about how the schemes operate and which employers are supportive.

GROWING UP: SPEAKING UP AND BEING HEARD

Being able to speak and clearly communicate your wants and needs is fundamental to being able to have control over your life. Many people with learning disabilities find this very difficult. Maybe they physically cannot speak, or are unused to being in a position where people really listen or even value what they have to say. This is when an *advocate* can make a dramatic difference to someone's life. Advocacy means standing by someone and speaking on their behalf with their permission. There are many organisations that offer and employ people to act as paid advocates.

Citizen Advocacy (CA) relies on a volunteer network of local 'well respected and valued citizens' willing to act on behalf of another more vulnerable person. A valued citizen is defined as someone who is richly connected to networks and associations in their own community. CA programmes focus on arranging and supporting relationships between people who otherwise would not meet. Often the relationship results in lasting friendship, which means that a new 'circle of friends' evolves around someone who is not in a position to facilitate this for themselves. People are brought together by the work of a CA Co-ordinator, again someone who is well connected to local community networks; this is the only paid position in the scheme. The fact that their time is given freely and unpaid gives Citizen Advocates a powerful voice. They can be truly independent, not bound by constraints imposed by any organisation. At the same time CA Co-ordinators do not identify themselves as being human service workers. Their primary aim is to work with people who are working to regenerate communities (Tyne, 1996).

Alongside and complementary to CA and other advocacy schemes is self-advocacy. Self-advocacy involves people with disabilities working on their own behalf. It is about organisations and groups *of* disabled people rather than *for* people with disabilities. The People First Movement is a prominent example. This network of disabled people has grown dramatically during the past ten years and local groups are forming all over the country. Another self-advocacy organisation is the British Organisation for Disabled People (BCODP). Both assist people with disabilities to get their voices and views heard.

CONCLUSION

Healthy, vigorous, vibrant communities, which welcome and include all their members, depend on disabled people and non-disabled people working together in equal partnership, using their individual and unique talents to benefit everyone.

The growing interest in inclusion has helped people appreciate that exclusion is a problem and not a natural state of affairs. However, for many people with learning disabilities and their families and friends, adult life is full of uncertainty and anxiety. In spite of innovative schemes and examples of good practice it seems that improvements are only available to a small minority. Many people with severe learning disabilities still live in large congregate settings. They are dependent on ageing parents. They have meaningless day-time activities. They have little control over their lives. Much depends on geography and who is in control of implementing the services locally. In 1996 a Mental Health Foundation Report presented some disturbing findings:

> Although people with learning difficulties are increasingly living in ordinary communities, many live in poverty, have little meaningful activity during the day, few friends and no real hopes for change in the future.
>
> (p.7)

Many people with severe learning difficulties have to rely on organised human services for the most fundamental things in their lives. All too often the building blocks of community life – a partner, family, friends and neighbours and neighbourhood – all seem quietly to disappear along with the chance for an ordinary life.

Government legislation of recent years has begun to recognise the legitimate grievances and difficult life circumstances of disabled people. Official rhetoric regularly refers to 'inclusion' and 'community'. Legislation allowing Social Services to implement Direct Payments Schemes so that disabled people can manage their benefit payments themselves to purchase the kind of care they want and employ their own assistants is but one positive example of how government policy can help improve quality of life for people with disabilities. Recent legislation (i.e. The Disability Discrimination Act, The 1989 Children's Act, The 1993 and 1996 Education Acts), and reports such as the Tomlinson Report on further education (FEFC, 1996) are helping to create a climate that promotes discussion about inclusion and building inclusive communities. These discussions promote the development of human services, and encourage investment in supporting families and individuals with disabilities to stay within their local communities. It is important to remember, however, that legislation alone will not ensure genuine inclusion because inclusion relies on people who have the energy, determination and commitment to make the process work. This chapter has focused on the importance of friendship and support systems – two of the most critical though often overlooked components in creating the opportunities for people with learning difficulties to participate fully in everyday life.

ACKNOWLEDGEMENTS

The author would like to acknowledge the works of John and Connie Lyle O'Brien. This chapter draws upon ideas they present in their 1996 book, *Members of Each Other: Building Community in Company with People with Developmental Disabilities*.

REFERENCES

Callahan, M. (1990) *What ever happened when 'Try Another Way' met the Real World*, Gautier, MS: Marc Gold and Associates.

Further Education Funding Council (1996) *Inclusive Learning: Principles and Recommendations*, Report of the Learning Difficulties and/or Disabilities Committee, London: FEFC.

Kinsella, P. (1993) *Supported Living: a New Paradigm*, Manchester: National Development Team.

Lister, T. (1992) *National Survey of Supported Employment Agencies*, Manchester: National Development Team.

Mental Health Foundation Committee of Inquiry (1996) *Building Expectations Opportunities and Services for People with a Learning Disability*, London: MHFC.

Mount, B. (1988) *What We are Learning from Circles of Support*, Manchester, CT: Communitas.

O'Brien, J. (1992) 'Members of each other', in J. Nisbet (ed.) *Natural Supports in School at Work and in the Community for People with Severe Disabilities*, Baltimore, MD: Paul Brookes.

O'Brien, J. and Lyle O'Brien, C. (1992) *Remembering the Soul of Our Work*, Madison, WI: Options in Community Living.

O'Brien, J. and Lyle O'Brien, C. (1996) *Members of Each Other: Building Community in Company with People with Developmental Disabilities*, Toronto: Inclusion Press.

Strully, J. and Strully, C. (1989) 'Friendship as an educational goal', in W. Stainback, S. Stainback and M. Forest (eds) *Educating All Students in the Mainstream of Regular Education*, Baltimore, MD: Paul Brookes.

Strully, J. and Strully, C. (1993) 'That which binds us: friendships as a safe harbor in a storm', in A. Novak Amado (ed.) *Friends: Connections between Persons with and without Disabilities*, Baltimore, MD: Paul Brookes.

Towell, D. (1997) 'Promoting a better life for people with learning disabilities and their families: a practical agenda for the new government', *British Journal of*

Learning Disabilities 25(3): 90–4.

Tyne, J. (1996) 'Advocacy: not just another subject', in R. Rose, A. Fergusson, C. Coles, R. Byers and D. Banes (eds) *Implementing the Whole Curriculum for Pupils with Learning Difficulties*, Revised edition, London: David Fulton.

Wertheimer, A. (1981) *Living for the Present*, London: Values into Action.

Wertheimer, A. (1992) *Real Jobs 1990–93*, Manchester: National Development Team.

Wertheimer, A. (1993) *Changing Lives*, Manchester: National Development Team.

Chapter 18

Quality of life as a consideration in the development of inclusive education for pupils and students with learning difficulties

Christopher Robertson

This chapter examines the concept of quality of life and its applicability to the education of pupils and students with learning difficulties. Christopher Robertson then considers how the concept relates to the process of inclusive education.

> She [Mrs Spud, the cleaner] says that everybody is different and that it is quite good indeed, and that we should all be happy and that, for every person is a very special person and that it is good to be different . . . as if there was no difference we would all be the same. And Mrs Spud told me not to worry about my brain because to be different is to be who you are. So, I do not believe that it was my dad's fault for the floozy, or mam's cos' I was unattended. I believe that I was supposed to be backward. I believe that it is all part of what is supposed to be, and when I was born God came and touched me on my head, down he came and touched my soft spot and made me, *me*.
>
> (Hall, 1997, emphasis added)

This quotation from a funny, moving and riveting radio drama captures one of the most important features that needs to be taken into account in furthering inclusive educational practice for pupils and students with learning difficulties. Spoonface, the young girl with autism speaking to us, knows the importance and value of being an individual and being different. She knows too that she has many difficulties, including learning difficulties and a terminal illness. As the dramatic monologue unfolds it becomes very apparent that Spoonface is both a unique individual with special qualities and a person like everyone else, who has to face day-to-day living as well as the more existential certainties that affect all living beings.

If inclusive educational approaches are to be valuable, they need to operate in ways which take the strongest possible account of individuals and their differences. At the same time, such approaches also need to consider common needs (Norwich, 1996), and the social and relational contexts in which these are met. In other words, the 'quality of life' of individuals should be paramount in the thinking of educationalists. The term quality of life implies a kind of life (i.e. the good life) and involves activities which go beyond schooling. However, as the philosopher John Dewey famously noted: schooling *is* preparation for life. The process of education must not lose sight of the need to prepare students for adult life. This chapter considers the usefulness of the concept of quality of life in the context of *inclusion* and its potential to contribute to the development of improved educational provision for pupils and students with learning difficulties. Two specific approaches to the process will be considered: (1) responsive inclusion; and (2) caring inclusion.

LEARNING DIFFICULTIES AND QUALITY OF LIFE

The concept of quality of life has both negative and positive connotations when it is used in the field of learning difficulties. Negatively, the right to have learning difficulties (to live) has been questioned in our, and many other, societies, because it is believed by some people that to have these difficulties must *de facto* mean that quality of life is irrevocably poor. Mittler (1988), Pfeiffer (1994), Stanworth (1989) and Williams (1995) are just a few of the authors who have expressed concerns about bio-ethical practice and the continuing presence of largely *unquestioned* eugenic perspectives, particularly in the medical profession and the sciences associated with it. If such perspectives are located strongly in powerful and influential professions, it is of course likely that their influence will impact on the views of other members of society, including those of educational professionals and parents.

In contrast to this arguably negative usage of the quality of life concept, a significant number of professionals (especially those involved in providing adult services) have utilised it systematically as a means to assess and improve life for people with learning difficulties. David Goode (1994) has drawn together a range of international theoretical approaches which focus upon what good measures of quality of life might be, but acknowledges that work in this field is still developing. Perry and Felce (1995) have produced a useful meta-analysis of formal quality of life measures and found them to be of some use in community-based staffed houses for people with learning difficulties. There is a tendency for these measures (and there are quite a lot of them about) to be assessment and diagnostic oriented in design and they do not appear to offer much in the way of guidance about how to set about enhancing the quality of life. Nevertheless, they are clearly emerging tools that could be used to improve quality of life in two possible ways. Firstly, they can be used to inspect and monitor the quality of provision, and therefore to protect the interests of people with learning difficulties. Secondly, they can be used to help *map* important aspects of activity that contribute to a good quality of life. Perry and Felce identify six quality of life domains which could valuably be measured:

- activity;
- autonomy and choice;
- housing quality;
- personal development;
- social and community integration;
- social interactions.

If the value of such measurements is that they safeguard the interests of people with learning difficulties, then it might be worthwhile to consider how they could be adapted for use in educational settings. Certainly, of the six domains highlighted above, five could be seen as immediately relevant to the furtherance of inclusion for pupils and students with learning difficulties. The domain of housing quality could also warrant serious consideration for use in the planning of transition to adulthood as pointed out in Chapter 17. If appropriately developed, quality of life measures could be incorporated into school inspection and monitoring systems, and be used at both the school and individual level. However, it should be remembered that these measures are not currently developed to a significant degree, that they could be used ineptly, and in reductionist ways, as managerial tools with limited and unhelpful purposes (Ball, 1990) that focus upon the patina of educational provision rather than its underlying quality. Taylor (1994) has cautioned against this kind of usage and suggested that quality of life measures need to be seen as *sensitizing concepts* rather than as closely defined prescriptive manuals.

Bearing these concerns in mind, it is perhaps worth noting that any quality of life measures should be used in conjunction with other assessment methods. It is also important for quality of life measures to move beyond the purely diagnostic, to a level where they are informing teaching and learning. Daniels (1996) refers to the empowering potential of quality of life approaches that go beyond measurement, and stresses the need for learners with disabilities and difficulties to be engaged in educational dialogue, rather than be seen as passive recipients of teaching. For some pupils and students with learning difficulties, this engagement may be especially difficult. Where this is the case, the central purpose of teaching will be to seek this engagement, and on the learner's terms. Examples of such approaches can be found in the work of Holm *et al.* (1994) and Ware (1994).

If quality of life concepts, measures and *dialogues* can usefully enhance the education of learners with significant difficulties, they should also further the practice of inclusion. This is because of their acknowledgement and valuing of social activity as the central component of life for the vast majority of people. In this regard, emergent quality of life perspectives can be seen to be resonant with a tradition in education generally that stems from the work of John Dewey. Dewey (1938) stressed the importance of both personal and social growth in children, and identified quality education as a combination of both of these. A consideration of the application of Dewey's work to the field of learning difficulties can be found in Dumbleton (1990) and Robertson (1997), who both suggest that a reappraisal of his work would be timely.

In the following sections two specific approaches to the inclusion process are considered. Both of these approaches incorporate a quality of life dimension, though this is not always overtly stated. The approaches are overlapping with each other, and should also be seen as inextricably linked to the quality of life domains highlighted in this section.

RESPONSIVE INCLUSION

If educational provision is to become more inclusive for pupils and students with a wide range of learning difficulties it will need to be responsive at both organisational and pedagogical levels (see Chapter 2). A number of concerns have been discussed in relation to the organisational level. Clearly, schooling as we know it will have to be considerably reshaped if the diverse needs of pupils with learning difficulties are going to be met in mainstream settings. This point is well made by Wedell (1995) who emphasises the importance of flexibility that will allow for different groupings of pupils, and the use of various locations for learning (including the home and special school environments). Such flexibility, he argues, is the only way forward in planning to meet widely diverse needs. Such organisational flexibility is of course linked to teaching too. This linkage, and the need for new developments in this area, is hinted at in the Labour government's White Paper on education (DfEE, 1997) where 'schools of the future' are discussed. The document argues that the time is ripe for innovations in teaching and learning:

> It is striking that so far the teaching and learning process has stayed remarkably stable in spite of the huge structural changes of the last decade or so. We believe that, as the pressure of international competition increases and we face up to the likely demands of the 21st century, we must expect change in the nature of schooling.
>
> (DfEE, 1997, p.43, point 23)

Whether consciously so, or not, this policy document has identified the importance of reviewing teaching and learning processes for all children and young people, including those with learning difficulties. As discussed in Chapter 7, some considerations we need to take account of if teaching and learning is to be more responsive are:

- A stronger recognition of the value of difference between pupils and students is needed if inclusive approaches to teaching are to be valued by teachers and other educators (Oliver, 1996); this awareness might be enhanced by good quality disability equality training.
- A curriculum that offers flexibility without excluding some pupils. An example of this is the Scottish 5–14 Curriculum Special Educational Needs Material Support for Learning (Scottish Consultative Council on the Curriculum – the SCCC, 1993).
- Approaches to teaching that are dialogical, and negotiated between pupils/students and teachers (Daniels, 1996). Such approaches have a strong tradition in East European and Russian practice, and owe much to the seminal work of Vygotsky (1978). They also have interesting similarities with the pedagogical practice and theory of Paulo Freire (1972; 1973). The application of such methods in the field of learning difficulties has been limited, but clearly has vital potential. Examples of interesting related work in this area are Ware's (1996) which emphasises the importance of responsive environments for people with profound and multiple leaning difficulties (PMLD); Nind and Hewett's (1994) focus upon interaction and communication for pupils and students with severe learning difficulties (SLD); and Watson's (1996) study of the value of reflection through interaction for pupils with moderate learning difficulties (MLD) and pupils in mainstream school. Danish work by Holm *et al*. (1994) also illustrates the empowering nature of responsive interaction in both educational and residential living settings. The potential for the use of all of these approaches is enormous, and it is especially interesting to note that they have a real value for all children and young people, not just those with learning difficulties.
- Responsive approaches to teaching also need to be studied in action. Lindsay and Thompson (1997) note this, and cite an example (Salisbury *et al*., 1995) of small-scale research which reveals the contribution of responsive pedagogy to inclusive practice. Consistent with the review in Chapter 2 five 'themes' that support inclusion are:
  - the active facilitation of social interactions;
  - detailed attention to the planning and organisation of seating, co-operative group work and collaborative problem solving (something which affected all children in class);
  - the involvement of children themselves in enhancing interaction, seeing them as a resource and as responsible for inclusion;

– the modelling of acceptance, by both teachers and pupils;
– specific and agreed school policies and practices.

Reflective practice in classrooms can certainly enhance the quality of life for pupils and students with learning difficulties. This practice needs to be connected to a wider range of educational activity in schools, or other educational settings. If this connection is not made, then success in one environment may not be replicated elsewhere. Responsive support across school life is something that inclusive education advocates have not always taken account of. Clegg (1993) has developed a conceptual framework for encouraging a focus upon the social interaction of people with learning difficulties. This framework is designed to encourage professionals to adopt a more social focus when considering the interests of people they work with, be they pupils, students or clients. Though the model devised by Clegg is a theoretical one, with implications for practice outlined for clinical psychologists rather than educators, it has the potential to enhance social relations in educational settings in powerful ways. This is because it focuses on the understanding of staffing and organisation, as much as it does on individuals with difficulties.

Quality inclusive education needs to be underpinned by responsiveness. Responsiveness is characterised not only by activity in individual classes, or study sessions, but by the way in which it pervades all practices in educational settings.

CARING INCLUSION

I have argued elsewhere (Robertson, 1997) that caring should have an important place in the education of pupils and students with learning difficulties. For some people, especially those with PMLD, specific care related to physical well-being is an essential part of life, and one which can be seen as a central part of daily life. Where this is the case the overlap between education and personal care is an important one, not to be ignored (Thornes, 1990). But care and caring can also be viewed as warranting a central place in the education of all children and be seen as a key value in furthering the development of inclusive education.

An exponent of the view that caring should constitute the core of the curriculum is Nel Noddings. In her book, *The Challenge to Care in Schools* (Noddings, 1992), she argues cogently that the curriculum for all children and young people should be organised around themes of care:

All students should be engaged in general education that guides them in caring for self, intimate others, global others, plants, animals, and the environment, the human-made world, and ideas. Moral life so defined should frankly be embraced as the main goal of education. Such an aim does not work against intellectual development or academic achievement. On the contrary, it supplies a firm foundation for both.

(pp.173–4)

There is much in Noddings' caring conceptualisation of schooling that echoes discussion in this chapter about the organisation of learning contexts, responsible and responsive approaches to inclusion. Her view of what we must do to create more caring schools which enhance the quality of life of all individuals is:

1. Be clear and unapologetic about our goal. The main aim of education should be to produce competent, caring, loving, and lovable people.
2. Take care of affiliative needs.

    – Keep students and teachers together (by mutual consent) for several years.
    – Keep students together where possible.
    – Keep them in the same building for considerable periods of time.
    – Help students to think of the school as theirs.
    – Legitimize time spent in building relations of care and trust.

3. Relax the impulse to control.

    – Give teachers and students more responsibility to exercise judgement.
    – Get rid of competitive grading.
    – Reduce testing and use a few well-designed tests to assess whether people can handle the task they want to undertake competently.
    – Encourage teachers to explore with students. We don't have to know everything to teach well.
    – Define expertise more broadly and instrumentally. For example, a biology teacher should be able to teach whatever mathematics is involved in biology.
    – Encourage self-evaluation.
    – Involve students in governing their own classrooms and schools.
    – Accept the challenge to care by teaching well the things students want to learn.

4. Get rid of program hierarchies. This will take time, but we must begin now to provide excellent programs for all our children. Programs for the non-college bound should be just as rich, desirable, and rigorous as those for the college bound.

- Abandon uniform requirements for college entrance. What a student wants to do or to study should guide what is required by way of preparation.
- Give all students what all students need: genuine opportunities to explore the central questions to human life.

5. Give at least part of every day to themes of care.

- Discuss existential questions freely, including spiritual matters.
- Help students to treat each other ethically. Give them practice in caring.
- Help students to understand how groups and individuals create rivals and enemies. Help them to learn how to be on both sides.
- Encourage a way of caring for animals, plants, and the environment that is consistent with caring for humans.
- Help students to care deeply for ideas that engage them.

6. Teach them that caring in every domain implies competence. When we care, we accept responsibility to work continuously on our own competence so that the recipient of our care – person, animal, object, or idea – is enhanced. There is nothing mushy about caring. It is the strong, resilient backbone of human life.

(pp.174–5)

I have quoted the above list to illustrate the comprehensiveness of Noddings' approach. I leave it to the reader to extrapolate how it might be put into practice. I do, though, think that a central thread in her work – the importance of relationships in the world – is an important feature of developing effective inclusive educational provision for pupils and students with learning difficulties. A critical appraisal of Noddings' theory, by Vandenburg (1996), identifies the emphasis on 'dialogical relations' in it as a great strength. This emphasis on relations has frequently been associated with Gilligan (1982), and a feminist perspective on education. Some male authors, though, have also written about the importance of this kind of dialectic (Freire, 1972; 1973; Buber, 1965), and it is also a notable feature of the educational philosophy of Rudolf Steiner (Hansmann, 1992).

The final point to make in this brief consideration of caring as a positive factor in the process on inclusion is that it is closely associated with quality of life. This is well illustrated by Robert Pirsig (1974) in *Zen and the Art of Motorcycle Maintenance*:

it occurred to me there is no manual that deals with the real business of motorcycle maintenance, the most important aspect of all. *Caring* about what you are doing is considered either unimportant or taken for granted.

(p.35, emphasis added)

And

by subtracting *Quality* from a picture of the world as we know it, he'd revealed a magnitude of importance of this term he hadn't known was there. The world can function without it, but life would be so dull as to be hardly worth living. The term worth is a quality term. Life would just be living without any values or purpose at all.

(p.216, emphasis added)

When thinking about a caring and quality education together, we are of course exemplifying the important symbiotic relationship between formal education and informal lifelong living and learning.

CONCLUSION

The two approaches to inclusion considered in this chapter – responsive and caring inclusion – are interconnected. While they may not coalesce to produce a whole, or anything remotely like a theory of inclusion, it is hoped that they will stimulate thinking about what might need to be done in a wide range of real-world educational settings if pupils and young people with learning difficulties are going to be able to enjoy good-quality lives as adults.

Implicit in this discussion of approaches has been the importance of responsibility in furthering inclusiveness. We live in a society which grapples with a plurality of values (Berlin, 1990; Williams, 1981), such as equality and individuality, and can never hope to achieve a *type* of inclusion which reconciles these completely. Indeed, to do so would be logically impossible. As educators our responsibility is to enable pupils and students with learning difficulties to grow into adults who can, as freely as possible, participate and make choices about how to live their lives. For some, such a capability may be problematic, but striving towards it should still be seen as the central pedagogic aim. At the same time, educators also need to avoid falling into the paternalistic trap of prescribing too closely what a good life might be for someone with learning difficulties, and this requires critical responsibility associated with continuing discussion and evaluation of practice. Paulo Freire (1973) makes this point well, describing critical, reflective and responsive pedagogy as:

characterised by depth in the interpretation of problems; by the substitution of causal principles for magical explanations; by testing of one's *findings* and by openness to revision; by the attempt to avoid distortion when perceiving problems and to avoid preconceived notions when analysing them; by rejecting passive positions; by soundness of argumentation; by the practice of dialogue rather than polemics; by receptivity of the new for reasons beyond mere novelty and by good sense not to reject the old just because it is old — by accepting what is valid in both old and new.

(Education: The Practice of Freedom, p.18)

The process of inclusion is not about ultimate ideological ends, or the seeking of identical forms of educational provision. Rather, it is about empowering people to be themselves, and this requires, above all else, a dialogue with the learner. Then we might be able to affirm with Spoonface Steinberg:

everybody is different and that it is quite good indeed . . .

ACKNOWLEDGEMENT

The author is grateful to Teachers College Press for permission to reprint extracts from: Noddings, N. (1992) *The Challenge to Care in School: an Alternative Approach to Education*, New York: Teachers College Press, pp.174–5.

REFERENCES

Ball, S. (ed.) (1990) *Foucault and Education: Disciplines and Knowledge*, London: Routledge.
Berlin, I. (1990) *The Crooked Timber of Humanity*, London: Fontana Press.
Buber, M. (1965) *Between Man and Man*, New York: Macmillan.
Clegg, J. (1993) 'Putting people first: a social constructionist approach to learning disability', *British Journal of Clinical Psychology* 32: 389–406.
Daniels, H. (1996) 'Back to basics: three R's for special needs', *British Journal of Special Education* 23(4): 155–61.
Dewey, J. (1938) *Experience and Education*, New York: Macmillan.
DfEE (1997) *Excellence in Schools*, London: The Stationery Office.
Dumbleton, P. (1990) 'A philosophy of education for all?', *British Journal of Special Education* 17(1): 16–18.
Freire, P. (1972) *Pedagogy of the Oppressed*, London: Penguin.
Freire, P. (1973) *Education: the Practice of Freedom*, London: Writers and Readers Publishing Cooperative.

Gilligan, C. (1982) *In a Different Voice: Psychological Theory and Women's Development*, Cambridge, MA: Harvard University Press.

Goode, D. (ed.) (1994) *Quality of Life for Persons with Disabilities: International Perspectives and Issues*, Cambridge, MA: Brookline Books.

Hall, L. (1997) *Spoonface Steinberg. A Radio Drama Monologue* (radio cassette), London: BBC (Radio Collection) Publications.

Hansmann, H. (1992) *Education for Special Needs: Principles and Practice in Camp Hill Schools*, Edinburgh: Floris Books.

Holm, P., Holst, J. and Perlt, B. (1994) 'Co-write your own life: quality of life as discussed in the Danish context', in D. Goode (ed.) *Quality of Life for Persons with Disabilities: International Perspectives and Issues*, Cambridge, MA: Brookline Books.

Lindsay, G. and Thompson, D. (eds) (1997) *Values into Practice in Special Education*, London: David Fulton.

Mittler, P. (1988) 'Quality of life and services for people with disabilities', in G. Fairbairn (ed.) *Ethical Issues in Caring*, London: Avebury.

Nind, M. and Hewett, D. (1994) *Access to Communication: Developing the Basics of Communication with People with Severe Learning Difficulties through Intensive Interaction*, London: David Fulton.

Noddings, N. (1992) *The Challenge to Care in Schools: an Alternative Approach to Education*, New York: Teachers College Press.

Norwich, B. (1996) 'Special needs education or education for all: connective specialisation and ideological impurity', *British Journal of Special Education* 23(3): 100–4.

Oliver, M. (1996) *Understanding Disability: from Theory to Practice*, Basingstoke: Macmillan.

Perry, J. and Felce, D. (1995) 'Measure for measure: how do measures of quality of life compare?', *British Journal of Learning Disabilities* 23(4): 134–7.

Pfeiffer, D. (1994) 'Eugenics and disability discrimination', *Disability and Society* 9(4): 481–99.

Pirsig, R. (1974) *Zen and the Art of Motorcycle Maintenance*, London: Bodley Head.

Robertson, C. (1997) 'I don't want to be independent: does human life need to be viewed in terms of potential autonomy. Issues in the education of children and young people with severe and profound and multiple learning difficulties', in M. Fawcus (ed.) *Children with Learning Difficulties*, London: Whurr.

Salisbury, C., Gallucci, C., Palombaro, C. and Peck, C. (1995) 'Strategies that promote social relations among elementary students with and without severe disabilities in inclusive schools', *Exceptional Children* 62: 125–37.

SCCC (1993) *Support for Learning Material* (esp. part 5, Developing the Curriculum for Pupils with Complex Learning Difficulties), Dundee: Scottish Consultative Council on the Curriculum.

Stanworth, M. (1989) 'The new eugenics', in A. Brechin and J. Walmsley (eds) *Making Connections: Reflecting on the Lives and Experiences of People with Learning Difficulties*, London: Hodder & Stoughton.

Taylor, S. (1994) 'In support of research on quality of life, but against QOL', in D. Goode (ed.) *Quality of Life for Persons with Disabilities: International Perspectives and Issues*, Cambridge, MA: Brookline Books.

Thornes, R. (1990) 'Towards a comprehensive system of care for dying children and their families: key issues', in J. Baum, F. Dominica and R. Woodward (eds) *Listen. My Child has a Lot of Living to Do*, Oxford: Oxford University Press.

Vandenburg, D. (1996) 'Caring: feminine ethics or maternalistic misandry? A hermeneutical critique of Nel Noddings' phenomenology of the moral subject of education', *Journal of Philosophy of Education* 30(2): 253–69.

Vygotsky, L. (1978) *Mind in Society: the Development of Higher Psychological Processes*, Cambridge, MA: Harvard University Press.

Ware, J. (1994) *Educating Children with Profound and Multiple Learning Difficulties*, London: David Fulton.

Ware, J. (1996) *Creating a Responsive Environment for People with Profound and Multiple Learning Difficulties*, London: David Fulton.

Watson, J. (1996) *Reflection through Interaction: the Classroom Experience of Pupils with Learning Difficulties*, London: David Fulton.

Wedell, D. (1995) 'Making inclusive education ordinary', *British Journal of Special Education* 22(3): 100–4.

Williams, B. (1981) *Moral Luck*, Cambridge: Cambridge University Press.

Williams, P. (1995) 'Should we prevent Down's Syndrome?', *British Journal of Learning Disabilities* 23(2): 46–50.

Author index

Subject index